D1552686

LUCID,
THE DATAFLOW
PROGRAMMING LANGUAGE

This is volume 22 in A.P.I.C. Studies in Data Processing
General Editors: Fraser Duncan and M. J. R. Shave
A complete list of titles in this series appears at the end of this volume

LUCID,
THE DATAFLOW
PROGRAMMING LANGUAGE

William W. Wadge

Department of Computer Science
University of Victoria
Victoria, British Columbia
Canada

Edward A. Ashcroft

SRI International
Menlo Park, California
United States of America

1985

ACADEMIC PRESS

(Harcourt Brace Jovanovich, Publishers)

London   Orlando   San Diego   New York
Toronto   Montreal   Sydney   Tokyo

ACADEMIC PRESS INC. (LONDON) LTD.
24–28 Oval Road
LONDON NW1 7DX

United States Edition published by
ACADEMIC PRESS, INC.
Orlando, Florida 32887

British Library Cataloguing in Publication Data

Wadge, William W.
    Lucid, the dataflow programming language.–
    (APIC studies in data processing)
    1. Programming languages (Electronic computers)
    2. Electronic digital computers–Programming
    I. Title   II. Ashcroft, Edward A.   III. Series
    001.64'24   QA76.7

Library of Congress Cataloging in Publication Data

Wadge, William W.
    Lucid, the dataflow programming language.
    (A.P.I.C. studies in data processing; no.)
    Bibliography: p.
    Includes index.
    1. Lucid (Computer program language)   2. Electronic
digital computers--Programming.   I. Ashcroft, Edward A.
II. Title.   III. Series.
QA76.73.L83W33   1985   001.64'24   84-15685
ISBN 0–12–729650–6 (alk. paper)

CONTENTS

v

PREFACE

When Academic Press first suggested that we might write a book about Lucid, we readily agreed. Producing a book would be relatively easy (we thought); we could simply collect a number of existing papers and reports, add a few editorial comments, and that would be that. Once that was taken care of, we could then move on to some more ambitious project. However, when we went back and reread the papers and reports, we realised that out initial plan was unworkable. Lucid was (and still is) a very new development; nevertheless, it had already evolved so much that the various papers we proposed to include had become incompatible. Some of the changes were of a detailed or technical nature, but on the whole they reflected a radical shift in the underlying motivation.

Lucid was born in 1974 at the University of Waterloo in Canada, where at the time both authors were teaching in the Faculty of Mathematics. The original goals in developing Lucid were very modest. We wanted to show that conventional, 'mainstream' programming could be done in a purely declarative language, one without assignment or **goto** statements. We felt then (and still do now) that real "structured programming" required first the elimination of both these features and that only then would program verification become a practical possibility.

Of course we knew that in principle any programming problem could be solved by using only recursion in a "functional" or "applicative" language such as LISP. We felt, however, that this approach was not really credible. The purely recursive solutions cannot (apparently) use iteration and therefore exclude most of the algorithms used in real, everyday programming. (Some exponents of recursive programming consider "tail-recursion" to be the same as iteration, but such programs, with their clumsy parameter lists, cannot really be used for everyday programming.) Languages such as LISP do, in fact, allow loops to be written—but only by allowing assignment back into the language (as LISP does with its

ix

PROG feature). Our goal therefore was to show that iterative algorithms could be expressed in a declarative (or "nonprocedural") language, without introducing 'dirty' features like PROG.

Our starting point was the observation that the information contained in the assignment statements

$$I := 1;$$
$$\vdots$$
$$I := I + 1;$$

could be conveyed by the declarations

$$\text{first } I = 1;$$
$$\text{next } I = I + 1;$$

The form of these declarations suggested that **first** and **next** could be used as operations and that these operations could be applied to expressions as well as simple identifiers. This in turn opened up the possibility that intuitively true equations like **next(x + y) = next(x) + next(y)** could be used to reason algebraically about dynamic aspects of programs.

At first, however, it was not clear what *values* were being equated. Work on Lucid came to a halt for several months until we finally realised that variables and expressions ought to denote infinite sequences (or *histories*) of individual data values.

Once this principle was established, we were, in fact, able to show that at least simple iterative algorithms could be expressed in a natural way by sets of equations. We were also pleased to confirm that reasoning about programs was indeed much simpler. One advantage, not the least, was that the language in which assertions were formulated was an extension of the programming language. The statements in a program were already true assertions about the values of variables in the program, and they constituted the axioms from which deeper properties could be derived.

This initial work did show that in principle iteration could be made respectable. The original Lucid was, however, a very simple language and could express only very simple algorithms. If we really wanted to displace the mainstream, imperative languages, we would have to show that more realistic applications could be programmed in the equational style. We therefore began considering extensions of the language which would allow us to attempt more ambitious problems.

The first feature added was nesting (of loops) and that proved to be relatively easy—we simply allowed the value of a variable to depend on more than one time parameter. (A simple infinite sequence could be thought of as a value which depended on one parameter, the position in the sequence, which we called "time".) After nesting, the most obvious step was to add arrays, but here things went awry. We spent a great deal of effort trying to find a simple algebra of arrays (along the lines of APL), with little success. We realise now that the main problem was our insistence that these arrays be finite, and of finite dimension. We knew that infinite arrays had much more pleasant properties, but we could not fit them into the conventional model of computation which still dominated our thinking.

We therefore suspended our work on arrays while we considered the other most obvious extension, namely, user-defined functions. This one extension proved to be the simplest of all; yet it was more powerful than we had ever expected. We discovered that functions defined by using the special Lucid operations can be thought of as filters (continuously operating processes which transform data streams). Our language now had a coroutine-like facility. Coroutines were known to be powerful programming tools but were thought to be very complicated. In Lucid, coroutines came almost for free!

The success of user-defined functions strengthened our confidence in the Lucid approach. Finally, we understood that there are other forms of repetition than those expressed by conventional imperative loops. We began to realise that underlying the new approach to programming was a new approach to computation itself—the dataflow approach. From then on, Lucid was not just a new way of expressing old algorithms. It became a new way of expressing new (dataflow) algorithms. In a sense, our original objective had become reversed. Originally, we wanted to preserve the conventional approach to computation by showing that it could be made mathematically respectable. Now, we attempted to show that the old way could be eliminated and replaced by a whole new world view.

Naturally, we make no claims to having discovered dataflow and the dataflow approach to computation. For this, many people share the credit, people such as M. McIlroy, J. Dennis and G. Kahn. We owe a special debt to the developers of UNIX,† who have provided practical proof that dataflow is a powerful programming technique.

The book as it now appears therefore bears little relationship to the book which we originally planned to write (or rather, assemble). The emphasis is now on Lucid as a practical tool, rather than as an object of formal study. We still believe that program verification is important and is much easier in a functional language, but we treat the subject very briefly and in a very informal way (transformation gets rather more attention). There seems little point in demonstrating the correctness of programs

---

† UNIX is a trademark of AT&T Bell Laboratories.

written in a language unfit for realistic problems, one which is based on an unworkable model of computation. The primary objective of this book is therefore to prove that dataflow is a real alternative to sequential/imperative computing and that dataflow algorithms can be expressed naturally and concisely in Lucid. We hope that we have succeeded, but we will let you, the reader, be the judge.

We would ask, though, that before you deliver your verdict you obtain the excellent pLucid interpreter (or "evaluator") written by A. Faustini† (based on a first draft by C. Ostrum). The language is rich enough to allow interesting applications to be programmed, and the error-handling is excellent. The interpreter is (like most interpreters) big and sometimes slow, but it is efficient enough to be usable for some applications. The example programs given in this book have all (except for those in extended Lucid) been tested and so should work for you as well. The only problem is that the present version of the interpreter is written in C and requires UNIX. Those of you who are forced to use older, more primitive operating systems unfortunately will have to wait a little while longer before you can gain first-hand experience to dataflow programming in Lucid.

We would like to thank the funding agencies that supported the development of Lucid, and the production of this book. Initially this was done completely by the Canadian Science Research Council (subsequently the Natural Sciences and Engineering Research Council), even after one of the two of us (Bill Wadge) moved to the University of Warwick, in England. Eventually he obtained funding from the Science and Engineering Research Council of the United Kingdom. We are grateful for the help of both these bodies.

Collaboration across the Atlantic is not the easiest thing, and the development of the language was probably slower than necessary. (It did, however, enable us to preface lectures about Lucid with the observation that it was being developed by an Englishman working in Canada and a Canadian working in England.) At present, Ed Ashcroft is at SRI International, in California, and Bill Wadge is at the University of Victoria, in British Columbia, Canada, and so now the authors are at least on the same side of the same continent.

We also would like to take this opportunity to thank the many people who have contributed to the development of Lucid and to the production of this book. These include (in alphabetical order) Thomas Cargill, Mansour Farah, Tony Faustini, Patrick Gardin, Christoph Hoffmann, Steven

---

† Contact A. Faustini, Department of Computer Science, Arizona State University, Tempe, Arizona 85297, USA.

Matthews, David May, Calvin Ostrum, Paul Pilgram and Ali Yaghi. Our special thanks go to Tony Faustini, Ali Yaghi and Steve Matthews, who wrote the pLucid manual and consented to having it included in the appendix. Extra special thanks go to Calvin Ostrum and Tony Faustini. Calvin became interested in Lucid as a second-year undergraduate student at Waterloo and single-handedly produced an interpreter, written in C, in his third year. This interpreter forms the basis of the pLucid interpreter, which Tony Faustini developed while a research assistant at Warwick. Tony also contributed greatly to the design of pLucid itself.

Finally, we would like to thank the many students at the Universities of Warwick, Waterloo and Victoria who registered in courses in which Lucid was taught. Some of them were cruelly treated by early versions of pLucid and its interpreter, but they showed that mere mortals are capable of writing dataflow programs.

December 1984   W. W. WADGE
Victoria, Canada   E. A. ASHCROFT

I INTRODUCTION

Lucid is a programming language, but it is very unlike any of the programming languages (BASIC, PASCAL, even LISP) with which the reader might already be familiar. A simple Lucid program which describes a computation involving rational numbers follows. The program computes a 'running' root mean square of its input; in general the nth number output is the *root mean square* (square root of the average of the squares) of the first n numbers input.

```
sqroot(avg(square(a)))
      where
        square(x) = x * x;
        avg(y) = mean
              where
                n = 1 fby n + 1;
                mean = first y fby mean + d;
                d = (next y − mean)/(n + 1);
                end;
        sqroot(z) = approx asa err < 0.0001
              where
                Z is current z;
                  approx = Z/2 fby (approx + Z/approx)/2;
                  err = abs(square(approx) − Z);
              end;
      end
```

Readers with some knowledge of mathematics (or even just algebra) can probably form a good guess as to how the program works, even if this is the first Lucid program they have ever seen. The program uses the function **square** to form the squares of the numbers input, the function **avg** to

1

generate a running average of these numbers and the function **sqroot** to generate the square roots of these averages.

The computations described by the above program can be understood as taking place in a simple network with three components connected in series.

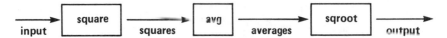

This network corresponds to the Lucid expression **sqroot(avg(square(a)))** and the three components correspond to the three functions defined in the program. The Lucid programmer would imagine an endless stream of input values coming in from the left, along the arc labelled 'input' (these are in fact the values of the variable **a**). These values pass through (and are transformed by) the three 'components' or 'black boxes' and are sent to the 'outside world' on the line labelled **output**. The output of the program is this last stream of values; this stream of values might be sent to a printer, or perhaps stored in a file, depending on how the program is being used. The 'particles' of data passing through this system are called 'datons', and the components through which they pass (and by which they are transformed) are called 'filters', by analogy with electronics.

The input values pass one by one through the first 'component' or 'black box' labelled **square**. The **square** component computes the squares of the values it receives, one by one as they arrive, and sends the squared values down the 'line' labelled **squares**—in the order the original values were received.

The squares travel down the line labelled **squares** until they encounter the second black box, the one labelled **avg.** This component receives these numbers one by one and with each one computes the average of all the inputs received so far. The new averages are sent one by one, as they are computed, down the line labelled **averages**.

These averages are fed into the third black box, the one labelled **sqroot**. This component calculates the square roots of the numbers it receives as it receives them, and passes these roots one by one down the line labelled **output** in the order they were produced.

Those readers who are mathematically inclined (or who have some knowledge of programming) can probably also guess how the individual components carry out their calculations. The definition of **square** is based on the obvious idea of multiplying together two copies of each input. The definition of the **avg** function uses a more sophisticated algorithm. It does not keep a running total of the values of its arguments; instead, it increments the previous value of the computed average by an appropriate amount. Finally, the function **sqroot** defined inside the program computes the square root of its argument (somewhat naively) by using Newton's method. It generates better and better approximations until the desired accuracy is achieved.

Naturally, the three components in this network can carry out their computations in parallel, i.e., they can all be working simultaneously. There is no need for the **square** filter to consume all its input and calculate all the squares before the **avg** filter can begin forming the averages. In general the **avg** filter can be processing one item while its upstream neighbour is preparing its next input and the downstream neighbour is working on its last output. The filters in the network may even work at different rates; there is no need to assume that their activities are synchronised, i.e., that they all read inputs simultaneously and produce outputs simultaneously. If some of the filters are capable of processing their data faster than others, the worst that can happen is that some are kept idle waiting for input or that datons begin to queue up on input lines waiting to be processed. Neither of these phenomena affect the final series of values output by the program. They affect only the *rate* at which these values are produced and the *resources* (such as space for storing queued datons) required to produce the output.

1. What Makes Lucid Run?

At this point the reader might begin to suspect that we are reading rather more into the program than is actually there. These suspicions are basically correct; the computational activity described is really only one *interpretation* of the program. Most conventional programming languages require the programmer to supply explicit information about any dynamic activity (such as the flow of data through a network) which the program is supposed to generate. The reader with experience in such languages would probably expect that dataflow networks will be described in some cumbersome and appalling jargon in which it is specified which lines are attached to which filters, which lines are input and output, initial contents of arcs, and so on. For example, something like

NETWORK DIVISION.
    CONNECT PROGRAM-INPUT TO SQUARE-INPUT
    CONNECT SQUARE-OUTPUT TO AVG-INPUT
    CONNECT AVG-OUTPUT TO SQROOT-INPUT
    CONNECT SQROOT-OUTPUT TO PROGRAM-OUTPUT

The Lucid programmer, however, does not directly manipulate lines and filters. Instead, the Lucid user specifies the *data* to be processed and the *transformations* to be applied. Consider, for example, the expression **sqroot(avg(square(a)))**. It is obvious from the expression itself that the transformation **square** is to be applied to the data **a**, that the transformation **avg** is to be applied to the result, and that a third transformation **sqroot** is to be applied to this second result. Furthermore, the expression itself (taken as a whole) denotes or represents the final result of applying all three transformations in the order indicated. Since this final result is the output of the program, there is no need for a separate 'output' statement or declaration. In the same way, the variable **a** (representing the original input to the filters) is not defined in the program. The data which the variable **a** represents is arbitrary (can be anything); it can therefore be taken as the input to the program.

We see then that the expression **sqroot(avg(square(a)))** contains (when taken with the auxiliary definitions following the **where**) all the information the programmer needs to provide. This expression, together with its accompanying **where** clause, specifies exactly *what* the output is to be—namely, the value of the expression. At the same time, however, it also specifies to a certain extent just *how* this output is to be obtained—namely, by applying in turn the transformations **square**, **avg** and **sqroot** to the input. There is therefore no absolute *need* to talk about boxes and lines directly; the network given above can be considered as simply a *graphical* representation of the given expression. And there is certainly no need to develop a second textual form (like the hypothetical 'program' given earlier) to specify a graph which itself is simply a two-dimensional specification of the original expression.

A program in Lucid is therefore simply an expression, together with definitions of the transformations and data (other than input) referred to in the expression. The output of the program is simply the data denoted by the program as an expression, i.e., the value of the program. Lucid has more in common with school algebra than with BASIC or COBOL.

At this point it is now the turn of the more mathematically inclined readers to be skeptical. Lucid certainly *looks* like conventional mathematics, but appearances can be deceptive. After all, many programming languages use mathematical notation but in a way that (as we shall see) is anything but conventional. Consider again the expression **sqroot(avg(square(a)))**. The filters **sqroot** and **square** can certainly be understood as conventional mathematical functions operating on numbers, but what about **avg**? What is the result of applying **avg** to a number? What is the 'average' of 8? In mathematics, the value a function returns is determined by the value given it, i.e., by its argument. According to the description given earlier, however, the **avg** filter supposedly *remembers* the average of the previous values and updates this remembered average every time it is given a new argument. Who ever heard of a mathematical function with a memory? Surely this is a dynamic concept peculiar to computer science.

The apparent contradiction disappears, however, if we recall that the 'data' transformed by a filter like **avg** is more than just a single number. The average filter, in the course of its working lifetime, accepts a whole *series* of numbers $s_0, s_1, s_2, \ldots$. This is the *total* input to the filter. In the same way, the filter does not produce just a single number, it produces another whole series $a_0, a_1, a_2, \ldots$. This is the *total* output of the filter. Therefore, if we want to think of the filter as computing a conventional mathematical function, then the function must be given as its argument the entire series $s_0, s_1, s_2, \ldots$ and must return as its result the entire series $a_0, a_1, a_2, \ldots$. It must be a function *from* the set of sequences of inputs *to* the set of sequences of outputs. It is not hard to see that there is in fact a sequence function f which specifies the input/output transformation performed by the **avg** filter. Given a series s, $f(s)$ is simply the series

$$\langle s_0, (s_0 + s_1)/2, (s_0 + s_1 + s_2)/3, \ldots \rangle$$

of averages (everything is simpler if we use only infinite sequences).

This is how Lucid resolves the apparent conflict between the static nature of conventional mathematics and the dynamic nature of programming. Expressions in Lucid really are expressions in the mathematical sense, and the functions referred to in the expressions really are functions in the strict sense of the word. Expressions have as their values not individual data items but sequences thereof; and functions map sequences to sequences. For the sake of uniformity even 'conventional' expressions and transformations denote sequences and sequence functions. Thus the expression **2 * 3** has the sequence

$$\langle 6, 6, 6, 6, 6, \ldots \rangle$$

as its value, and the transformation **square** corresponds to the function which maps

$$\langle s_0, s_1, s_2, \ldots \rangle \qquad \text{to} \qquad \langle s_0^2, s_1^2, s_2^2, \ldots \rangle$$

We have already seen that an expression in Lucid can be thought of as denoting the output of a network of filters involving the transformations referred to in the program. The value of such an expression is an infinite sequence, one which can be thought of as a complete record or history of all the individual values produced by the network, in the order they were produced. If the expression in question is a program, the infinite sequence is a record or history of the entire output activity of the program. For example, if the value of a program P is the infinite sequence $\langle 2, 3, 5, 7, 11,$

13, ...⟩ of all prime numbers (in order), then P can be thought of as a program which lists or enumerates the primes. When such a prime generating program is run it will produce the number 2 first of all, then 3, then 5, 7, 11 and so on—although not necessarily at a constant rate.

The statements appearing in the Lucid program, for example,

mean = first y fby mean + d;

really are equations, and they specify the value which the variable has in the region of the program in which the definition is valid. The value of a variable is also an infinite sequence of data items, one which can be thought of as a complete record of the values produced by the network corresponding to the expression on the right hand side of the definition. (In thinking this way we must not assume that these values are produced at constant rate, or that the production of these values is synchronized with that of other variables or of the output.)

A program may use variables which have no definitions in the program (and which do not, like **y** in the rms (root mean square) program, serve as 'dummy' arguments in function definitions). These variables are called *input* variables; the value of a program will in general depend on the values of these variables. The values given the input variables constitute the input to a Lucid program. These values are also infinite sequences, and can be thought of as a complete record of all the data items fed into the program in the order in which they were entered. Again, one must not assume that the rate at which data items are read in as input by a program is necessarily constant or that it is necessarily the same as the rate at which data items are written out as output.

In the rms program above there is only one input variable, namely the variable **a**. If the input to the example program (i.e., the value of **a**) is the sequence ⟨3.5, 3.2, 3.9, 4.1, 3.8, ...⟩, then the output (i.e., the value of the program as an expression) is the sequence ⟨3.5, 3.35, 3.54, 3.69, ...⟩. Thus, for example, the third number output is 3.54, which is $\sqrt{(3.5^2 + 3.2^2 + 3.9^2)/3}$. This is just what one would expect from the network described above.

In a sense the 'dynamic' aspect of Lucid is an illusion. Lucid is really just a calculus of static histories. Obviously we go to some lengths to preserve the illusion: by using suggestive names (like **next**), by using the ordinary symbols (like +) to denote the pointwise operations on sequences, and above all by avoiding explicit reference to sequence indices. This 'illusion' is absolutely indispensable as a programming aid. It is almost impossible to write programs while using a strictly static viewpoint, i.e., while interpreting Lucid's history sequences as just another data type like strings or lists. For that matter, the dynamic viewpoint is not all that illusory. A Lucid program will eventually be run, and the implementation will probably involve dataflow or some simulation of dataflow. We could just as easily argue that the static, infinite histories are 'illusory' and that the actual operational activity is the 'reality'. The dataflow interpretation of Lucid is no more illusory than the interpretation of a set of differential equations in terms of a dynamically changing system. The main difference is that the 'time variable' in calculus varies continuously, whereas Lucid's 'iteration time' changes discretely.

2. Imperative Programming

The rms program comes out very differently when written in an imperative language like PASCAL, even when roughly the same approach is used. The following PASCAL program corresponds more or less to the Lucid program given in the preceding section. It performs the same task; i.e., it repeatedly reads in rational numbers and repeatedly writes out the root mean square of all its input 'to date'. Like the Lucid program, it is intended to run indefinitely.

```
program rms(input, output);
var mean,a: real;
    n: integer;
function square(x: real): real;
begin
  square := x * x
end;
function newavg(y: real): real;
var d: real;
begin
  n := n + 1;
  d := (y - mean)/n;
  mean := mean + d;
  newavg := mean
end;
function sqroot(Z: real): real;
var approx: real;
    err: real;
begin
  approx := Z/2;
  err := abs(Z - approx * approx);
  while err > 0.0001 do
  begin
```

(continued)

```
            approx := (approx + Z/approx)/2;
            err := abs(Z − approx * approx)
        end;
        sqroot := approx
    end;
    begin
        n := 1;
        read(a);
        mean := square(a);
        writeln(abs(a));
        while true do begin
            read(a);
            writeln(sqroot(newavg(square(a))))
        end
    end.
```

There are some obvious similarities between the Lucid program and the PASCAL 'version' just given. Both languages use variables (i.e., 'identifiers' like **approx**) and allow expressions [such as $(x - mean)/n$] to be built up with arithmetic and other operations—much as in conventional mathematics. In both languages variables are thought of as taking on a whole series of data items as their values, and not just one single data item as in ordinary algebra. Also, both languages allow the programmer to define something like the functions of ordinary mathematics, using 'dummy arguments' in much the same way as they are used in ordinary mathematics. In short, both languages are notationally much like ordinary mathematics but with an extra 'dynamic' aspect. This dynamic aspect reflects the fact that programs are intended to bring about computation, and computation is an inherently dynamic activity. Both use at least the notation of mathematics to specify a dynamic process.

The two languages are, however, very different. They appear more similar than they really are because PASCAL and Lucid use similar mathematical symbolism, but these symbols are used in very different ways. The statements in an imperative language like PASCAL are commands, not definitions. The most basic command of all is the assignment statement, and all imperative languages are based on some form of assignment. Assignment statements such as FORTRAN's $x = b + c$ or PASCAL's $x := b + c$ superficially resemble definitions (in the form of equations) as found in mathematics, but in fact they are very different. In PASCAL an identifier denotes a *storage location*. These storage locations can be thought of as 'buckets' capable of holding one data item at a time. In general a storage location will contain different items at different times during the computation. Any given item, however, will remain in the location until the computer (under the control of the program) removes the old value and replaces it with a new one.

An assignment statement is an order to a machine to perform just such an 'update' on the storage location named on the left hand side of the assignment statement. The machine 'executes' an assignment command by evaluating the expression on the right hand side and placing the result in the named storage location. The name of the location being updated may itself appear on the right hand side, as in the PASCAL assignment **mean := mean + d**. A statement of this form certainly makes sense as a command. This statement orders the machine to increase the value stored in location **mean** by the amount stored in location **d**. Interpreted as a definition, however, the statement is nonsense (unless the value of **d** happens to be 0, in which case it is pointless).

Imperative languages have other kinds of basic commands (such as input/output statements) but no simple command can accomplish much on its own. The imperative languages therefore have in addition a large number of "control structures" for building up complicated commands out of simpler ones. These 'constructs' allow the imperative programmer to specify that a number of simpler commands are to be 'executed' in a particular order; or that one command is to be executed repeatedly until some condition is true; or that one of a number of commands is to be executed with the choice depending on the outcome of a corresponding number of tests. In addition, the imperative programmer is allowed to give names to certain commands so that they can be 'called' by using these names. These "procedures" can be called with parameters, and can also return results (in which case they are called "function procedures" or simply "functions").

In short a PASCAL program specifies, in great detail, exactly *how* the desired values are to be computed—and not just *what* these values must be. Imperative programmers think of the computer as executing the program by jumping around the text of the program, executing and re-executing the program's assignment statements in the order specified by the program's control structure. The programmer in an imperative language is concerned primarily with specifying the *action* which a machine is required to perform, rather than with the *values* (data) which the machine is required to produce.

Lucid programs do have statements which somewhat resemble assignment statements. Some of the 'assignments', such as **x = a + b**, seem conventional enough, but others such as

$$\textbf{i = 1 fby i + 1;} \quad \text{or} \quad \textbf{d = x − next x;}$$

use mysterious 'temporal' operators not found in conventional languages. On the other hand, even the most harmless assignments such as $k = 2 * k + 1$ give totally unexpected results in Lucid. Within a given 'block' only one 'assignment' to any particular variable is allowed, and (strangest of all) the order of the statements within the given block is irrelevant—does not affect the meaning of the program. In Lucid the definition is the only kind of statement; there are no read or write statements, no **goto** statements, no **do**, **while** or **for** statements, no **if** statements—in short, no control statements of any kind. Lucid allows programmers to define their own functions, but there are no calling conventions (or rather, exactly one). Functions are incapable of having side effects. They really are functions, in the mathematical sense of the word. Furthermore, since there are no commands and no side effects, there are no procedures.

Lucid retains some of the dynamic concepts used by the PASCAL programmer (iteration), adds others (filtering), but completely drops the idea of "flow of control". In the PASCAL program above, the successive values of the variable **approx** are generated by the execution of two assignment statements (the second one being executed over and over again). In the Lucid program, however, the entire series of values of the corresponding variable **approx** is specified by the single definition of the variable in question. It makes no sense to say that a machine has reached a certain textual point in the execution of a Lucid program—in fact the word "execution" itself is not really appropriate. A Lucid program is an expression, and its output is its value (as an expression). A machine which is running a Lucid program is therefore *evaluating* it, not executing it.

3. Control Flow versus Dataflow

The differences between the Lucid and PASCAL version are more profound than just the differences between two languages. The designs of the two languages reflect the structure or "architecture" of the machinery which is used to implement the language. The different approaches of Lucid and PASCAL reflect two fundamentally different modes of computation, i.e., two very different ways of computing the results desired.

Programs in an imperative language like PASCAL are intended to be run on what are known as "von Neumann" machines (named after the mathematician John von Neumann). A von Neumann machine consists of a small processor attached to a big memory,

mean	23.07854
a	8.6000
n	7
approx	13.5
d	0.036

CPU

this memory being a vast collection of storage locations. Data items are fetched one by one from the memory, are sent to the central processing unit (CPU) in which the actual computation is performed, and then the results are returned one by one to their 'cells'. The basic philosophy of the von Neumann machine is that data is 'normally' at rest. Often the analogy of a bank security box or even a jail is used. The data items are safely locked up in individual cells and are processed one at a time. The CPU is controlled by a program which is itself usually stored in the memory. A program is a series of "machine instructions" which specify which of a small number of basic operations (such as fetching the contents of a given location, performing a multiplication, storing a result in a given location) the CPU is to perform. The CPU normally executes the instructions in the order they are stored in memory, but some special instructions can alter this order so that (for example) a part of the program is executed repeatedly. The two fundamental concepts of the von Neumann architecture are those of "command" and "storage location"; it is on these same concepts that the design of the imperative languages is based.

One alternative form of computation, which we call "dataflow", is based on the principle of processing the data while it is *in motion,* 'flow-ing' through a dataflow network. A dataflow network is a system of *nodes* and *processing stations* connected by a number of communication chan-nels or *arcs.* The network given for the rms program is very simple; but in general the processing stations may have more than one input and/or output port, they will not be connected sequentially (in a line), and the network may even have loops in it. There are a number of research groups throughout the world working on dataflow machines and architectures. See, for example, Dennis, Misunas and Leung (1977), Davis (1978), Kel-ler, Lindstrom and Patil (1979), Arvind and Kathail (1981) or Watson and Gurd (1982).

Dataflow, even as we have just defined it, is a very vague term and includes endless variations on the general principle of processing data while it is in motion. One particularly simple and important class is what we call *pipeline* dataflow. In a pipeline net the datons flow down the arcs in exactly the order they are produced; there is no 'overtaking', and no labelling of datons with time information. Nodes in a pipeline dataflow net are not required to produce output at the same rate at which it is con-sumed. We will be especially interested in a restricted form of pipeline dataflow which we call "functional" or "pure" pipeline dataflow. In this kind of dataflow the filters in a net are required to be *functional*; a filter is functional if the entire history of its output is determined by the entire history of its input. Functionality implies that (roughly speaking) there is no randomness in the filter and that the rate of arrival of input to the filter affects only the rate of production of the output.

The first clear statement of the 'pipeline dataflow' was given by Con-way (1963) more than twenty years ago. The use of dataflow as a program-ming or program structuring technique has been developed by a number of workers, including McIlroy (1968), Kahn and MacQueen (1977) and Yourdon and Constantine (1979). In 1974 Gilles Kahn made an extremely important discovery [see Kahn (1974)], namely that the behaviour of a pure pipeline functional net is exactly described by the fixed point of a corres-ponding set of equations. [Faustini (1972) established the validity of the "Kahn principle" for a very general operational model.] Kahn's work stimulated a further interest in the theoretical aspect of dataflow, mainly in the problem of extending his approach to handle nets with nonfunc-tional nodes.

The dataflow approach to program construction (McIlroy calls it "plumbing") has proved to be very effective. The great advantage of the dataflow approach is that 'modules' interact in a very simple way, through the pipelines connecting them. The modules are well insulated from each other in the sense that the *internal* operation of one cannot effect that of another. This is not the case in ordinary programming languages like PASCAL; the body of a procedure can contain assignments to parameters and even to globals (variables external to the procedure and not in the parameter list). As a result, the modules (procedures) in an apparently simple PASCAL program (like the RMS example) can pass information to each other in a very complicated manner.

The dataflow approach to programming has already been tested in practice. The "shell" language of the popular UNIX operating system is based on the concepts of "pipeline" and "filter" (the result of McIlroy's influence). A UNIX pipeline is essentially a linear dataflow network (i.e., without loops and without branching). The form of dataflow provided in UNIX is therefore very limited, but nevertheless it is still very powerful. The interface between filters is very 'narrow' (a stream of characters) and so it is easy to combine them without the danger of interference and side effects. Very often a problem can be solved entirely within the shell language itself, without the need to "descend" into a 'high-level' language like C. Yourdon and Constantine have produced a formal dataflow methodology (which they call "transform analysis") and applied it to a number of significant applications. Their method involves two separate stages; in the first (which they call "program analysis") the analyst produces a (pipeline) dataflow net that performs the necessary computations; then in the second stage (which they call "program design") the net is translated into the language at hand, usually COBOL.

Lucid represents an attempt to extend the success of the dataflow methodology by freeing it from its dependence on imperative languages like C or COBOL (or the UNIX shell language itself, which also allows commands). There are already a number of dataflow languages, but most of them (in particular the "single-assignment" languages) are still heavily influenced by the von Neumann view of computation. There are also a number of pure nonprocedural languages (basically variations on LISP) but they are oriented towards the 'recursive function' style of programming, rather than towards dataflow. Lucid is intended to be a clean, nonprocedural language which is nevertheless intended to be used in conjunction with a dataflow approach to programming. Our goal is to simplify as much as possible the "system design" phase; as we have already seen, a Lucid program is basically just a textual form of a dataflow graph.

We certainly admit that most programmers will find Lucid strange and even 'unnatural' in comparison with other 'mainstream' programming languages. The reader may even wonder whether such an unconventional language has any future at all, given the human and material resources invested in the 'conventional' approach. The reader might even question our wisdom in devoting an entire book to such a strange language which until recently did not even have an implementation capable of running other than the simplest examples. There is hardly a community of eager Lucid users anxiously waiting to find out more about the language.

Whatever the current state of affairs we do not, however, admit that Lucid or the definitional approach is *inherently* strange or unsuitable for human/machine communication. In our opinion, programmers find the approach to be strange only because they have very little experience in using it. Is it really so 'natural' to think of a computation as a long, linearly ordered sequence of one-at-a-time changes to the values associated with some collection of variables? Students learning a language like FORTRAN often find it very difficult to grasp the fact that FORTRAN statements are commands. Those with a mathematical background are often totally confused by so called "statements" such as $x = x + 1$ which contradict everything they ever learned about the symbol $=$.

The question that should be asked is not which approach is stranger compared to which, but rather which approach is better. The decimal number system at first seemed very strange by comparison with roman numerals, but was eventually adopted because it made calculation so much easier. The algebraic system of notation itself took many centuries before it gained acceptance. In 1545 Cardano described his algorithm ("rule") for solving the cubic $x^3 + px + q$ as follows [quoted in Smith (1929), p. 206]:

> Cube the third part of the number of "things", to which you add the square of half the number of the equation, and take the root of the whole, that is, the square root, which you will use, in the one case adding half the number which you just multiplied by itself, in the other case subtracting the same half, and you will have a "binomial" and "apotame" respectively; then subtract the cube root of the apotame from the cube root of the binomial, and the remainder from this is the value of the "thing".

Cardano undoubtedly considered his procedural (imperative!) formulation to be very 'natural' and 'conventional'. A modern-day mathematician, however, can express Cardano's solution far more concisely as

$$u^{1/3} - v^{1/3} \quad \text{where} \quad u = d^{1/2} + q/2,$$
$$v = d^{1/2} - q/2,$$
$$d = (p/3)^3 + (q/2)^2,$$

and the reader is spared the details of one particular sequence of calculations which yields the value of the expression.

The imperative, procedural approach to algebra was abandoned hundreds of years ago (even though algebra has always been closely connected with computation, for example, of roots of equations as above). In modern computer programming, however, the imperative view has been the dominant one since the invention (during World War II) of the modern electronic digital computer. All of the most important programming languages are based on the imperative view. There are, of course, a few languages (such as LISP) which use a more or less definitional approach, but they have always remained 'minority interest' languages with limited areas of application. The vast majority of working programmers have practically no opportunity to use, and no experience with, any form of definitional programming.

The imperative approach has certainly proved to be a success, if we take popularity as our measure of success. Almost all programs being written today are imperative. By the same measure, of course, both the roman numeral system and the procedural approach were just as successful in mathematics. During the Renaissance, however, these systems were put to far greater use than ever before. The rapid advance of science required that mathematicians apply the old procedural algebraic notation to far more complex problems. At the same time the great expansion of trade and industry required that computations be performed by large numbers of ordinary people untrained in the intricacies of the 'conventional' number systems. The old notational systems, which had proved adequate for over a thousand years, began to reveal fundamental defects. Eventually, they were replaced by entirely new systems based on radically different principles such as positional notation or referential transparency.

4. The Problems with the Imperative Approach

In recent years the imperative approach to programming languages has shown increasing signs of strain. The conventional 'mainstream' programming languages are now being used for tasks which are far more complicated than ever before, and by far more people than ever before. The first von Neumann machines (those produced in the early 1950s) could perform only a few hundred operations (such as additions) per second. A program was usually the work of a single programmer and was considered big if it was more than a few dozen lines long.

Modern machines can now perform hundreds of thousands of operations per second. Some current software systems involve millions of lines of code, the product of years of labour on the part of hundreds of programmers and systems analysts. The basic principles of the von Neumann languages and machines have remained unchanged since 1952—or at least since the introduction of ALGOL in 1960. It is hardly surprising, then, that by 1985 the descendants of FORTRAN and the EDSAC are showing their age.

The most obvious sign that something is wrong with the von Neumann approach is the explosive and exponential growth in the complexity of these machines and languages—especially the languages. There are now literally hundreds of imperative languages in active use. Of course, it is only to be expected that different applications might require different languages. These languages, however, employ essentially different ideas even when the same domain of application is intended. There is even a large number of supposedly "general purpose" languages— ALGOL, PL/I, ALGOL 68, PASCAL, BASIC. These languages in particular are supposedly intended for roughly the same applications, are supposedly based on the same concepts (variables and the assignment statement), and claim to be "machine independent". Nevertheless each somehow manages to be unique in its own way and incompatible with its colleagues. There is no practical way of translating programs from one of these languages to another.

The mushrooming complexity of the von Neumann approach is reflected in the state of the individual languages themselves. The more ambitious of the general purpose languages (especially PL/I) have assumed colossal proportions. A language like PL/I offers thousands of features, options and defaults all subject to thousands of restrictions and constraints. It is almost inconceivable that any one person could know all or most of PL/I; its 'manual' is a set of volumes each the size of a telephone book.

A number of language designers have rejected the linguistic 'overkill' approach and produced modest languages such as PASCAL. These languages have on the whole been more successful, but in the end always prove to be deficient in some vital respect. The process of simplification always seems to go one step too far. There is always some useful, perfectly natural, and apparently harmless statements or programs that the user is strictly forbidden to write. In PASCAL, for example, you can write a program to sort an array of 100 numbers, and you can write a program to sort a array of 200 numbers, but you cannot write a single program that will sort an array of arbitrary length.

Of course, it always seems that these restrictions can easily be lifted. A little loosening of the type system, a simple extension of the concept of array, extra features for multiprogramming ... and very quickly the language is no longer simple. The general trend seems to be that a language which is simple but too restrictive to be useful gets extended until it becomes a bloated monster too cumbersome to be useful. ALGOL swelled up to become ALGOL 68, FORTRAN was inflated to PL/I (and again FORTRAN 77), and now PASCAL has spawned ADA. The golden mean between restrictiveness and generality seems impossible to obtain. The language designers may have had their successes, but after a quarter of a century FORTRAN and COBOL are still by far the most widely used languages.

A second, related problem with the von Neumann languages is their lack of precise specifications. The manuals usually give the syntax (what programs are allowed) unambiguously and in great detail but give only an approximate and informal treatment of semantics (what the programs do). The supposedly exhaustive telephone book manuals describe what happens only in the most common cases, and then only in very informal language. Any really complicated question (especially one involving the interaction of different features) must be referred to the local compiler— or to a local 'guru' who knows the compiler well. Programmers often write short 'experimental' programs to discover how the language works. The situation was well described by Dijkstra (1976, p. 202):

> Since then we have witnessed the proliferation of baroque, ill-defined and, therefore, unstable software systems. Instead of working with a formal tool, which their task requires, many programmers now live in a limbo of folklore, in a vague and slippery world, in which they are never quite sure what the system will do with their programs. Under such regretful circumstances the whole notion of a correct program— let alone a program which has been proved to be correct—becomes void. What the proliferation of such systems has done to the morale of the computing community is more than I can describe.

The third symptom of the von Neumann disease is an inevitable consequence of the first two: unreliability. The programs do not work! It is almost impossible to write an imperative program longer than a dozen lines or so without introducing some kind of error. These "bugs" prove to be extremely hard to locate, and programmers can easily end up spending far more time in "debugging" a program than they spent in designing and coding it. Error-free software is, as a result, enormously expensive to produce. In a large system it is practically impossible to remove all the bugs. Some of the subtler errors can remain dormant for years (say, in a seldom used part of the program) and then suddenly 'come to life' with catastrophic results. Of course human beings will always make mistakes, no matter what language is used. But the features that have been found by experience to be most error prone (**goto** statements, side effects, aliasing) are suggested naturally by the imperative approach and are difficult to do without.

Finally, we should mention a fourth weakness of von Neumann systems, one which has only recently become apparent but which may prove to be the most serious of all: they are inefficient. Experienced programmers may find this statement hard to believe. They will admit that the languages are complicated, poorly specified, and even error prone; but inefficient? If nothing else they let the programmer get close to the machine and so supposedly allow the programmer to make the best use of the hardware. In fact this need to stay close to the machine is responsible for all the problems with von Neumann languages. Simplicity, reliability, user-friendliness and so on all suffer in the name of efficiency. If von Neumann systems are not efficient, what are they?

The criticism of inefficiency, however, is directed more towards the machines than at the languages. A von Neumann machine is capable of performing only one operation at a time; if the logic of a given problem allows thousands of results to be calculated in parallel, the von Neumann machine will perform the calculation at a rate thousands of times slower than that which is possible in principle. The imperative languages may be well suited for getting the most out of a von Neumann machine, but they necessarily reflect the sequential nature of these machines.

Christopher Strachey pointed out a simple but striking example of this kind of efficiency: matrix multiplication. As he pointed out in the discussion, which appears after Landin (1966, p. 166),

> One inconvenient thing about a purely imperative language is that you have to specify far too much sequencing. If you wish to do a matrix multiplication, you have to do n cubed multiplications [by the obvious method; the matrices being dimension n by n]. If you write an ordinary [i.e., imperative] program to do this, you have to specify the exact sequence in which they are all to be done. Actually, it doesn't matter in what order you do the multiplications as long as you add them together in the right groups.

This drawback did not seem too important in the days when processors were expensive pieces of hardware and represented a major portion of the cost of the machine. But now, large-scale integration has made processors relatively cheap. There is no technical or economic reason why we cannot build machines with thousands of processing units. The problem is, how to organise the activity of these processors so that they can cooperate on the same task.

To be fair, our criticism of the von Neumann machine is really a criticism of a particular view of systems architecture, that a computer system is centred around a single monstrous von Neumann machine. In fact, von Neumann machines may prove to be useful components of systems for a long time time to come. One can, for example, connect a large number of modest-sized von Neumann machines in a network in such a way that they can cooperate on the same program. This is certainly one way of avoiding the von Neumann bottleneck. Of course, many researchers are working on entirely new machine architectures (such as dataflow or reduction machines) which process data in very different ways. At any rate, when we criticise "von Neumann languages" what we are criticising are the conventional sequential/imperative languages based on a view of computation as taking place on a single von Neumann machine.

Of course in principle there is no reason why an imperative language like FORTRAN could not be implemented on some sort of parallel or distributed architecture. There would be no point in doing so, however, if the implementation merely simulated the steps of a single, conventional sequential machine. Most of the computing power of the 'parallel' machine would lay idle. A really worthwhile (say) dataflow implementation of FORTRAN would require a stage of sophisticated program analysis to detect hidden parallelism. But then we would find ourselves in an absurd situation in which the programmer and the implementation work at cross purposes. The language forces the programer to code up his algorithm in a rigourously sequential form; then the implementation has to 'crack' this code and recover the original parallel algorithm! Naturally many have tried to solve this last problem by adding features for 'parallelism' to the imperative languages. The resulting creations, however, are even more complicated, and the interplay of the new features with the other aspects of the language only aggravates the problems discussed earlier.

Reynolds (1970) once said that the challenge facing language designers is that of producing a language which is simple, general and efficient (i.e., in which it is fairly easy to write efficient programs) all at the same time. The designers of the conventional, imperative school have so far failed to meet this challenge. PL/I, for example, is general and efficient but not simple. PASCAL is simple and efficient but fails to be general enough in certain crucial aspects. APL is simple and general but not efficient. Finally, ADA is not simple, and it remains to be seen whether it will be either general or efficient.

5. Some Suggested Solutions

Even the most enthusiastic supporter of imperative languages will admit that something is very wrong. There are, however, a number of different attitudes regarding the "software crisis" and the "parallelism problem". Here are some of the more common points of view (slightly parodied).

First there is what we might call the Clint Eastwood outlook. According to this "rugged Western" point of view, programming is a demanding and difficult activity, and always will be, but still "a programmer's gotta do what a programmer's gotta do". According to the 'Cowboys' the actual problem is a shortage of *real* programmers who are clever enough and tough enough to get the job done. The Cowboys learned programming the hard way, through long hours 'in the saddle' (i.e., at the terminal) and expect everyone else to do the same. If you make mistakes, it is 'yer own darned fault'. Cowboys generally distrust 'book larnin' (theory) and 'new-fangled' languages. They sneer at 'greenhorns' who complain that PL/I is too big or that C is too low level. To them, PL/I does not have enough features and C is not dirty enough. What they want is even more powerful tools which allow them to get even closer to the computer and make it 'dance'.

The Cowboys certainly deserve our admiration. The best of them (the real Straight Shooters) can produce impressive software that ordinary programmers are too 'chicken' even to try. Nevertheless, we have to ask ourselves whether or not there are enough really tough Wranglers to go around. There almost certainly are not, and we have to resign ourselves to the fact that most software will be written by ordinary, humble Trail Hands—not by the Wyatt Earps of the terminal.

Next we have what we call the "Mr. Wizard" school of thought. The Wizards are in many ways the opposite of the Cowboys, but they agree on one thing: programming and programming languages are inherently very complex. The problem, as the Wizards see it, is that we lack a good theoretical/mathematical understanding of these languages. The Wizards have searched through many a dusty tome of ancient lore. The have learned the Arts Magical, the Logyck Symbolyck and the Calculus of Lambda. They have conjured up the mighty names of Tarski, Church and Curry.

The ultimate dream of the Wizards is a system for formal program verification. This would allow programmers (assisted by Wizards) to produce airtight proofs that given programs are correct—no matter how appallingly bad the language or program might be. Program verification is therefore a kind of philosopher's stone which will turn base programs into gold. As John McCarthy (1965, p. 219) said,

> The prize to be won if we can develop a reasonable mathematical theory of computation is the elimination of debugging. Instead, a programmer will present a computer-checked proof that the program has the desired properties.

The problem, of course, is that no amount of Wizards' wand waving changes the basic nature of the von Neumann languages. The Wizards did succeed in producing formal specifications—but these specifications also took on telephone book proportions, full of incomprehensible lambda calculus expressions. Similarly, proving the correctness of 'real' programs has also turned out to be impractical. The Wizards ran into trouble with the 'dirty' features (side effects, **goto** statements, aliasing) mentioned. Of course, these are exactly the features the Cowboys love the most.

There is a third group, however, which views the antics of the Cowboys and Wizards with self-righteous disdain. The members of this group are wild-eyed fanatics, the Preachers of the gospel of structured programming.

The Preachers subscribe to a computer science version of the doctrine of Original Sin. They believe that human beings are born with an inherent tendency to be careless and make mistakes (the sin of Sloth), and to undertake tasks that are beyond the meager powers of their mortal minds (the sin of Pride). The wages of sin are, of course, bugs. If bugs (and software problems in general) are to be avoided, programmers must abandon their evil ways and adopt the way of the righteous. Programmers are exhorted to adopt some rigourous discipline (methodology) of programming whose rituals will prevent the software from being possessed by evil spirits.

The disciples of structured programming have indeed achieved important successes in the fight against bad software. Nevertheless the evil that lurks within the hearts of men and women has proved harder to vanquish than was expected. Abstention plays an important role in the Preachers' teachings—abstention from features like **goto** statements and pointer variables, those forbidden apples that tempt programmers into wickedness. Programmers, however, have great difficulty in avoiding these forbidden fruits, as we have already noticed. The Preachers dream of a pure and holy language from which all wicked features shall be banished. In practice, though, the designers of these 'structured programming' languages are always in the end forced to compromise their principles in the name of efficiency. The faithful are therefore faced with a terrible but unavoidable dilemma: they can choose to be virtuous and write programs that are correct but inefficient, or they can choose to be wicked and produce programs that are efficient but bug ridden. "Why," the Preachers must ask themselves, "does the Devil have all the fast programs?"

There is, however, a fourth and more optimistic point of view which shares the Preacher's low opinion of unaided human capabilities but which offers a more down-to-earth solution. We are referring to the "we have the technology" school of thought.

The Boffins agree that human weakness is the root cause of the software crisis, and that therefore mere humans cannot produce software naked and unarmed. The armament the Boffins offer, however, is physical and mechanical, not moral and spiritual. Their goal is to supply the programmer with a complete selection of powerful programming tools: structured editors, diagnostic compilers, clever type checkers, and sophisticated debugging systems. Their aim is to produce a kind of Bionic Programmer, a technologically enhanced Superhero who can battle the bugs on equal terms.

There is no denying, of course, that the ingenious devices found on the 'programmer's workbench' can be extremely useful. The problem is that they can amplify programmers' weaknesses as well as their strengths. The gadgets in the Million Dollar Programmer's utility belt can just as easily allow their user to produce colossal bug infested programs and then allow him to waste stupendous quantities of resources in debugging. Could the superprograms produced by the new generation of Superprogrammers breed a new race of terrifying superbugs? Will programmers need even more powerful tools as a result? Will these tools generate even more terrifying bugs? There could be no end to the process!

The ambitions of what we call the "DIY" or "Mr. Fixit" school are by contrast far more modest. According to this point of view, the software crisis is the result of serious flaws in the imperative languages. These flaws are not, however, the result of weaknesses inherent in the whole von Neumann approach; but rather the product of design error. All that is needed is a little tinkering, a few new parts here and there, the removal of a few troublesome features, and all will be well.

Now it is certainly true that the imperative languages can be improved, and often fairly simple changes can bring great benefits. The problem is that one change leads to another—and an improvement in one area can have disastrous consequences in another. We have already seen that tinkering with ALGOL and FORTRAN has not always been successful. This is especially true when an attempt is made to bolt on features for 'concurrency' or even 'dataflow'.

6. Honest, Folks, We Was Just Funnin'

It seems that in the last few pages we have mortally offended almost every computer scientist working in programming languages. At this very moment a lynch mob of enraged Cowboys, Wizards, Preachers, Boffins and Handymen is gathering outside. They have momentarily forgotten their own (often bitter) disputes and are united in their determination to drag us down the street to the old hangin' tree.

The reader probably does not have very much sympathy for us. After all, have we not just finished dismissing as futile almost every attempt to solve the software crisis? And have we not added insult to injury by portraying honest researchers as half-crazy comic book characters?

In actual fact our satire is directed at only a small minority of the people who might seem to be the target. For example, most people who work on program verification or semantics are fairly sensible. They think their work is important (which it is) but are under no illusions that (say) new semantic descriptions of existing languages are going to solve the software crisis. They do not really deserve to be called Wizards.

In the same way, most programmers/software engineers are well aware that programs will be constructed by people who for the most part are mere mortals. They know that expert, close-to-the-machine programming is not the universal remedy for software development problems—quite the opposite. Even clever people know that too much cleverness can kill. These people are not true Cowboys.

Similarly, most supposed "Boffins" know that a good environment is no remedy for a bad language; and most alleged "Preachers" know that a good methodology can not overcome a really bad system.

Our criticism is directed instead against the small minority who are convinced that the particular problems they deal with lie at the root of the software crisis. The true Wizards, for example, are convinced that the lack of formal tools is at the source of all the problems with imperative languages. In the same way, the real Boffins are convinced that the real problem is the lack of a proper programming environment.

They are all convinced that they have the solution, but they are all wrong. They are wrong because they do not place the blame where it belongs, on the basic design of the machinery being used. Instead, they think that the problem is with the *way* in which the machines are used. They do not see the problem as being a technological one. The various approaches are very different and even to some extent incompatible, but they have this in common: they are proposing *soft* solutions (i.e., software, mathematics, methodologies) to a *hard* problem.

One group of researchers is conspicuously absent from our blacklist. We have had nothing bad to say about people designing new kinds of machines. We could, of course, have lampooned them as the Repairmen—fanatics who think they can solve the software crisis with a soldering iron. After all, they can be just as convinced as any Cowboy or Preacher that their work is the key to the future!

The difference, though, is that they are right. The problem at the root of the whole software crisis *really is* the problem of machine architecture. We do not mean to say that each individual new architecture proposed is bound to work. On the whole, however, the hardware researchers are following the only path that will lead to a solution. Computer scientists in the 'soft' half of the subject (semanticists, methodologists, language designers) have a choice to make.

On the one hand, they can devote their skills and energies to trying to make the old sequential/imperative approach last a little longer. Those that make this choice are the Cowboys, Wizards, Preachers, Boffins and Handymen.

The other choice is to try to help the search for new machines and forms of computation. This choice means devoting the skills and energies to discovering the new kinds of semantics, methodologies, languages and so on that will be appropriate to the new generations of computers. Those that take this path are choosing the future, and their efforts, we claim, will prove to be neither futile nor ridiculous.

There is, of course, a third possibility: to try to ignore the issue and develop semantics, methodologies, verification systems, etc., which are 'independent' of particular forms of computation. This can be done— much work in (say) verification of imperative languages can be easily adapted to nonprocedural languages as well. Nevertheless, researchers cannot avoid the issues forever. Those who imagine that they are taking no stand are often victims of unconscious prejudices (such as the conviction that computation is inherently sequential). Researchers who try to avoid the fundamental controversies in their subject risk seeing their lifetime's work prove in the end to be irrelevant.

7. Nonprocedural Languages

It should be apparent by now that imperative programmers and language designers have a love–hate relationship with the machine. On the one hand, they want to get away from the machine, to be abstract, high level, structured, mathematical, problem oriented. At the same time, they feel an overwhelming urge to get close to it, to control the details of the computation and make the program as efficient as possible. Of course, the features and fixes that allow the programmer to get close to the machine are exactly those which cause all the trouble. These are the features that the Greenhorns come to grief with, that the Wizards have trouble analyzing, that the Preachers denounce as evil and that the Home Handymen are forever repairing.

The difficulties with imperative languages have led many to reconsider the 'love' aspect of the relationship with the machine. They have been tempted to reject the most basic principle of programming languages, namely, that they are somehow inherently dynamic because they are intended to specify computation, a dynamic activity.

The two essentially dynamic features of a language like PASCAL are assignment and control flow; so naturally many began wondering if they should not be eliminated. This radical solution gained credibility after the crudest form of control flow, namely, the **goto** statement, was forced to retire in disgrace.

It has been known for a long time that neither assignment nor control flow are truly necessary, that it is possible to write programs in a purely static, mathematical language. Some fifty years ago, Church showed that any computable numeric function could be expressed in the Lambda Calculus (a very simple formalism for defining functions). Later Kleene showed that the same was true of a simple language whose only 'construct' was recursive function definition. One of the first high-level languages invented was LISP, the 'pure core' of which has neither assignment nor control flow; indeed LISP was based in part on the work of Church and Kleene.

There is general agreement that the nonprocedural languages (i.e., languages without assignment or control flow) are in many respects far superior to the imperative languages. Nonprocedural languages are *referentially transparent*; the value of an expression appearing in a program depends only on the values of the subexpressions, and not on (say) the order in which these subexpressions are evaluated. In particular, functions (or "function procedures") really represent functions in the ordinary sense of the word. The value returned by a function is determined by the value of the arguments and is independent of the 'time' at which the function is 'called'. In other words, mathematical symbols (like $+$) are used exactly as they are in conventional mathematics. The notation used by nonprocedural programmers is that of conventional mathematics, modified for use by programmers.

The Wizards are, of course, delighted with nonprocedural languages, because they can use the techniques of conventional mathematics to reason about programs. There is no need to develop whole new formalisms to make mathematical sense of nonmathematical notation. For example, the law of substitution of equals for equals holds: if the function $f(x, y)$ is defined by the user by the expression $x - 2 * y$, then any expression of the form $f(A, B)$ can be replaced by $A - 2 * B$. The semantics of nonprocedural languages (at least of those considered in this book) are extremely easy to specify. The meaning of an expression is the result of applying the indicated function or operation to the meanings of the subexpressions, and the meaning of a recursive definition is its least fixed point (most general solution).

The Preachers, too, are ecstatic. There are no **goto** statements in a language like ISWIM, and not even any **for** loops. Nor are there any side effects; for example, the expression $f(x) - f(x)$ (involving integers) always has the value 0 (provided the computations terminate). Referential transparency obviously makes the top down approach much easier, and function definitions and **where** clauses are excellent structuring tools.

Nevertheless, nonprocedural languages have always been considered (especially by Cowboys) to be fatally flawed; they are (supposedly) inherently inefficient. The root cause of this (alleged) inefficiency is their lack of iteration. Since nonprocedural languages are purely definitional, the values of variables cannot change, at least within the range of the program where a given definition is in force. As Dijkstra (1965, p. 215) said,

> Despite its elegance a serious objection can be made to such a programming language [without assignment or control flow]. Here the information in the stack can be viewed as objects with nested lifetimes and with a constant value during their entire lifetime. Nowhere ... is the value of an already existing named object replaced by another value. As a result the only way to store a newly formed result is by putting it on the top of the stack; we have no way of expressing that an earlier value now becomes obsolete, and the latter's lifetime will be prolonged, although void of interest. Summing up: it is elegant but inadequate.

Dijkstra's judgement was certainly confirmed by the experience with the older, more conventional nonprocedural languages (primarily LISP). For many applications LISP is extremely well suited, but for others, especially the more prosaic, the LISP solution is unacceptably slow. In fact the developers of LISP quickly added a number of 'impure' features (including PROG for real iteration) which improve the performance but destroy referential transparency.

Recently, however, researchers have discovered a possible solution to the problem of inefficiency. The weakness underlined by Dijkstra is not in *inherent* weakness; it is a weakness of a *particular* method of implementing a *particular kind* of nonprocedural language. There are two assumptions implicit in Dijkstra's criticism. The first assumption is that the program is run on a von Neumann machine, using the conventional ALGOL runtime stack approach. The second assumption is that the basic data objects (the arguments of functions) are finite—collections of 'machine words' which will be piled up on the stack. Now new nonprocedural languages have appeared which allow the arguments of functions to be *infinite* objects (for example, the list of *all* prime numbers). These new languages are still respectable and mathematical—mathematicians have been reasoning about infinite objects for hundreds of years. Nevertheless they allow new styles of programming and new methods of implementation (by reduction machines, lazy evaluation, dataflow) which avoid the difficulties mentioned by Dijkstra, which make use of iteration as well as recursion and which allow many processors to cooperate in the evaluation of a single program. Nonprocedural languages may one day compete with FORTRAN in efficiency as well as elegance.

It may well be possible, then, to program efficiently without iteration—using only recursive definitions instead. This encouraging development has, however, led some to completely renounce iteration altogether. They accept uncritically the dogma that nonprocedural languages cannot have iteration; in fact they extend it to an even more general principle, that nonprocedural programming is inherently independent of *any* operational or dynamic considerations. They consider this lack of 'dynamism' to be a positive virtue. They feel that the dynamic/operational ideas are the source of all problems in programming languages. This mystical, visionary approach to programming represents what we might call the "fool on the hill" point of view: the programmer must not burden his language and his mind with pedestrian details of mere computation; instead he should be up on the hill ("sitting perfectly still") away from the hustle and bustle of mere computation, contemplating static, eternal mathematical objects. Of course programs have to be implemented, even implemented efficiently, but that (according to the "Mystics") is *entirely* the concern of the engineers—of mere tradesmen, so to speak. Programmers, according to this view, need not know anything about how the program is to be run—they should understand it from the mathematical point of view alone.

The Mystics are especially strongly represented in the current "functional programming" community. One particularly extreme sect believes that functions are clean and high level and worthy of the programmer's attention, but that their arguments (humble data objects) are dirty and low level and to be avoided. Mere data objects are, to the adherents of this sect, so unspeakably common that they consider it to be demeaning even to talk of them. Their languages therefore have no names for these objects; variables and expressions can denote only functions. Some dataflow languages are in this category as well. In these languages dataflow is purely an implementation technique, an operational concept which would only offend the refined sensibilities of the nonprocedural programmer.

Adherents to this philosophy often justify themselves on the supposedly obvious grounds that real ('pure') mathematics deals essentially and inherently with *static* objects, and that change and dynamic activity are alien to the mathematical spirit. As Christopher Strachey (1971, p. 77) once said,

> ... the use of imperatives (or commands) in programming introduces variables, and mathematics in general does not recognise the existence of variables in this sense, that is, values varying over a period of time. In its traditional branches mathematics deals only with static situations. Even the calculus, which is concerned with the approaches of objects to a limit, deals with the subject in terms of a series of fixed values.... In programming, on the other hand, we deal with time-varying variables by the very nature of the process; a program is essentially a schedule of changes.

(Strachey was not, incidentally, defending the mystical point of view. Rather, he was exhorting the Wizards to develop the new, dynamic mathematics necessary for the understanding of the assignment statement.)

But is it really true that mathematics is inherently static? Is it really true that mathematicians have never dealt with values which change with time? Nothing could be further from the truth! When calculus was first developed it was on a very operational basis. Newton introduced his fluxions, quantities which *change with time*. Later, of course, the calculus was formalised using the notion of limit (or, more recently, the notion of infinitesimal). Nevertheless the calculus is still in essence the study of changing quantities—in fact, of smoothly changing quantities. The basic principle of mathematics has always been to study the dynamic by means of the static, by continually generalizing the notion of quantity. Long ago the dynamic concept of 'taking away', for example, was formalised by means of the negative numbers, and in the same way 'dividing into parts' was formalised using the rationals. Mathematics has always been to a large extent the study of various forms of change.

Physicists and engineers would have great difficulty accepting Strachey's definition of the calculus as concerned with "the approaches of objects to a limit". People who actually use differential equations normally use very operational concepts—speed, acceleration, density and so on—in their work. It would never occur to them that dynamic thinking might be 'low level' or confusing. Nor do they see any real contradiction between the dynamic and the static point of view. Instead, they see the two approaches as being opposite but *complementary*, and in harmony. If the mathematics is modelling (or specifying) a dynamic situation, why not think dynamically? To do otherwise would certainly be foolish!

The Mystics acknowledge the basic problem (unsuitability of the von Neumann architecture) but want to solve the problem by ignoring it. The Mystics just do not want to know how their programs are run—or at least think that programmers should not know. Because the semantics of their languages can be given without reference to operational ideas, they think they can wash their hands of the whole problem. They say to the engineers, 'Here's the semantics of the language, go and implement it, you can use any method you want, you're not stuck with von Neumann architecture'. The Mystics think that language design can be completely machine independent!

8. Lucid, the Well-Balanced Language

In Lucid we are trying to restore to programming the same harmony between the static and the dynamic which is found in other branches of applied mathematics.

Lucid is in fact a nonprocedural language but it is in no way based on a purely static view of computation. Lucid statements are just equations, but the resemblance between some of these statements and assignment statements is not just superficial and syntactic. The variables in a clause really can be thought of as having values which change with time. The functions defined by a user do in fact denote correspondences between infinite sequences of datums; yet they really can be thought of as filters. The resemblance between a Lucid expression like **sqroot(avg(square(a)))** and the corresponding UNIX pipe

$$\textbf{square} < \textbf{a} \mid \textbf{avg} \mid \textbf{sqroot}$$

is deeper than the syntax would indicate. Lucid's temporal operators allow programmers to realize iteration and dataflow computation (filtering or 'plumbing') directly and in a natural way.

The Lucid programmer specifies exactly the output (meaning) of the program but only suggests or indicates the computations to be performed. The programmer has the benefits of operational thinking but not the drawback: namely, worries about details such as which particular order to perform operations in, rates of flow of data, capacities of buffers, protocols and so on. The 'implicit' approach gives the implementation more freedom as well. Lucid allows the programmer to avoid specifying unnecessary sequencing; this gives much greater scope for carrying computations out in parallel.

Lucid in particular has one great advantage over other 'dataflow languages': the programmer is not totally restricted to dataflow (and even less to a single dataflow paradigm) and can think in terms of other operational concepts as well. In particular, the programmer can understand some statements as specifying an *iterative* algorithm. By this we mean that the programmer can think of some variables as denoting stored (remembered) values which are repeatedly modified in the course of the computation. For example, the equations

$$\textbf{i} = \textbf{1 fby i} + \textbf{1;}$$
$$\textbf{f} = \textbf{1 fby f} * \textbf{i;}$$

can certainly be understood as specifying a dataflow network; but in this particular case the dataflow view is somewhat unnatural. Equations like the above are much more easily interpreted in terms of an iterative activity that initalises both **i** and **f** to 1, then repeatedly updates these values. On each step of the iteration the new value of **i** is the old value of **i** plus one, and the new value of **f** is the old value of **f** times the old value of **i**.

The objection could be made, of course, that iteration is not dataflow, and so has no place in a dataflow language. We would agree with the premise, but not the conclusion. Why should not a dataflow programmer have access to other 'modes' of computation? Why should everything be reduced to 'pure' dataflow? It is our belief that dataflow works best when supplemented with other forms of computing, such as iteration. This is true on the physical as well as on the conceptual level. We see nothing *inherently* wrong with a dataflow network which has filters with memory which process their input according to some iterative algorithm (the **sqroot** filter in the example program is a case in point). On the other hand, it may in fact be simpler for a machine to do everything through 'pure' dataflow. The important point is that Lucid does not force either the programmer or the implementation to make a choice between dataflow and (say) iteration. In fact, it is quite possible that the programmer's view of the computation (what we might call the 'virtual implementation') can be very different from the actual implementation. The actual implementation might not use any data flow at all. (In fact there exist many useful Lucid programs that cannot be implemented using only iteration and pipeline dataflow.)

Nevertheless, Lucid is still a "dataflow language" because (i) Lucid programs (at least the vast majority) can be written, read and understood using the pipeline dataflow model of computation and (ii) pipeline or other forms of dataflow can be used very effectively to implement these programs. The Lucid approach differs from that of some other dataflow languages (i) in that Lucid is a rigourously nonprocedural (in fact functional) language with a static, denotational semantics; but at the same time (ii) programmers are encouraged to think operationally, in terms of dataflow; yet (iii) the programmer does not need to understand the actual implementation, at least in any detail; and (iv) other forms of operational activity (i.e., modes of computation other than pipeline dataflow) are available to programmer and implementer alike.

The Lucid approach offers the possibility of finally achieving both efficiency and efficacy (simplicity and generality). The programmer has some control ("influence" would be a better word) over the way in which the computations are to be performed. The programs need not be inefficient. At the same time, since the operational side is only indicated, not specified, the programmer is spared the chore of planning the entire computation in all its grotesque detail. Programmers therefore have no need of extra 'dirty' features, of all those levers, handles and switches which the imperative programmers need to control their machine. The language can therefore remain relatively simple.

Many people, of course, are skeptical of our approach—they feel that it is too good to be true. We have seen that the root cause of all the trouble with imperative languages is the contradictory attitude to the machine; a desire to get away from it and to get close to it at the same time. Many think that this is a general phenomenon which occurs with all languages and systems—the eternal dilemma facing the programmer and language designer. Some of them (mainly Cowboys) think Lucid will fail because it is too simple and mathematical, because it is not close enough to the machine, does not allow pointer variables, error exits or run time rewiring of the dataflow net. Others (some of the Mystics) also think Lucid is doomed, but for the opposite reason. They think Lucid is dirty because it is based on dataflow, that it is too close to the machine (whether or not the machine in question is a von Neumann machine). They feel that we've betrayed the principles and 'gone Cowboy' by emphasising operational ideas. It has even been said that Lucid is not "functional"—in spite of the fact that Lucid statements are genuine equations, and in spite of the fact that Lucid function variables denote genuine functions.

Needless to say, we do not share these opinions. It is certainly true that imperative languages find it impossible to be high level and efficient at the same time. We do not agree, however, that this dilemma is just another example of the supposedly eternal, tragic but unavoidable disparity between nice clean idealistic theory and hard, dreary dirty practice. We feel there is a simpler explanation.

In many writings on programming it is made to seem that the job of a programmer is to make some given machine do something; the language is the way which the human communicates to the machine the activities which are to be performed. This picture is very misleading. Machines are not just *given*; nor do they exist to please the programmers. Languages are not the tools by which programmers communicate arbitrary desires to computers. Machines exist to *solve problems*; to simulate an airplane in flight, to control a refinery, to compute the gas bill. The role of programmers in this context is to communicate the problem to the machine—the programming language is their tool. The reason that the programmer wants to get *away* from the machine is to get *closer* to the problem. The difficulty with von Neumann machines is that they are *too far* from the problems. They are just not suitable for the work which they have to perform.

Many applications quite naturally suggest computations with a large degree of parallelism (most kinds of numerical analysis) and/or data flowing through a network (most forms of accounting). The von Neumann machine (or rather, a system consisting of one such machine) is suited for neither form of computation, and it is the poor programmer with his overburdened language who has to fill the gap. It is not enough for the programmer to merely indicate how the computation is to be performed, and then leave the details for some optimising implementation. The distance is too great between the kind of computation required and the kind of computation being offered. The programmers must take charge of the details of the computation themselves and apply their human intelligence to this task. The language designers must therefore provide *both* problems oriented and machine-oriented features. Since the problems and the machines are so ill-matched, it is not surprising that the resulting languages are unhappy compromises. The imperative language designers are trying to do the impossible—to solve a hardware problem through software. The software crisis is really a hardware crisis!

New languages cannot resolve the crisis unless they are accompanied by new machines as well. If we had a genuine dataflow machine available, the gap between the machine and many applications would be drastically narrowed. For those applications a language based on dataflow can therefore be close to the problem without being so far from the machine that the latter is used inefficiently. The programmer could be relieved of the burden of *specifying* the computation and only have to indicate it instead. That makes it possible for the language to be nonprocedural and not have extra, dirty features.

Our view, therefore, is that new languages and new machinery must be developed together. This is the view taken by the famous Japanese "fifth generation" project. In the words of Shunichi Uchida (1982, p. 1),

> The computer systems of today, however, are still based on the von Neumann model of computation, although all kinds of improvements have been made since the first generation. Essentially, all that has happened is that software systems have been extended to cope with new and sophisticated applications. The software systems used in current computers have become too large and complicated to maintain good productivity, reliability, and maintainability. And hardware systems based on conventional architectures are also approaching their limits in terms of improvements in computing power and memory space to support these complicated software systems.

The Japanese project is based in large part on the language PROLOG and the idea of computation as logical deduction. Programmers using PROLOG do not have to supply an exact recipe for producing the data desired. Instead, they present a collection of logical assertions about the required data. The PROLOG implementation automatically searches for the data which satisfies the requirements. The searching really amounts to investigating the logical consequences of the assertions given by the programmer. For example, a PROLOG programmer might type

path(Coventry, Reading, X)

(here **X** is a variable) and the PROLOG implementation might eventually answer

X = [Coventry, Birmingham, Oxford, Reading].

From this answer the programmer can conclude that

path(Coventry, Reading, [Coventry, Birmingham, Oxford, Reading])

is a logical consequence of the other statements in the program. These statements (not shown here) might axiomatise the notion of a path from one town to another in (say) the railway network. The programmer is not required to give an explicit path-finding algorithm. Instead, the implementation finds a path by searching for something that the program implies is a path. With PROLOG, computation is a form of controlled deduction.

PROLOG is a good example of a well-balanced language. A PROLOG program (at least a program in 'pure' PROLOG) can be understood statically, as a collection of assertions in first-order logic. At the same time programmers can understand the statements as rewrite rules to be used by (say) a depth-first searching algorithm. The two views are basically complementary. A PROLOG programmer needs to understand something of the search strategy in order to make the programs reasonably efficient, but he does not have to know all the details of every aspect of the behaviour. If he is concerned only with the correctness of his program, then the static statements-as-assertions semantics is enough.

The Japanese research group has undoubtedly made a wise decision in studying PROLOG. PROLOG is well suited to some of the Artificial Intelligence applications the Japanese group has in mind. However, we strongly doubt that PROLOG is destined to be the *only* fifth generation programming language. Certainly, the importance of intelligent knowledge-based systems (IKBS) and AI applications will increase in the years to come. Certainly, PROLOG and similar languages will be used more and more. Nevertheless, there will always be a great deal of more straightforward, 'bread-and-butter' computation to be performed (such as accounting and numerical analysis). PROLOG is not at all well suited for this kind of problem. For example, PROLOG programmers are not allowed to define their own functions, and even the arithmetic operations are not really respectable. The AI and IKBS applications themselves will involve a lot of well determined, cut and dried computation, in addition to PROLOG-style searching and backtracking. It remains to be seen how much PROLOG can do on its own, without the assistance of other languages and forms of computation. The Japanese group is certainly aware of the limitations of inference computation and is investigating dataflow architectures and languages (Lucid included) as well. It may be that in the future 'inference' programming languages (such as PROLOG) and dataflow languages (such as Lucid) will be used in cooperation. PROLOG could be used to interface with the end user (it is very simple) and to program the more 'exotic' applications. Lucid, on the other hand, would be used to program a dataflow machine to carry out the more conventional, behind-the-scenes computations.

Of course, PROLOG and Lucid can both be implemented on von Neumann machines. (PROLOG is easier to implement this way than Lucid.) With a little work a tolerably efficient optimising compiler could be produced which would accept a reasonable subset of Lucid. For many applications the degree of efficiency would be adequate or at least the inefficiency would be compensated for by the advantages of using a clean nonprocedural language. For other applications, however, such as systems programming, it is fair to say that no nonprocedural language could ever compete with C—they are simply not close enough to the (von Neumann) machine. By the same token, no imperative language (even run on a dataflow machine) should be able to compete with a dataflow language run on a dataflow machine.

The fools on the hill have only gone half the way; they have rejected one, unsuitable, form of computation without wholeheartedly adopting any other. They have left what they see as the filth and corruption of the decadent von Neumann approach in the valley below but have yet to cross the mountains. They have yet to commit themselves to the prophets of a new millenium of computing. They remain waiting on the mountain, not yet ready to descend into the land of milk and honey on the other side.

9. Lucid—The Dataflow Programming Language?

The title of this book was deliberately made ambiguous. The phrase "Lucid, the dataflow programming language" could mean "Lucid, which is a dataflow programming language (like many others)". But it could also mean "Lucid, the one and only dataflow programming language". We have left the title in its ambiguous form because we feel that, in a sense, both readings are appropriate.

The reader should by now understand the grounds on which Lucid itself can be considered a dataflow (programming) language. What is not clear are the grounds on which it could be considered *the* dataflow language.

There are in fact quite a number of dataflow languages already in existence. If by the term "dataflow language" we mean a language in which a programmer can write programs which specify dataflow computations, it is possible to classify these languages as follows.

(i) *Conventional Imperative Languages, such as FORTRAN.* It is in fact possible to compile imperative programs to 'run' on a dataflow machine. The most simple-minded compilation algorithms take no advantage of the parallelism offered by the dataflow architecture. More sophisticated techniques involve analysing the program to detect hidden parallelism (hidden, that is, by the sequential nature of the language) but it remains to be seen how successful this technique can be. It is certainly worth trying, considering the huge amount of effort that has been invested in writing imperative programs. But the long-term prospect must be that FORTRAN and company will be gradually phased out, to be replaced by proper dataflow languages.

(ii) *Enhanced Imperative Languages, Such as ADA.* It is possible to add features to conventional imperative languages which allow the programmer to set two or more computations operating at the same time. These new features are based on various operational ideas, for example, on communicating processes (CSP), on coroutines (Kahn–McQueen) or on the idea of filters and pipelines (UNIX). Certainly, these languages could take advantage of a dataflow architecture. Many of them are very close in spirit to Lucid, in that the programmer is intended and encouraged to think operationally in terms of dataflow. Unfortunately, the enhanced languages tend to be even more complicated than ordinary imperative languages, which are already bad enough. Also, the new features are sometimes based on the concept of a common central store, something which is completely alien to the dataflow approach to computing. Even those based more directly on dataflow can still be strange, complex and hard to use. We cannot believe that these 'enriched' languages represent the wave of the future. Instead of adding features for forcing parallelism, we should be removing features (like the assignment statement) which force (or at least encourage) the programmer to specify unnecessary sequentiality.

(iii) *Restricted Imperative Languages, for Example, Single-Assignment Languages Such as ID.* It has been known for a long time that certain restrictions on the use of the assignment statement can make it much easier for an implementation to find and exploit parallelism in a program. Even with the restrictions it is not too hard to write programs— single-assignment programming is like very rigorous structured programming. The single-assignment languages were the first really successful dataflow languages, if by successful we mean that (a) it is possible to write significant programs correctly without undue effort and (b) the programs can take good advantage of a dataflow architecture without a great deal of sophisticated preprocessing and program analysis. Nevertheless, it is hard to believe that the single-assignment languages are the wave of the future. The assignment statement is a hangover from the von Neumann approach to computation. Why restrict it? Why not eliminate it completely?

(iv)   *General Purpose Functional Programming Languages, Such As SASL, FGL or Lispkit.*   These languages, from which assignment has been banned, are modernised and sanitised versions of LISP. The list is normally the main kind of data structure. These languages can also be successfully used as dataflow languages, especially if infinite lists are allowed. If these infinite lists are used to represent histories (as they often tend to be), then programming in these languages can be very much like programming in Lucid. The problem with these languages is that (as we see it) they are still too general. Lists do not have to be used as histories, they can form much more complicated structures. The elements of lists can be arbitrary objects, and functions can be applied to (and yield) arbitrary objects. It is our belief that the programmer pays a heavy price for this generality. A general LISP-like language is much harder to implement, and certain techniques (such as tagged-demand interpretation) are not applicable. The generality affects the programmer as well as the implementer. A Lucid programmer can think of **x** and **y** as values varying with time, and write their (varying) sum as **x** + **y**. A LISP-ish programmer, however, is forcibly reminded that **x** and **y** really denote infinite objects and must write something like

```
componentsum(x, y)
  where
  componentsum(x, y) =
      cons(car(x) + car(y),componentsum(cdr(x), cdr(y)))
  end
```

Of course, we could (a) impose restrictions on the kinds of programs written; and (b) preprocess the program or extend the meanings of symbols like + to include componentwise summation of lists. This would take us to the final category in our list.

(v)   *Special Purpose Dataflow Functional Languages, Namely, Lucid.*   Lucid can therefore be seen as an attempt to anticipate the evolution of dataflow languages from the conventional languages, through the single-assignment and LISP-like functional languages. We feel it has some claim to be *the* dataflow language because in terms of this evolution it is the most advanced. We certainly do not claim that it is the only dataflow language. Nor would we wish to characterise other dataflow languages as necessarily being "failures". We do feel, however, that Lucid is the one dataflow language that has most thoroughly rejected the old von Neumann form of computation, and embraced dataflow in its place. Lucid is *the* dataflow language of the future.

II ISWIM AND ALGEBRAS

Lucid is a definitional language; the statements in a Lucid program are equations defining streams and filters, not commands for updating storage locations. Lucid is unusual in this sense, but not unique. The first definitional language, namely McCarthy's LISP, was designed more than some twenty-five years ago, in 1960.

A LISP program (or at least a program in LISP's 'pure' subset) is simply a set of definitions of side-effect-free functions, together with an expression (using some of these functions) whose value is required. The pure 'core' language contains no imperative features, and the semantics is therefore referentially transparent (in that the value of an expression depends only on the value of its subexpressions). Unfortunately, programs written in the pure subset were sometimes very cumbersome to write and unacceptably inefficient to run. Later versions of the language had extra imperative features (such as the PROG construct and the operations REPLACA and REPLACD) added to improve efficiency. Side effects became possible, and were immediately ruthlessly exploited. Referential transparency was therefore lost, and with it much of the mathematical elegance of the language. The considerable savings in time and space made possible by these 'dirty' features helped give rise to the belief that purely applicative, functional languages are intrinsically inefficient and that imperative features are essential to any language, and are even inherently natural.

After this brief glimmer of hope (for a purely functional language) was extinguished, several years elapsed before another definitional language appeared. This next language, Landin's ISWIM, was introduced in his famous 'The Next 700 Programming Languages' (Landin, 1966). Landin's aim was to show that purely functional languages need not be notationally cumbersome. The problem with LISP was that expressions often became very large, deeply nested and therefore (especially given LISP's use of parentheses) extremely difficult to read. Landin solved this problem by inventing the "**where** clause". A **where** clause is an expression together with a set of 'auxiliary' definitions of variables used in the expression. For example, the ordinary expression

$$((-b + sqrt(b * b - 4 * a * c))/(2 * a)) *$$
$$((-b - sqrt(b * b - 4 * a * c))/(2 * a))$$

can be rewritten using a **where** clause as

> **r1 * r2**
>   **where**
>   **r1** = (−b + sqrt(d))/(2 * a);
>   **r2** = (−b − sqrt(d))/(2 * a);
>   **d** = b * b − 4 * a * c;
>   **end**

Note that **d** occurs in the expressions defining **r1** and **r2**, with its value being given by the third definition in the **where** clause. (Actually, Landin would have used the word **whererec**, for reasons which will be explained later. In fact, all the following 'ISWIM' clauses would, following Landin's conventions, be written with **whererec**.) Landin proposed a number of syntactic variations on the above notation; we could also write

> **let d** = b * b − 4 * a * c **in**
>   **let r1** = (−b + sqrt(d))/(2 * a)
>   **and r2** = (−b − sqrt(d))/(2 * a) **in**
>   **r1 * r2**
>   **end**
> **end**

An ISWIM program is simply an expression, and its output is its value (considered as an expression). (Input will be discussed later.) The official syntax of ISWIM is an abstract one—what is specified is the collection of parse trees and not a collection of strings. The designer of a particular member of the family is allowed some freedom in the concrete (string) syntax. In this book we will use fairly conventional concrete syntax, with familiar operations (such as addition) denoted by familiar symbols (such as +) used as infix operators, and with function application indicated by the usual parentheses and commas notation. Obviously, in designing ISWIM, Landin merely adapted and made precise some common notational conventions of ordinary mathematics.

ISWIM allows functions to be defined by equations, in the obvious way, as in the following clause:

```
dist(P, Q)
  where
  dist(A, B) =
    sqroot(sumsq(xcoord(A) − xcoord(B),ycoord(A) − ycoord(B)));
  sumsq(x, y) = x * x + y * y;
  end
```

A defining expression in a **where** clause can (as above) use other functions or variables defined in the clause. The expression defining a function can even use the same function, so that recursive definitions like that of **fac** in

```
fac(6)
  where
  fac(n) = if n < 2 then 1 else n * fac(n − 1) fi;
  end
```

are possible. Mutually recursive definitions, like those of **pow**, **evenpow** and **oddpow** in

```
pow(B, E)
  where
  evenpow(x, n) = pow(x * x, n/2);
  oddpow(x, m) = x * evenpow(x, m − 1);
  pow(x, n) = if n eq 0 then 1
    elseif odd(n) then oddpow(x, n)
        else evenpow(x, n)
      fi;
  end
```

are also permitted. There is no requirement that a variable or function be defined before it is used. In general, the order of the definitions in a clause is irrelevant; permuting the sequence of definitions has no effect on the meaning of the clause.

The right-hand sides of definitions in a **where** clause can, as in

```
Z * A
  where
  A = 5;
  B = 5;
  C = Z * Z
    where
    A = 3;
    Z = A + B;
    end;
  end
```

themselves involve **where** clauses. In general, the definition which applies to a given occurrence is the one in the innermost enclosing clause. For example, in the definition of **Z** in the above expression, the relevant value of **A** is 3 while that of **B** is 5. The ISWIM programmer can write nested, hierarchically structured programs much as in PASCAL. The scope conventions are, as we shall soon see, exactly those of PASCAL or ALGOL.

Here is an ISWIM program which prints the 100th prime.

```
primeno(100)
  where
  primeno(I) = if I eq 1
        then 2
        else nextprime(primeno(I − 1)) fi;
  nextprime(Q) = if isprime(Q + 1)
        then Q + 1
        else nextprime(Q + 1) fi;
  isprime(P) = nodivsgt(2)
    where
    nodivsgt(k) = k * k > P or
        (P mod k ne 0 and nodivsgt(k + 1));
    end;
  end
```

This program is written in what we might call "integer ISWIM": the individual variables denote integers, and the function variables denote functions over the integers. The arithmetic, relational and logical symbols as +, > and **and**) have the usual meanings, with 0 and 1 playing the role of the truth values *false* and *true*, respectively.

The language described by Landin (1966) is more elaborate and powerful than we have indicated so far. For one thing, he actually had two kinds of **where** clause, a recursive one, indicated by the word **whererec**, and a nonrecursive one, indicated by the word **where**. In the nonrecursive clause, the auxiliary definitions are valid only in the expression at the head of the clause (we call this expression the *subject* of the clause). Landin's ISWIM was also higher order: functions could have other functions as their arguments. Finally, Landin added a 'dirty' imperative feature, the "program point", apparently to make the language more efficient and to make it easier to translate imperative languages into ISWIM.

Our language Lucid is based directly on Landin's, but not exactly on the language as presented in 1966. For one thing, our **where** clauses are all really **whererec** clauses; since the recursive option is the default (in fact, the only) one, there is no need to indicate it explicitly. We therefore use only the word **where**, even though in the original ISWIM this indicated a nonrecursive clause.

Furthermore, Lucid is a first-order language; functions cannot be used as the arguments of other functions (the reasons for this restriction, and the possibilities for its removal, are discussed in a later chapter). The version of ISWIM on which Lucid is based is therefore also first order.

Finally, Lucid is a strictly nonprocedural language with no 'dirty' features; the version of ISWIM on which it is based must therefore not have program points.

To make this distinction clear we will use the name "ISWIM 66" for historical ISWIM, as introduced in 1966, with its nonrecursive clauses, higher-order functions and program points. We will use "ISWIM" to refer to a cleaned-up, modern version (which we describe only informally) in which imperative features are removed and all **where** clauses are recursive. Finally, we will use the (more modest looking) name "Iswim" for the first-order subset of ISWIM on which Lucid is based. We will not use ISWIM 66 at all in this book.

1. Algebras

One of the most commonly asked questions about a programming language is, 'What data types does it have?' In other words, what kinds of data objects do programs in the language manipulate? Typical answers to this question would refer to integers, reals, booleans, strings, records, lists, complex numbers, arrays, tables and so on. However, the answer to the question 'What data types does Iswim have?' is "any".

Although this answer is correct, it does not mean that Iswim is a single, unimaginably huge language in which all conceivable data types are already available. Rather, what we mean is that Iswim is a *family* of languages, each member of which is determined by a choice of underlying data structures. The different members of this family look very similar; they are identical in what we might call, after Wilkes, their "outer syntax". This uniformity is possible because the basic feature of Iswim—the **where** clause—is independent of any considerations of data types and operations. Iswim separates what Landin (1966) calls "a way of expressing things in terms of other things" and "a basic set of given things" Each member of the family is (in Landin's words) "a point in a well-mapped space".

The coordinates of any point in the Iswim space is just the collection of given or primitive things. This set of primitive things consists of a set of data objects, a collection of operations over this set and a collection of symbols denoting objects and operations. In other words, a member of the Iswim family is determined by an *algebra*. Given an algebra A, the member of the family determined by A is *Iswim(A)*.

We can make this slightly more precise as follows. By a *signature* we

mean a collection of individual and operation constants (these are symbols) together with a *rank* or *arity* for each operation constant. Given a
signature *S*, an *S-algebra A* consists of a set of data objects (called the
universe of *A*) together with a collection of elements of the universe and
operations over the universe, one element for each individual constant
and one operation of the appropriate arity for each operation symbol.
Since we will need to solve arbitrary recursive definitions of individuals,
we require also that the universe have the structure of a *domain* (cpo) and
that all the operations provided by the algebra be continuous. In other
words, the coordinate of a member of the Iswim family is a *continuous*
algebra.

To illustrate these ideas we present a very simple algebra *Z* of integers
with arithmetic operations. The individual constants in the signature are **0**
and **1**. The operation symbols and their arities are as follows:

abs	*1*
eq	*2*
ne	*2*
and	*2*
or	*2*
+	*2*
−	*2*
*	*2*
div	*2*
<	*2*
>	*2*
mod	*2*
if−then−else	*3*

The universe of *Z* (which must be a cpo) is the set of all integers
together with the special object ⊥. The object ⊥ lies (in the ordering of the
elements of the universe of *Z*) below all the integers; but the integers
themselves are incomparable in this ordering. The partial ordering therefore looks like

and for obvious reasons ⊥ is sometimes called "bottom".

The operations which Z assigns to these symbols are as follows (in general, k_A is the operation which algebra A assigns to an operation k in its signature):

abs$_Z$ returns the absolute value of its argument if it is an integer, otherwise $\perp$.

not$_Z$ returns 0 if its argument is 1, 1 if its argument is 0, otherwise $\perp$.

eq$_Z$ returns 1 if both arguments are integers and equal, 0 if they are integers and unequal, $\perp$ otherwise.

ne$_Z$ returns 0 if both arguments are integers and equal, 1 if they are integers and unequal, $\perp$ otherwise.

and$_Z$ returns 1 if both its arguments are 1, 0 if the first argument is 0 or if the first argument is 1 and the second argument is 0, and $\perp$ otherwise.

or$_Z$ returns 0 if both its arguments are 0, 1 if the first argument is 1 or if the first argument is 0 and the second argument is 1, and $\perp$ otherwise.

$+_Z$ returns the sum of its arguments if they are both integers, otherwise $\perp$.

$-_Z$ returns the difference of its arguments if they are both integers, otherwise $\perp$.

$*_Z$ returns the product of its arguments if they are both integers, otherwise $\perp$.

div$_Z$ returns the integer quotient of its arguments (the remainder is discarded) if they are both integers and the second is positive; otherwise the result is $\perp$.

$>_Z$ returns 1 if its arguments are integers with the first greater than the second; returns 0 if the arguments are integers with the first less than or equal to the second; returns $\perp$ otherwise.

$<_Z$ returns 1 if its arguments are integers with the first less than the second; returns 0 if the arguments are integers with the first greater than or equal to the second; returns $\perp$ otherwise.

mod$_Z$, given arguments x and y, returns $x - ny$ if x and y are integers and $y > 0$ and n is the greatest integer such that $ny < x$; returns $\perp$ otherwise.

if–then–else$_Z$ returns its second argument if its first argument is 1; its third argument if its first argument is 0; $\perp$ otherwise.

The algebra interprets **and** and **or** as logical conjunction and disjunction, respectively, with the integers 0 and 1 representing truth and falsity, respectively. The value $\perp$ is used as the result of applying operations to unsuitable operands (such as dividing by 0), but apart from that has no apparent use. Its real significance will be explained later.

The language $Iswim(Z)$ is therefore "integer Iswim" (recall that this language was mentioned earlier).

A more interesting example is the 'POP' algebra P, which will be the most important index algebra used in the book. P is based on (some of) the data types and operations provided by the language POP-2 (Burstall, Collins and Popplestone, 1971). The universe of P consists of numbers (including rationals), strings, words (which are like LISP atoms), lists, and two special objects for error and end-of-data situations. The pLucid manual in the appendix describes these objects and operations in detail. It also gives a concrete syntax, which follows that of POP-2 as closely as possibly.

Here is a program in *Iswim(P)* (the member of the Iswim family determined by the 'POP-2' algebra P).

```
perms([a b c d])
   where
      perms(L) = if L eq []
            then [[ ]]
            else allinserts(hd(L), perms(tl(L)))
         fi;
      allinserts(x,J) = if J eq []
            then []
            else inserts(x, hd(J)) ⟨⟩ allinserts(x, tl(J))
         fi;
      inserts(x, M) = if M eq []
            then [%[%x%]%]
            else (x :: M) :: h(hd(M),inserts(x, tl(M)))
               where
                  h(m, K) = if K eq []
                        then []
                        else (m :: hd(K)) :: h(m, tl(K))
                     fi;
            end
         fi;
   end
```

The program outputs a list of all permutations of the list $[a\ b\ c\ d]$. The concrete syntactic conventions are those of pLucid; for example, :: denotes the list constructor operation.

2. The Syntax of Iswim

The language *Iswim(A)*, its (abstract) syntax and semantics, is entirely determined by the algebra A. The Iswim family is simple enough that we can give here, in a few paragraphs, a reasonably precise specification.

Given an algebra A, its signature determines the syntax (class of legal programs) of $Iswim(A)$. An $Iswim(A)$ program is one in which the expressions are built up from nullary variables and from individual constants (nullary operation symbols) in S. Expressions are built up by applying operation symbols in S to the appropriate number of operands, by applying function variables to argument (actual parameter) lists and by forming **where** clauses. The individual and function variables defined in a **where** clause are called the *locals* of the clause. The only syntactical restrictions necessary are to ensure the following:

(i)   that each local of a clause has only one definition in the clause;

(ii)   that each local of a clause is used in the clause with the same arity as its definition; in other words, that the number of "actual parameters" of a function call must be the same as the number of formal parameters of the innermost enclosing definition (in particular, if a local is defined in a clause as an individual variable, it must be used in the clause as an individual variable);

(iii)   that the formal parameters of a definition are distinct from each other and from the function being defined;

(iv)   that the formal parameters of a definition are used as individual variables in the right-hand side of the definition; and

'(v)   that each operation symbol in S is used with the arity prescribed by S.

We make this more precise as follows. Given any signature S, an *S-ranking* is an object which extends S by assigning a rank to all possible variables as well as to the operation symbols in S (variables assigned rank 0 are intended to be used as individual variables). Given a signature S and an *S-ranking* r, an Iswim *r-expression* is one in which the constants and variables are used in a manner consistent with r (inside a **where** clause a variable may be redefined and used with a different arity).

In general a *r-expression* is

(i)   an individual symbol, i.e., a constant or variable to which r assigns the value 0;

(ii)   a function variable or operation constant k together with a sequence $F_0, F_1, ..., F_{n-1}$ of operand or argument r-expressions, n being the arity which r assigns to k; or

(iii)   a **where** clause consisting of a r'-expression (the subject) and a set of r'-definitions (the body), r' being any ranking differing from r at most in the ranks assigned to the variables defined in B. The definitions in B must be compatible; i.e., there cannot be more than one definition of the same variable.

An *r-definition* consists of a variable (which is being defined), a sequence of individual variables (the formal parameters) and a r' expression (the right-hand side), r' being a ranking identical to r except that the r' assigns rank 0 to each of the formal parameters. The formal parameters must be distinct from each other and from the variable being defined. The length of the formal parameter list must be the rank which r assigns to the variable being defined.

An *Iswim(A)-program* is an *r-expression*, where r is the ranking which extends the signature of A by assigning the rank 0 to all variables. Programs are therefore allowed to have free (undefined) variables, but only if these variables are used as individuals (not as functions).

3. The Semantics of Iswim

The semantics of Iswim is even easier to specify than the syntax. We need the notion of an interpretation; interpretations correspond to rankings in the same way that algebras correspond to signatures. Given a signature S, an S-algebra A and an S-ranking r, an A, r-interpretation is a mathematical object which extends A by giving meanings to the individual and function variables as well as to the constants—meanings consistent with the rank information supplied by r. Given I, we can recover r and S; it therefore makes sense to speak of "the signature of I" or "the universe of I".

Given an algebra A with signature S, the value of an *Iswim(A)* *r-expression* E with respect to a *r-interpretation* I is defined as follows:

(i) If E consists of an individual variable or constant c, then the value of E with respect to I is the value which I assigns to c;

(ii) if E consists of an *n*ary operation constant or function variable a together with operand expressions or actual parameters $F_0, F_1, ..., F_{n-1}$, then the value of E with respect to I is $g(v_0, v_1, ..., v_{n-1})$, where g is the operation over the universe of A which I assigns to a, and each v_i is the meaning of F_i with respect to I;

(iii) if E consists of a **where** clause then the value of E with respect to I is the value of the subject of E with respect to the least interpretation I' such that (a) each definition in the body of E is true with respect to I' and (b) I' differs from I at most in the values it assigns to variables having definitions in the body of E.

A definition of an individual variable is true with respect to an environment iff both sides have the same value with respect to the environment; in other words, iff the value the interpretation assigns to the variable is the value of the right-hand side with respect to the interpretation in question. A definition of a function variable is true iff both sides have the same value for all values of the formal parameters; in other words, iff both sides have the same value with respect to any environment differing from the original one at most in the values assigned to the formal parameters of the definition. The ordering on the collection of interpretations is that induced by the ordering on the universe of A, and by the corresponding ordering on the collection of operations of a given arity over universe of A;. An interpretation I' therefore lies below an interpretation I iff each value which I' assigns to a variable lies below the corresponding value assigned by I. The least interpretation in a set of interpretations is the one which lies below all the others.

Now we see why the universe of the algebra Z had the extra object $\perp$. The semantics of Iswim require that the collection of all interpretations be partially ordered, so that there is a *least* solution of the equations in the clause. The ordering on the class of interpretations is induced by that on the operations over the universe of Z, and this ordering in turn is induced by that on the universe of Z (in which $\perp$ is at the bottom). It would not be possible to base Iswim on a conventional notion of algebra (without the partial ordering and $\perp$). The problem is that some equations (like **f(x) = f(x) + 1**) have *no* conventional solution, whereas others (like **f(x) = f(x)**) have more than one. The object $\perp$ is not, however, just a meaningless gimmick added to make a definition work. This object has a very simple operational interpretation: it represents the 'result' of a computation that never terminates. For example, the function defined by

f(x) = if x eq 0 or x eq 1 then 1 else f(x − 1) + f(x − 2) fi;

yields (according to the Iswim semantics) the value 5 (the fourth Fibonacci number) when given the argument 4, but yields $\perp$ when given -1 as its argument. This is in accord with our operational intuitions about recursion (see below). There are many solutions of the definition above, including ones in which the value of **f(− 1)** is 197! Nevertheless, we would be very surprised if an Iswim implementation produced this value—we would want to know where it came from. In a sense, the *least* solution of a definition can be thought of as the one which does not involve any 'arbitrary' values which are not obtainable from the definition by direct computation. Since the equation above specifies no such value for **f(−1)**, $\perp$ is the 'result' returned by the least solution.

An *Iswim*(A) program may, as we saw earlier, have free (undefined) variables. This means that a program may have no meaning on its own— we have to supply values for the free variables. These extra values are the *input* to the program. (Iswim input is therefore 'named' or 'labelled' input.)

More precisely, let A be an algebra and let T be an *Iswim*(A) program with input (free) variables. An *input* to T is a function (necessarily finite) which assigns to each input variable an element of the universe of A. Let r be the ranking which extends the signature of A by giving rank 0 to all variables (thus T is an r-expression). The *output* of T given input i is the value of T with respect to any A, r-interpretation I such that the value I gives to any input variable V is $i(V)$.

4. A Sample Program

To help illustrate how the formal semantics coincides with the informal idea of the body of a **where** clause being 'auxiliary definitions', consider the expression

$$
\begin{aligned}
&\textbf{C + A} * \textbf{Z} \\
&\quad \textbf{where} \\
&\qquad \textbf{A} = 5; \\
&\qquad \textbf{B} = 5; \\
&\qquad \textbf{C} = \textbf{Z} * \textbf{A} + 1 \\
&\qquad \quad \textbf{where} \\
&\qquad \qquad \textbf{A} = 3; \\
&\qquad \qquad \textbf{Z} = \textbf{A} + \textbf{W} * \textbf{B}; \\
&\qquad \quad \textbf{end;} \\
&\quad \textbf{end}
\end{aligned}
$$

given earlier. Le r be a ranking which assigns the rank 0 to all variables, and let I be a Z, r-interpretation which assigns the value 9 to Z, the value 7 to W, and the value 0 to all other variables. Let us use the formal semantics to determine the value of this expression with respect to I.

Clause (iii) of the definition tells us that this value is the value the expression $\textbf{C} + \textbf{A} * \textbf{Z}$ has with respect to the 'least solution' J of the equations in the body. It is not hard to see that J must be an interpretation identical to I, except that it assigns the values 5, 5 and 115 to the variables $\textbf{A}$, $\textbf{B}$ and $\textbf{C}$. (Since $\textbf{A}$, $\textbf{B}$ and $\textbf{C}$ are the only variables defined in the clause, J must agree with I on the value it assigns to all other variables.)

The expression $\textbf{C} + \textbf{A} * \textbf{Z}$ consists of the binary operation constant $+$ and the two operand expressions $\textbf{B}$ and $\textbf{A} * \textbf{Z}$. By clause (ii), then, the value of $\textbf{C} + \textbf{A} * \textbf{Z}$ with respect to J is the result of applying Z's interpretation of $+$ to the values of the two operand expressions (i.e., to their values with respect to J). The value of the first is, by clause (i), the value which J assigns to $\textbf{C}$, namely, 115. The value of the second is easily seen to be 45 (because J assigns the values 5 and 9 to $\textbf{A}$ and $\textbf{Z}$, respectively) and so the final result is 160.

To check that J is a solution to the three equations in the body of the outer **where** clause, we need to verify that in each case the value of the left-hand side with respect to J is the same as the value of the right-hand side with respect to J. For the first two equations this is obvious, but for the third we have to calculate the value of the inner **where** clause with respect to J.

Clause (iii) tells us that this is in turn the value that the subject expression $\mathbf{Z} * \mathbf{A}$ has with respect to the least solution K of the definitions in the body. It is not hard to see that K differs from J only in that it assigns $\mathbf{A}$ and $\mathbf{Z}$ the values 3 and 38, respectively. The value of the subject expression is therefore 115.

This confirms that J is a solution of the equations in the outer clause; because 115 is also the value that J assigns $\mathbf{C}$. Of course this does not prove that J is the least solution; but the definitions are nonrecursive and so have a unique solution.

The expression given above is in fact a program, because the free (undefined) variables are used as individuals. Our calculations therefore show that the output of this program is 160 whenever its input is $\{(\mathbf{Z},9), (\mathbf{W},7)\}$ (that is, whenever the input value of $\mathbf{Z}$ is 9 and the input value of $\mathbf{W}$ is 7).

5. The Operational Semantics of Iswim

The formal semantics of Iswim are simple and precise. This 'least fixed point' specification can be used as a standard against which implementations are judged to be correct and complete. It can also be used to reason *about* the language, for example to prove that certain transformation rules (such as those given in Chapter VI) are correct. The formal definition does not, however, serve as a very good guide for reading and writing programs, and cannot be used directly to implement the language. Fortunately, a large subclass of the Iswim family can be understood and/or implemented using relatively conventional concepts.

The 'conventional' model is based on the idea of interpreting the definitions of individuals as assignment statements and the definitions of function variables as function procedure declarations. This point of view is applicable whenever the universe of the algebra parameter is (like Z) a collection of 'ordinary' finite objects, plus $\perp$.

The definitions in a **where** clause body may appear in any order, and so we cannot expect to be able to execute them like assignment statements and get a sensible result. However, in *Iswim(Z)* and in similar languages, recursive definitions of individual variables are pointless because any variable so defined will (almost always) have the value $\perp$. If we disallow circular definitions, it is then not hard to see that there must be at least one way to reorder the definitions so that any variable appearing on the right-hand side has already been defined by an earlier definition (or else is a global of the clause). For example, in the expression

$$X + Y$$
where
$$C = A + B;$$
$$X = C * C - D;$$
$$D = A - B;$$
$$Y = C + D * D;$$
end

we cannot interpret the body as a series of assignment statements: the second statement cannot be executed because the value of **D** required is that computed by the statement following. But we can reorder the definitions as follows:

$$X + Y$$
where
$$C = A + B;$$
$$D = A - B;$$
$$X = C * C - D$$
$$Y = C + D * D$$
end

Now we can imagine that the evaluation of the clause proceeds as follows: the four definitions are executed in order, then the subject expression is evaluated using the resulting 'stored' values. After the evaluation, the original values of the local variables (**C, D, X** and **Y**) must be restored.

Now suppose that some **where** body has a definition of the form

$$f(X, Y) = P - Y$$
where
$$Q = X + Y;$$
$$R = X - Y;$$
$$P = Q * R;$$
end

and that elsewhere in the body an expression of the form **f(5, A − B)** occurs (in a position where the above definition is relevant). We can then interpret the definition as a procedure declaration, think of the expression **f(5, A − B)** as a call to this procedure, and imagine that such calls are executed much as they are in ALGOL or PASCAL. In other words, we would imagine that the formal parameter **X** is temporarily given the value 5, that **Y** is temporarily given the difference of the values of **A** and **B**, that the procedure body of **f** (the expression on the right-hand side of the definition of **f**) is executed, that the result is returned as the result of the call and that the original values of the formal parameters are then restored.

The 'conventional' model on the whole gives a correct interpretation of the special object ⊥. Consider, for example, the program

f(3) where f(n) = n ∗ f(n − 1); end

If we use our procedural semantics as a guide, we would not expect to get any output at all from this program. The 'call' to **f(3)** would generate a call to **f(2)**, which would generate in turn a call to **f(1)**, then to **f(0)**, **f(−1)**, **f(−2)**, ..., *ad infinitum*. It may seem as if the procedural semantics fails (because it produces no value) but in fact it works perfectly! The formal semantics implies that **f** is the function which always returns ⊥ as its value; thus ⊥ is the output of the whole program. The procedural semantics is therefore correct, provided we interpret ⊥ as meaning 'nontermination' or 'no output.'

This is exactly the true significance of ⊥. The object ⊥ is the 'output' of a program which runs forever and never produces anything. This object is the static, denotational value which corresponds to the dynamic, operational activity 'nontermination.' The various rules for combining ⊥ can all be explained quite naturally in terms of this interpretation. Consider, for example, the fact that the sum of 3 and ⊥ is ⊥. Suppose that a computation involves adding two values, that the (sub) computation for the first value yields 3, but that the computation for the second runs forever without yielding a result. The 'value' of the sum must therefore be ⊥, and this is exactly the (extended) sum of the two values 3 and ⊥.

6. Calling and Binding in Iswim

Care must be taken in applying the procedural interpretation, for otherwise mistakes can be made concerning the scope rules. One must be especially careful about the correct interpretation of function definitions involving global variables.

The right-hand side of a definition of a function variable definition may contain occurrences of variables which are not formal parameters and for which there are no relevant definitions in the right-hand side itself. Variables used in this way, like **B** and **C** in

f(X, Y) = X + B ∗ Y + C;

are called the *globals* (global variables) of the function definition. Whenever a language allows 'procedure bodies' with global definitions, a subtle question arises as to the meaning to be given to a global during the execution of a call that takes place in a context in which the global has a meaning. For example, in

> **f(3, U)**
>   **where**
>   **B = 7;**
>   **C = 5;**
>   **f(X, Y) = X + B ∗ Y + C;**
>   **U = P − Q**
>   **where**
>   **Q = 2;**
>   **B = 3;**
>   **P = f(B, Q);**
>   **end;**
>   **end**

consider the inner 'call' of **f**. What should the result be? What value should **P** have?

If we naively follow the 'sequential' interpretation of Iswim described above, we would simply give **X** and **Y** the values 3 and 2 and evaluate the expression **X + B ∗ Y + C**. What value does **B** have when we start the evaluation? The variable **B** has clearly been assigned the value 3 just before this call was executed. It would be only logical to expect that the value of **B** is still 3, and that the result of the call is therefore 3 + 3 ∗ 2 + 5, i.e., 14. On the other hand, when the call to **f** in the subject is executed, we would expect that the value of **B** would be 7, after the execution of the first statement in the body. A little calculation shows that the final value expected should be 92.

This reasoning is in error. The formal semantics of Iswim implies that the value of the clause is 148. This is exactly the number that results if we assume that **B** has the value 7 (not 3) during the execution of the inner call to **f**.

This example illustrates one of the pitfalls in using a conventional, procedural view of Iswim. The formal semantics of Iswim implies that the language has what is called "static binding"; this means that the global variables take their values from the environment or context in which they are defined, not the environment in which the function is called. Since the function **f** above is defined in a clause in which the global **B** is defined to be 7, this is the value in effect no matter where the function is used. Static binding can be rather hard to understand in terms of the sequential imperative interpretation of Iswim—even though some genuine imperative languages like PASCAL or ALGOL have static binding as well.

On the other hand, if we interpret Iswim in a purely declarative way, and think of definitions as equations which are true (for all values of the formal parameters, if any), then static binding is completely natural. Consider the definitions

$$C = 5$$
$$B = 7;$$
$$f(X, Y) = X + B * Y + C;$$

The first says that the value of **C** *is* 5 and the second says that the value of **B** *is* 7. The third says that the value of **f(X, Y)** *is* the value of **X + B * Y + C**, no matter what values **X** and **Y** might have. However, since we already know that **B** and **C** have values 5 and 7, respectively, we can conclude that the value of **f(X, Y)** is that of **X + 7 * Y + 5**, no matter what the values of **X** and **Y** might be.

The declarative view of Iswim leads to the right answer because it is much closer to the formal semantics of Iswim. Iswim interpretations associate *values* with individual symbols and *functions* with function variables. The assignment/calling model of Iswim is misleading because it associates a 'procedure body' (not just a function) with a function variable. A procedure body is text (an expression) which can have occurrences of global variables; but a real mathematical function is not text (it is instead a correspondence between sets of values) and cannot have 'global variables.'

There is another subtle issue concerning functions for which the imperative interpretation of Iswim can prove somewhat misleading. Consider the program

    f(3, 4)
        where
        f(X, Y) = if X < 1 then 0 else f(X − 1, f(X, Y + 1)) fi;
        end.

What is its output? According to the formal semantics (and the declarative interpretation), the answer should be 0. The variable **f** has been defined as the function of two variables which always returns 0; this function is the only solution of the equation. The imperative interpretation, however, suggests that the call to **f** never terminates and that the output of the program is therefore ⊥. The problem, according to the imperative view, is that the call to **f(3, 4)** generates a call to **f(3, 5)** which generates calls to **f(3, 6)**, **f(3, 7)**, **f(3, 8)** and so on. It is in fact true that this program, when transcribed into PASCAL, will run for ever as it generates deeper and deeper nested calls.

The trouble with the naive imperative approach to function calling is that it assumes that the body of a procedure really needs the values of all the actual parameters before a result can be produced. The naive method simply calculates all these values before executing the procedure body itself. In fact, it would be quite useful to be able to define a function whose result does not necessarily depend on all the values of the parameters—although it may not be possible to say ahead of time exactly which of them will be needed for a particular result. Suppose, for example, that a PAS-CAL programmer was annoyed at the language's lack of an **if–then–else** expression and tried to fill the gap with a **cond** function defined as

```
function cond(P : bool; X, Y : integer) : integer;
   begin
      if P then cond := X else cond := Y
   end;
```

then tried to write an assignment-free version of the factorial function as follows:

```
function fac(n : integer) : integer;
   begin
      fac := cond(n < 1, 1, n * fac(n − 1))
   end
```

The plan will not work; no call to **fac** ever produces any value at all, because an attempt will be made to evaluate **n * fac(n − 1)** *before* **n** is tested to see if it is less than 1.

In Iswim, however, this idea works—the users can define their own choice functions. The output of the program:

```
fac(3)
   where
      fac(n) = cond(n < 1, 1, n * fac(n − 1))
         where
            cond(p, x, y) = if p then x else y fi;
         end;
   end
```

is (according to the formal semantics) the number 6. The reason is that the value of **cond(p, x, y)** is always equal to that of **if p then x else y fi**, even if the value of **y** is ⊥—in other words, even if **y** is the 'result' of a computation which never terminates. Of course, the naive imperative view would suggest that the above program never produced any value at all. The naive view is simply wrong.

It should be apparent, then, that a sequential imperative view of *Iswim*(Z) is inappropriate and even (if followed naively) wrong. It is possible, however, to patch up the interpretation and use it as the basis for a completely correct but still conventional implementation. We need to ensure that binding of globals is dynamic (this is not too difficult). But we also need to ensure that function parameters are called 'by name' (evaluated as needed) rather than 'by value' (evaluated beforehand). This is much more difficult, but not impossible—ALGOL has call by name available as an option. Still, the imperative view is not to be recommended, even if it can be made to work. It is simply not in the 'spirit' of Iswim.

7. Lazy Evaluation

There are, however, other operational (dynamic) interpretations of Iswim that are more appropriate. These methods *evaluate* the program instead of running it, and the various parts of a program are evaluated as required. The evaluation techniques are called 'lazy' because they never do any more work than is absolutely necessary. In particular, they do not automatically evaluate the actual parameters of a function call. The lazy evaluation techniques are more faithful to the mathematical semantics. In fact, with a little care the can be made completely correct: they produce exactly what the formal semantics specifies.

The first of these might be called the 'demand-driven' interpretation. In this method demands for the values of parts of the program (initially the whole program) generate demands for values of subexpressions. The demands propagate through the program like an infection, then gradually the required values start flowing back in the opposite direction. To evaluate an expression which is (say) the sum $E_1 + E_2$ of two subexpressions E_1 and E_2, the evaluating machine evaluates E_1 and E_2 (possibly in parallel), then adds the two results. To evaluate an expression consisting of an individual constant, the evaluator returns the value assigned to the constant by the parameterising algebra. To evaluate an expression consisting of a individual variable, the evaluator looks up the appropriate definition of the variable and evaluates its right-hand side. If the variable in question is a formal parameter of a function definition, it locates the corresponding actual parameter and evaluates it. To evaluate an expression of the form **if** C **then** E_1 **else** E_2 **fi**, it evaluates C then evaluates either E_1 or E_2, according to the truth value of C. Finally, to evaluate an expression of the form (e.g.) $\mathbf{f}(E_1, E_2)$, it looks up the definition of $\mathbf{f}$ and evaluates the right-hand side.

Of course, demand driven evaluation is a little more complicated than this informal description would indicate. Nevertheless, it is not particularly difficult to implement, and is completely correct. (The pLucid interpreter described in the manual in the appendix uses a demand driven evaluation scheme. [*Iswim(P)* is a sublanguage of pLucid.]) The demand driven model is suitable as a programming aid, up to a point. The demand driven view does not require that definitions be presented in an executable order. In fact it encourages a more top-down approach to writing programs: you write first an expression whose value is the desired output, but which uses variables and functions. This expression will be the subject of a **where** clause. Then you write the definitions of the **where** body as required, so that the definition of a variable *follows* its use. A demand driven interpreter would therefore proceed through the definitions in much the same order as they were written (not that this would be of any particular help). This 'define as needed' approach yields a much better style of programming and is much more in the definitional spirit of Iswim.

There is also another nonsequential way of implementing Iswim programs. The idea is to use the rules for program manipulation, to be discussed in Chapter VII, and gradually transform the source program into its output. The transformation method uses the definitions in the program as rewrite rules. If the strategy for choosing the reductions to be performed is carefully defined, the implementation will not attempt to evaluate an expression whose value is not definitely needed.

This method (*reduction* computation) is quite simple but cannot be recommended unreservedly as a programming aid. The intermediate expressions can be very large and complicated and bear very little relationship to the original program. The method is primarily syntactic; a programmer who thinks exclusively in terms of syntax looses the advantage of having an understanding of the Iswim semantics. The programmer should think of a function definition as defining a function—a 'device' that transforms *data*. We do not recommend thinking of a definition as a rewrite rule which transforms *text*. There is more to computation than symbol manipulation.

Both these alternate operational models respect the meaning of $\perp$ in their own way. Consider, for example, the definition

$$X = X + 1;$$

whose least (indeed only) solution is $\perp$. A demand driven interpreter will cycle endlessly because each demand for a value of **X** leads directly to another demand for **X**. And a reduction implementation will endlessly replace **X** by **X + 1** and generate the series

$$X + 1, (X + 1) + 1, ((X + 1) + 1) + 1, \ldots .$$

In both cases the computation never terminates, and this is exactly the operational activity that corresponds to $\perp$.

Finally, we should point out that the programmer may wish to avoid using any dynamic model at all. Iswim's greatest strength is that its official semantics is strictly static, and uses the well-understood concept of function. If the programmer is not concerned about efficiency (performance) of the program, there is no real need to think in terms of operational concepts at all. If the programmer is exclusively concerned with correctness, then the purely static semantics is adequate on its own, because it completely specifies the output of a program.

In general, however, a programmer cannot ignore questions of performance (otherwise there would be no programs, only specifications). A programmer is forced to think in some operational terms and formulate the program to reduce the amount of resources required to 'run' it. But this does not mean that the programmer need worry about every tiny detail of the implementation or that he/she need understand the workings of *every* part of it. Even in very practical programming there will be parts of the program best understood purely declaratively. Furthermore, the correctness of even the most practical and efficient program depends only on its denotational (static) semantics, and can be considered without any reference to operational ideas. The term "abstractness" means essentially independence from problems of representation or implementation. The formal, denotational semantics of Iswim is therefore an abstract semantics, and must be understood by anyone who wishes to use the language.

8. Infinitary Programming

Our discussion of the Iswim family has so far been limited to members of the family parameterised by an algebra of conventional, finite objects. We have seen that an Iswim of this form corresponds more or less to a purely recursive subset of a conventional imperative language like ALGOL. With this restriction Iswim programming is essentially a very rigorously restricted or structured form of conventional programming.

There is no inherent reason, however, to restrict ourselves to languages indexed by such 'conventional' algebras. There are many interesting and useful members of the Iswim family indexed by algebras whose elements are not finite objects. These languages are far richer than mere subsets of conventional languages, and they make possible entirely new approaches to programming.

One interesting example of a member of the Iswim family is that based on an algebra H which is like the POP-2 algebra P but whose universe contains infinite as well as finite lists. Lists may be infinite, and their components can be arbitrary elements of the universe of H (in partic-

ular, the components may in turn be lists). This idea can be made somewhat more precise with the following "domain equations" defining the
universe H_0 of H in terms of the domain D of non-list POP-2 data objects:

$$L = 1 + H_0 \times L \quad\text{and}\quad H_0 = D + L.$$

The first says that a 'hyperlist' (element of the domain L) is either empty
(there is only one empty list) or else consists of an element of H_0 (its head)
and a hyperlist (its tail). The second says that an element of H_0 is either an
element of D (a string, a number, a word etc.) or a list. The equations
specify only the universe H_0 of H, not H itself, because they do not
specify any operations over H. However, the usual list operations (denoted by the symbols **hd**, **tl**, **::**, and so on) are easily defined once the
solution to the equations is available.

These domain equations do, in fact, have a solution in which there are
lists of infinite length. The only price we must pay is that the domain H_0
contains a rich variety of partial objects as well. In the domain D the only
partial (nonstandard) object was $\perp$ itself—all the other objects were normal, healthy strings, words, integers, etc. In H_0, however, we must allow
'mixed' lists; that is, lists in which some (but not necessarily all) of the
components are $\perp$. Also, we must allow lists that 'tail off' after some
point—lists which finally yield $\perp$ when **tl** is applied often enough. Finally,
since a component of a list can be any other list, we must allow lists with
components which are 'partial lists'; not to mention lists with components
which are lists with components which are partial, and so on. In short, the
domain H_0 allows an infinite variety of shades of gray between the 'pure
white' of the total objects and the 'jet black' of $\perp$.

One great difference between programming in $Iswim(H)$ and programming in $Iswim(A)$ with A an algebra of 'finite' objects is the following: it makes sense to give recursive (circular) definitions of individual
variables. Another difference is that it also makes sense to give recursive
function definitions without a terminating condition—the evaluation runs
'forever', which is fine, because the 'result' is intended to be infinite.

Consider, for example, the definition

$$\mathbf{X = 1 :: X;}$$

In $Iswim(P)$, this definition would associate the value $\perp$ with **X**, because
P has only finite lists and no finite list satisfies the equation. In $Iswim(H)$,
however, there is an infinite solution: the list

$$[1\ 1\ 1\ 1\ 1\ 1\ 1\ 1\ 1\ 1\ 1\ 1\ 1\ 1\ 1\ 1\ 1\ 1\ 1\ 1\ 1\ 1\ 1\ 1\ 1\ 1\ 1\ 1\ 1\ 1\ 1\ 1\ 1\ 1\ 1\ \cdots\ ]$$

of infinitely many 1's (space does not permit a complete rendering of this
list). Moreover, it is the *least* solution to this equation and is therefore the

value associated with the variable **X**. The following 'nonterminating' definition

$$\textbf{bump(X)} = \textbf{hd(X)} + \textbf{1} :: \textbf{bump(tl(X))};$$

defines a perfectly sensible function. It expects an infinite list of numbers as its argument, and returns as its result the infinite list formed by increasing each component of its argument by 1. Then the definition

$$\textbf{nats} = \textbf{0} :: \textbf{bump(nats)};$$

defines **nat** to be the infinite list

[0 1 2 3 4 5 6 7 8 9 10 11 12 13 14 15 16 17 18 19 20 21 22 23 24 ⋯]

of all natural numbers. This list is the least (in fact the only) solution to the equation.

Algebras with infinite objects permit a very different style of Iswim programming, one that can produce some very elegant (if unconventional) programs. Here is an *Iswim(H)* program whose output (value) is the infinite list.

[2 3 5 7 11 13 17 19 23 29 31 37 41 43 47 51 53 ⋯]

of all prime numbers.

```
       P
        where
        nats = 1 :: bump(nats)
           where
           bump(X) = hd(X) + 1 :: bump(tl(X));
           end;
        P = 2 :: primesin(tl(tl(nats)))
           where
           primesin(L) = if isprime(hd(L))
                         then hd(L) :: primesin(tl(L))
                         else primesin(tl(L)) fi;
           isprime(n) = nodivsin(P)
              where
              nodivsin(Q) = (q * q > n) or
                            ((n mod q ne 0) and nodivsin(tl(Q)))
                            where
                               q = hd(Q);
                            end;
              end;
           end;
        end
```

The program works by removing all nonprimes from the infinite list of natural numbers. The test for primeness uses the infinite list **P** of all primes which is being constructed.

There already exist a number of interpreters for 'infinitary' members of the Iswim family. The best known (and first to appear) are Turner's (1979) SASL and Henderson's (1980) Lispkit. These languages are based on the original, higher order language—they are variations on ISWIM, rather than Iswim. One of the authors (WWW), together with some colleagues at the University of Warwick, has implemented just such a 'Lambda Calculus' language, based on the algebra H described earlier. The language [which is essentially $Iswim(H)$] is called PIFL (POP-2 Influenced Functional Language) and has been used for an undergraduate functional programming course.

PIFL is a 'companion' language of pLucid—it is based on the same algebra and uses the same syntactic conventions. As a result, there is a large overlap between the two languages (in PIFL **where** is recursive); many PIFL programs are (syntactically) also pLucid programs and produce the same output. The intersection between pLucid and PIFL is (roughly) first-order PIFL, i.e., $Iswim(P)$. (It is not exactly $Iswim(P)$ because in PIFL recursive definitions of lists do not always yield $\perp$.) We will use the name "pIswim" to refer to $Iswim(P)$—in other words, to first-order, finitary PIFL. We will also make use of $Iswim(H)$ (first-order, infinitary PIFL) and for this language will use the name "HyperpIswim." pIswim is therefore a sublanguage of pLucid, and HyperpIswim is a sublanguage of PIFL. The examples in this section are all HyperpIswim programs and (therefore) PIFL programs as well.

It should be apparent that members of the Iswim family which allow computations with infinite objects require more sophisticated implementations. The conventional, sequential interpretation which (barely) covers a language like $Iswim(P)$ breaks down completely when faced with a language like $Iswim(H)$. In particular, recursive definitions of individual variables, though perfectly sensible and usable, make no sense at all when considered as assignment statements.

The other two methods of implementation (namely, reduction and demand driven) do, however, extend. The reduction method is the simplest to extend; we need only use equations such as

$$\textbf{hd}(X :: Y) = X;$$

which tell us how to rewrite expressions involving operations on infinite data. The PIFL interpreter works in more or less this way, as do the implementations of SASL and Lispkit.

The demand driven method also extends, although here we have to be more careful, It is not possible to demand the value of an expression if that value is infinite; instead, we must demand only *part* of that value, namely, as much as we need to satisfy other partial demands. In the course of a computation we may return to demand more and more parts of the same value, but we will never need *all* of the value at once (this is how the pLucid interpreter works). There is, however, no general demand driven interpreter because the notion of what constitutes a 'part' of an object depends on the nature of the objects in question.

III THE LANGUAGE LUSWIM

The simple language Iswim is surprisingly powerful, in spite of its simplicity. It does lack, however, one extremely useful 'feature' found in even the most primitive imperative languages—iteration. In general it is difficult to formulate iterative algorithms in Iswim—algorithms which are based on *repetition*, on the strategy of doing the same thing over and over again. It can be done (and some of the methods will be discussed later), but not in any simple or natural style valid for all members of the Iswim family. Iswim favours instead the recursive, divide-and-conquer approach to computation.

As a simple example, suppose that we want to write a program which repeatedly inputs integers and prints out a running average of these numbers. In other words, each time it reads in a number it outputs the average of all numbers input so far. If the first number input is 3, the first number output will be 3; if the second input is 5, the second output will be 4 (the average of 3 and 5); if the third number input is 10, the third number output will be 6 (the average of 3, 5 and 10), and so on.

This is quite easy to do in PASCAL:

```
program avg(input, output);
var n, s, x : real;
begin
  n := 0; s := 0;
  while true do begin
    read(x);
    s := s + x;
    n := n + 1;
    writeln(s/n)
  end
end.
```

But, of course, the PASCAL program makes essential use of *assignment* (to initialise and update **s** and **n**) and *control flow* (to cause the updating assignments to be repeatedly executed).

There is clearly no pIswim program that can perform this task, not with the meaning of 'input' and 'output' given in the last chapter. The input of a pIswim program is a set of data objects, one for each free variable. The output of a pIswim program is a single data object. There can be no running average program in pIswim because no pIswim program is capable of 'ongoing' input/output activity. We could run the same program over and over again, but in this case it would be of no help because the number input at any particular point would still determine the corresponding output. For example, if at any time an input of 3 is followed by an output of 3, then at any other time an input of 3 must produce the same value. This obviously is not the case with the above PASCAL program. Suppose that the PASCAL program inputs 3, then 9, then 3 again. The first 3 produces a 3 as the corresponding output, but the second 3 produces 5. We conclude that the running average program cannot be formulated in pIswim, even with a generous reinterpretation of the notion of input.

This sort of reasoning has led some to conclude that nonprocedural languages like Iswim are inherently static, and that therefore programs in these languages are unable to perform repetition and certainly unable to interact with the user. The PASCAL program works because it has 'memory'—something apparently banned from Iswim.

1. Iteration through Sequences

Of course, Iswim is simply algebraic notation slightly adapted, and so the above argument seems to imply that algebra and mathematics in general is incapable of describing 'dynamic' activity like that engaged in by the above program. Once this point of view is carried to this its logical conclusion, however, it is finally seen to be ridiculous. A mathematician would have no difficulty at all specifying the running average computation in a simple algebraic form. The conventional mathematical description might be as follows:

Let $x_0, x_1, x_2, \ldots$ be the numbers input. Then the numbers output are $a_0, a_1, a_2, \ldots$, where $a_n = s_{n+1}/(n + 1)$ and $s_n = x_0 + x_1 + x_2 + \cdots + x_{n-1}$.

The flaw in the reasoning which lead to the ridiculous conclusion is that there is something inherently operational and dynamic about inputting rationals over and over, as opposed to inputting a single rational. It is true that "repeatedly inputting rationals" is an operational concept; but then so is "inputting a rational". When a rational is input it happens at some particular time and place, and using some particular representation. This does not stop us, however, from abstracting (by forgetting time, place and manner) a mathematical object, namely, the rational which was input. In other words, there is nothing to stop us from abstracting "the input" from an "act of inputting". Inputting one rational after another is also a dynamic notion, but we can still abstract a mathematical object from such activity. The mathematical object extracted is the *entire sequence of rationals* which is input. This is the meaning of the phrase

let $x_0, x_1, x_2, \ldots,$ be the numbers input

The same can be said for output: outputting one rational after another is dynamic, but we can abstract from such an act the output, also an infinite sequence.

A continuously operating program like the above therefore has an infinite sequence of rationals as its (total) input, and another infinite sequence of rationals as its (total) output. For example, if the input to the running average program is $\langle 1, 3, 5, 7, 9, \ldots \rangle$ (the odd numbers in increasing order), then the output is $\langle 1, 2, 3, 4, 5, \ldots \rangle$ (the natural numbers in increasing order). The running average program is in fact deterministic after all: the (total) output is determined by (is a function of) the total input. Moreover, the input/output function is easily specifiable in 'static' mathematical notation.

All this suggests that programs like the above could be written in a member of the Iswim family in which infinite sequences of data objects are allowed and in which appropriate operations on sequences are available. Then the mathematical specification given above could be turned into a proper program.

As a matter of fact, sequences can be represented, in a limited way, in pIswim itself. We can represent them as functions. The sequence $\langle x_0, x_1, x_2, \ldots \rangle$ is represented by any function f such that $f(n) = x_n$ for all n (the other values of f are irrelevant). Then if f represents the input to the running average program, the following definitions

a(n) = s(n + 1)/(n + 1);
s(n) = if n < 1 then 0 else f(n − 1) + s(n − 1) fi;

ensure that **a** represents the desired output. To make this idea work, however, we would need to devise a new I/O convention which would allow functions to be input and output. Also, if we wanted to have iterative programs that had user defined functions as well, we would have to have some way of distinguishing functions which are representing sequences from functions that really are functions. This would cause even more complications. The sequences-as-functions approach is not really practical.

A more plausible alternative is HyperpIswim, namely, the language *Iswim(H)*, where *H* is an algebra like *P* but containing infinite as well as finite lists (HyperpIswim was introduced in the preceding chapter). We could adopt a simple input/output convention for infinite lists which would permit ongoing I/O. We could restrict programs to have only one input variable, and give to this variable as its value the infinite list of all (finite) data items input. In the same way, if output is an infinite list of finite objects, then the program is deemed to be outputting these values one after another. Given these conventions about I/O, the running average can be programmed as

```
a
    where
    a = quot(tl(s), tl(n));
    s = tot(x, 0);
    n = nums(0);
    end
    where
    quot(p, q) = hd(p)/hd(q) :: quot(tl(p), tl(q));
    tot(h, k) = k :: tot(tl(h), hd(h) + k);
    nums(k) = k :: nums(k + 1);
    end
```

(the function **quot** divides two lists componentwise).

It should be apparent that quite a wide range of iterative algorithms can be expressed in HyperpIswim. We have therefore demonstrated, at least in principle, that iteration can be expressed in *some* members of the Iswim family.

This approach to iteration is not, however, very convincing. The resulting programs are notationally very cumbersome, especially in comparison with PASCAL or even with conventional mathematical notation. The approach is semantically cumbersome as well. PASCAL programmers writing a simple running average program would certainly not think in terms of infinite objects (let alone functions on infinite objects, like **tot**); and they would hardly consider running average to be a problem requiring list manipulation in any form. Yet HyperpIswim programmers are forced to think of infinite lists, even for a simple problem like this.

It would not be exactly obvious, to someone seeing the program for the first time, that an iterative algorithm is being used. The names **hd** and **tl** do not have dynamic connotations. How are we to know when a list 'really is' a list, and when it is a representation of a variable history. What if we wanted to write an iterative list algorithm? Any problems humans have in understanding 'iterative' HyperpIswim could be even worse for machines.

2. Luswim: The Abstract Approach to Iteration

The problem with the HyperpIswim approach to iteration through sequences is that it is not *abstract*. The programmer is forced to use one particular *representation* of sequences (the representation as lists). As a result, lists and their operations are 'overloaded'. It is not surprising that the approach is cumbersome (because the programmer is forced to consider details of the representation) and ambiguous (because there is no way to tell how a particular list is being used). The same problems would arise if we tried to represent sequences as functions.

What we need is not another representation of sequences, but sequences themselves. In the context of the algebraic approach, this means asking the question "What are the appropriate operations on sequences?" To put it another way, suppose that we were going to do a lot of iterative programming in HyperpIswim (representing sequences as lists). We should try to be abstract, write a sequence package, and then use only packaged operations when iteration is intended. What operations would be included in the package?

One powerful operation is what we might call "subscripting". The subscripting operation expects a sequence x and a natural number i and returns the ith element x_i of x. The mathematical formulation of running average uses only subscripting plus ordinary arithmetic operations. We could, following Arsac (1977) and others, design a programming language based on the conventional notation. There are, however, serious disadvantages to such an approach. For one thing, definitions need subscripted variables on the left-hand side, and that means that our language cannot be a member of the Iswim family. Another problem is that programming with subscripts tends to obscure the fact that our sequences are meant to be histories of dynamic activity. Almost every expression the programmer writes will involve a number of subscripts, and this can prove to be very tedious. Finally, there is the problem that the unrestricted use of subscripts can make possible programs that do not have a simple iterative interpretation.

The trouble with subscripting is that it is *too powerful*. Using only subscripting forces programmers to do too much of the work by themselves; and at the same time, it allows them to do too much, and too easily. In this respect programming using subscripts is very much like programming in assembly language. What we need are a number of simpler, less general operations which permit a higher level approach to using sequences.

The simplest operations are those involving only arithmetic operations, performed pointwise (component by component). One example is pointwise division, already used in the above example. Another simple operation is the one that throws away the first value of a sequence—represented by **tl** in HyperpIswim. This is the function we will call *next*; given any sequence x,

$$next(x) = \langle x_1, x_2, x_3, \ldots \rangle$$

As it turns out, we need only one more operation, one which will allow us to define sequences by recurrence, but without subscripting. This is the function we will call *fby* (for "followed by"); given a rational x and a sequence y,

$$fby(x, y) = \langle x, y_0, y_1, y_2, \ldots \rangle$$

If we let **sum** denote the pointwise version of addition and **quot** that of division, then our running average program is

```
next(quot(s, n))
  where
  s = fby(0, sum(s, x));
  n = fby(0, sum(one, n);
      where
        one = fby(1, one);
      end;
  end
```

(here the symbol **next** denotes the function *next*, and **fby** denotes the function *fby*).

This is much better, but can still be improved upon. We have still been forced to think up a new set of names for the pointwise versions of the data operations (and for constant sequences). Also, programs are very clumsy because we are forced to use functional (prefix rather than infix) notation for arithmetic operations on sequences. For example, if in another program we wanted the components of the sequence **z** to be the sums of the squares of the corresponding components of the sequences **x** and **y**, we would have to write

$$\mathbf{Z} = \mathbf{sum(product(x, x), product(y, y))};$$

Also, we have to keep around two versions of every constant—for example, we have the single number **1** but also the sequence **one** of ones.

These problems can be resolved very simply—we banish individual data objects from the language and use only the corresponding constant sequences. We make everything a sequence, and then use infix notation and the old symbols (like **1** and **+**) to denote the corresponding sequences and sequence operations. We redefine *fby* so that its first argument is also a sequence—it places the first component of its first argument in front of its second argument. Finally, we use **fby** as an infix and **next** as a prefix operation symbol.

Here is the running average program in the new notation

> **next s/n**
> **where**
>   s = 0 **fby** s + x;
>   n = 0 **fby** n + 1;
> **end**

These decisions are remarkably easy to formalise. Given any (continuous) algebra A, $Luswim(A)$ is simply $Iswim(Lu(A))$, where $Lu(A)$ is the unique algebra L such that

(i)   the signature of L is that of A plus a unary operation symbol **next**, and a binary symbol **fby**;

(ii)   the universe of L is the collection of all infinite sequences of elements of the universe of A;

(iii)   the partial order on L is the pointwise order induced by the order on A; if x and y are in the universe of L, $x \sqsubseteq_L y$ if $x_i \sqsubseteq_A y_i$ for all i;

(iv)   Any symbol o in the signature of L denotes the pointwise operation on sequences corresponding to its denotation o_A in A; in other words,

$$o_L(x, y, z, \ldots)_t = o_A(x_t, y_t, z_t, \ldots)$$

(v)   The operations $\textbf{next}_L$ and $\textbf{fby}_L$ are $next$ and fby, where

$$fby(x, y) = \langle x_0, y_0, y_1, y_2, \ldots \rangle, \qquad next(x) = \langle x_1, x_2, x_3, \ldots \rangle$$

The objection could be made that the user is now forced to use sequences where at least before (in HyperpIswim) they could be avoided. In fact the effect is quite the opposite. The Luswim user can now think in terms of *dynamically changing* type 0 (data) objects rather than static, invariant type 1 (infinite) objects. This is the whole point of Luswim (and Lucid). Programmers who do not understand the dynamic, operational significance of Lucid 'histories' will have great difficulties. Lucid is NOT a language for manipulating infinite sequences. It is a language for expressing iterative (and more generally, dataflow) algorithms.

3. Iterative Programs in Luswim

The language $Luswim(A)$ allows us to write 'iterative' programs because it allows us to write programs which we can think of (and even implement) in terms of iteration. Of course, a $Luswim(A)$ program is really just an

Iswim program, and its meaning is therefore defined in terms of a purely static concept—namely, that of least fixed point. Nevertheless, no harm (and much good) can come of using the alternate, operational semantics, provided it is used correctly, i.e., as long as it is consistent with (gives the same answers as) the static history-function semantics. The iterative, operational viewpoint is based on the interpretation of nullary variables (and expressions) as representing values which change with time, rather than as histories; in other words, as dynamic objects rather than as static objects. Sometimes it is useful to keep in mind the entire history of a nullary variable when developing a program, but sometimes it can be very distracting. *Luswim(A)* is not intended to be *thought of* as a member of the Iswim family, with 'facilities' for manipulating infinite histories. Instead, *Luswim(A)* is best thought of as an 'extension' of *Iswim(A)* which has iteration as well as recursion. The data types and operations of *Luswim(A)* are 'really' just those provided by *A* itself.

The simplest Luswim definitions are those in which a single nullary variable is defined in terms of itself alone, by means of a simple **fby** expression. For example, if **i** is defined by the equation

$$\mathbf{i = 1\ fby\ 2 * i + 1;}$$

we can think of the values as being generated by an iterative process in which (i) the initial value given to **i** is 1; and thereafter (ii) on each iteration the new value given to **i** is twice the old value plus one (This and all the following examples are in *Luswim(P)*, *P* being the POP-2 algebra.) Thus repeated 'execution' of this iterative process results in **i** taking on the values

$$1, 3, 7, 15, \ldots$$

In general, we may have two or more nullary variables defined in this way (using **fby**) but in terms of each other. For example,

$$\mathbf{f = 1\ fby\ f + g;}$$
$$\mathbf{g = 0\ fby\ f;}$$

We can think of mutually recursive equations like these as an iteration in which the variables (in this case **f** and **g**) are updated together. It is extremely important to realise that in cases like this the formal semantics requires us to think of the updates being performed simultaneously but in step. We must imagine that the variables are all initialised at the same time, and that on each iteration the new values are computed and assigned simultaneously. In other words, we must imagine that the values of the variables never get 'out of step' with each other as they do in imperative loops. In the case of **f** and **g** defined as above, for example, the generation of the values of **f** and **g** involves (i) initialising **f** and **g** to 1 and 0, respectively, and (ii) on each iteration computing the new values of **f** and **g** as being the old value of **f** + **g** and the old value of **f**, respectively.

The idea of variables being initialised and updated in step is not easily captured in sequential imperative languages like PASCAL. The best we can do is simulate the effects in a sequential way. For example, the PASCAL simulation of the last two definitions would consist of a never-ending loop which continually changes the values of **f** and **g**. The program

```
          f
            where
            f = 1 fby f + g;
            g = 0 fby f;
            end
```

does not correspond to the PASCAL program

```
program fib(output);
var f, g : integer;
begin
  f := 1; g := 0;
  while true do
  begin
    write(f);
    f := f + g;
    g := f
  end
end.
```

Nor does it correspond to the program

```
program fib(output);
var f, g : integer;
begin
  f := 1; g := 0;
  while true do
  begin
    write(f);
    g := f;
    f := f + g
  end
end.
```

(in which the order of the assignment statements in the body of the loop has been reversed).

If PASCAL had a multiple assignment statement we could express the algorithm for generating the values of **f** and **g** as

```
program fib(output);
var f, g : integer;
begin
  f, g := 1, 0;
  while true do
  begin
    write ln(f);
    f, g := f + g, f;
  end
end.
```

Of course, the multiple assignment would have to be simultaneous. All the expressions on the right-hand side of the assignment would have to be evaluated before any change could be made to any variable on the left. We can achieve the correct effect in standard PASCAL only by using extra variables, e.g.,

```
program fib(output);
var f, g, newF, newG : integer;
begin
  f := 1; g := 0;
  while true do
  begin
    write (f);
    newF := f + g;
    newG := f;
    f := newF;
    g := newG
  end
end.
```

The values of **f** and **g** which should be computed are therefore

f 1 1 2 3 5 8 ...,   **g** 0 1 1 2 3 5 ...

Nullary variables like **f** and **g**, which are defined using **fby**, can be called loop variables. Sometimes a nullary variable will be defined directly in terms of other variables which may be defined using **fby**. Such variables, like **w** in

```
v
  where
    v = 1 fby (v + w)/2;
    w = 100/v;
  end
```

can be thought of as 'auxiliary' variables, whose values are recomputed, from the values of the 'genuine' loop variables, on each step. The 'old' value of a variable like **w** is not needed in the computation of the new (and so it need not be initialised).

Another Luswim program which illustrates the differences with PAS-CAL is the following, which generates the running sums of the factorials of the positive integers:

```
s where
  i = 1 fby i + 1;
  f = 1 fby f * (i + 1);
  s = 1 fby s + f * (i + 1);
end
```

The (or at least one) corresponding PASCAL program would be

```
program fac(output);
var i, f, s : integer;
begin
  i := 1; f := 1; s := 1;
  while true do
  begin
    write (s);
    i := i + 1;
    f := f * i;
    s := s + f
  end
end.
```

In the PASCAL program, the occurrence of **i** in **f := f * i** refers to the *new* value of **i**, because **i** has just been updated. In the Lucid version, all occurrences of **i** must be though of as referring to the *old* value (the value **i** has at the beginning of the iteration step). Therefore, the Lucid program contains the expression **f * (i + 1)** instead of **f * i**.

These examples illustrate an analogy between Luswim and PASCAL which is suggestive but can be misleading. In particular, the statements (definitions) in a Luswim program are equations, not assignment statements, and any attempt to understand them as assignments can cause great confusion. For one thing, the order of statements in Luswim programs is irrelevant, but if we tried to change the order of the corresponding statements in the body of the PASCAL loop, they would behave very differently. Even when an analogous PASCAL program exists, it cannot in general be obtained just by changing = to :=, keeping the order of statements the same.

We will see that not all Luswim programs correspond to **while** loops in PASCAL, and it is also true that not all PASCAL programs directly correspond to Luswim programs. The main difference, of course, is that the order of Luswim equations is irrelevant, whereas in general the order in which assignment statements are executed is very important.

In a PASCAL program a variable may be the subject of more than one assignment statement. At one point in the program there might appear the statement $x := y + 1$, and later on $x := a * b$. A Luswim clause, however, cannot include both the corresponding equations ($x = y + 1$ and $x = a * b$) because in a clause a variable can have at most one definition. In a PASCAL program the commands which can affect the history of values of a particular variable can be scattered throughout the entire program, while in Luswim all the information is collected in one place, in the definition of the variable.

Both Luswim and PASCAL allow definitions and assignments, respectively, which are self-referential, i.e., in which the variable being defined or assigned to appears in the right-hand side expression. There are important differences, however, in the way in which self-reference is interpreted. In PASCAL the assignment $x := x + 1$ simply causes the value of x to be increased by one. The corresponding equation $x = x + 1$ can appear in a Luswim program, but not usefully: it defines x to be its own numerical successor and any attempt to calculate a value for x results in a nonterminating computation. The reason is that in PASCAL the occurrences of x on two sides of the assignment symbol implicitly refer to values of x at different times ('before' and 'after'). On the other hand, Luswim definitions assert the equality of the values on either side at the same point in time. For example, the definition $x = a + b$ asserts that for each time t the value of x at the time t is the value of $a + b$ at time t. The Luswim definition $x = 1$ **fby** $x + 1$ can (as we have seen) be thought of as specifying repeated assignments of $x + 1$ to x; in terms of histories, it implies that the value of x at time t is the value of $x + 1$ at time $t - 1$ for all positive t. The 'before–after' effect is due not to equality, but to the operation **fby**; the value of a **fby** expression at a given (nonzero) time depends on the value of the right operand one 'instant' earlier.

4. Variables in PASCAL and Luswim

The difference between the Luswim and PASCAL approaches to iteration stands out even more clearly when we consider 'realistic' PASCAL programs. All but the simplest PASCAL programs use a wide variety of mathematically (if not operationally) complicated features—**for** loops, **if** statements, procedures, side effects, **var** parameters, subscripted assign-

ment, pointer variables and so on. Underlying PASCAL (and all imperative languages) is a view of variables (i.e., varying entities) as passive
objects subject to the unpredictable whim of the programmers. The basic
principle (with some restrictions) is that the programmers should be
'free', at any place in the program or at any time during its execution, to
'do' anything they want to a variable. In Luswim, on the other hand, the
programmer specifies once and for all, in the definition of the variable,
everything which is going to happen to it. The programmer imagines that
values of a variable will be generated by a self-sufficient device capable of
performing the steps of a computation without anyone having to issue any
commands at all. It is possible to think iteratively and operationally without thinking imperatively.

We could, of course, devise 'improvements' to Luswim which would
give it a more imperative 'flavour' and allow Luswim imitations of other
PASCAL features to be added. When Lucid was first developed, the
language allowed inductive definitions: instead of defining a variable by a
single equation with **fby**, two equations could be used. One equation
could be used to define the **first** value, and another could be used to define
the **next** (succeeding) values. The equation

$$i = 1 \text{ fby } i + 1;$$

could be replaced by the equations

$$\text{first } i = 1;$$
$$\text{next } i = i + 1;$$

Inductive definitions still make sense mathematically—the equations still
have a least solution, even though individually they are not definitions of
variables. The supposed 'advantage' of writing the definitions in this form
is that they now can indeed be thought of as assignment statements.

Eventually we decided that the 'advantages' offered by this approach
were illusory. The problem with inductive definitions was that they actually encouraged people to think of Lucid in terms of assignment, with
disastrous results. For example, people tended to write things such as

$$\text{next } x = x + 1;$$
$$\text{next } x = x + 2;$$

under the impression that this would result in **x** being changed twice per
iteration. In the end we realised that we had only ourselves to blame for
misunderstandings like these. We had misled people into believing that
Lucid was not really all that different from a language like PASCAL.

It is certainly true that Luswim is a very restricted language (though
not as restricted as it might seem), and later we will consider some exten-

sions. The significance of any extension, however, lies not in the details of the features being added but in the direction in which the language is evolving. The trouble with adding inductive definitions is that it represents a step backwards in the direction of the imperative philosophy. With the introduction of inductive definitions programmers can once again distribute information about a variable to some extent—even if not throughout the program. In reality, however, Lucid originally had inductive definitions; but they were removed (as we explained) and the function **fby** added instead. This was an important step away from the imperative viewpoint.

The mistakes we (the authors) made when developing Lucid can almost all be attributed to our underestimating the potential of the nonprocedural approach. Many people feel that only imperative languages are the 'real thing' and nonprocedural languages can never be anything but pallid and impractical imitations. This deeply ingrained attitude affects even the designers of nonprocedural languages, and produces a tendency on their part to try to simulate one imperative feature after another, to show that their language can 'handle', for example, shared variables or error interrupts.

The problems with imperative languages mentioned in the introduction (enormous complexity, lack of formal specifications, difficulties in expressing parallelism and so on) are products of the imperative philosophy itself, and are caused by the clash of imperative features (like assignment) with declarative features (like recursion). If the designers of nonprocedural languages try to borrow imperative features, they will end up borrowing the problems as well. Nonprocedural languages will succeed by developing the strength of the nonprocedural approach, not by imitating the weakness of the imperative. When first designing Lucid, for example, we worried for some time because the usual one-update-at-a-time array algorithms (e.g., for sorting) appeared somewhat inelegant in Lucid. Finally it occurred to us that perhaps this sort of strict sequentiality is not such a good idea in the first place.

Even in a simple nonprocedural language like Luswim, one can begin to appreciate the potential of the nonimperative approach. Using only **next** and **fby** (plus the data operations) one can write reasonable and understandable programs, which nevertheless do not correspond to simple **while** loops. Programs which correspond to **while** loops are based on the conventional notion of "variable" and use the special Lucid operations in a very restricted way. In such 'conventional' programs **next** does not appear at all, and **fby** appears exactly once for each 'loop variable'. On the other hand, the formal specification of $Luswim(A)$ (i.e., $Iswim(Lu(A))$) places no restrictions whatsoever on the expressions which may appear in right-hand sides. Many of these formally acceptable definitions (such as **x** = **next x**) are completely senseless. These 'senseless' programs usually specify the value ⊥, which in many ways acts as a 'default value'. On the other hand, there are many different (and perfectly sensible) ways in which the Lucid operations can be used.

The operation **next**, for example, can be used to give the effect of a 'look ahead' which allows us to refer to the value a variable will have after the execution of the current iteration. In the factorial sum program the variable **s** (which accumulates the sums of the factorials) was defined as

$$s = 1 \text{ fby } s + f * (i + 1);$$

and not

$$s = 1 \text{ fby } s + f;$$

because **s** is the sum of all factorials generated so far, up to and including the present one. The new value of **s** must therefore be the present value of **s** plus the new value of **f**, i.e., the present value of **s** plus the present value of **f** * (**i** + **1**). In PASCAL we can avoid writing **f** * (**i** + **1**) by a clever ordering of assignment statements. In Lucid, reordering the definitions is (as we explained) pointless; instead, we simply write

$$s = 1 \text{ fby } s + \text{next } f;$$

and nothing could more clearly express the way in which **s** is to be updated. In the same way, we could write

$$f = 1 \text{ fby } f * \text{next } i;$$

If we think of variables in the Pascal way, this use of **next** is hard to understand—how do we know what value will next be assigned to **i**? On the other hand, if we think of variables as varying values produced by autonomous processes, there is no problem. We can easily imagine that the new values of **f** are available sooner than those of **s**.

In the example just given, this calculation of **next i** can be carried out symbolically—it is simply the second operand (**i** + **1**) of the **fby** expression which defines **i**. The operation **next** can therefore be 'massaged' out of this particular program. This yields exactly the program given previously, which (we maintain) is somewhat less clear. Lucid's 'temporal' operations make it much easier for programmers to use (and to convey) the operational significance of their programs.

It would be very difficult, if not impossible, for an imperative language like PASCAL to incorporate an operation like **next**. According to the imperative viewpoint, the machine waits passively for commands to be obeyed. How can such a witless slave be expected to predict what it will next be ordered to do with a particular variable?

In the example programs just cited it was possible (if not desirable) to remove the operation **next**. This was so because (roughly speaking) the operation was not used to define a variable in terms of its own future; in the revised factorial sum program, for example, **s** was defined in terms of the future of **f**, **f** is defined in terms of the future of **i**, but **i** is defined in terms of previous values of **i** only. [This notion is made more precise in Wadge (1981).]

It is possible, of course, to write legal Luswim programs in which a variable is defined in terms of its own **next** value. Usually, such a definition specifies only the value ⊥. Sometimes, however, such programs can produce sensible results. The program

> **howfar**
> > **where**
> > > **howfar = if x eq 0 then 0 else 1 + next howfar fi;**
> > **end;**

is quite legal. If the values of **x** are of integers, the value of this expression at any point in time is the amount of time which will elapse before the value of **x** is next 0. For example, if **x** takes on the values

$$1, 6, 4, 0, 9, 2, 1, 4, 3, 0, 6, ...$$

then the program takes on the values

$$3, 2, 1, 0, 5, 4, 3, 2, 1, 0, ...$$

These values are (naturally enough) computed by 'looking into the future'. This program cannot be understood as an iterative process in the way we have been doing. Of course, an implementation of Lucid based on iteration (say, a compiler) might decline to accept such a program.

The operation **fby** also has more potential than is revealed by its use in transcribing while-like programs. We can use two **fby**'s in a single expression to specify explicitly the first two values of a variable. For example, the value of the expression

$$\textbf{1 fby 3 fby 5}$$

(**fby** associates to the right) is $\langle 1, 3, 5, 5, 5, ... \rangle$. In the Fibonacci program

> **f**
> > **where**
> > > **f = 1 fby f + g;**
> > > **g = 0 fby f;**
> > **end**

the variable **g** is defined in terms of the variable **f** only. We can eliminate **g** from the program by replacing the occurrence of **g** in the definition of **f** by the expression **0 fby f**. In the resulting program

$$f$$
$$\textbf{where}$$
$$f = 1 \textbf{ fby } f + (0 \textbf{ fby } f);$$
$$\textbf{end};$$

f is defined directly in terms of itself. In general, the value of the expression

$$(\textbf{x fby y}) + Z$$

is equal to that of

$$(\textbf{x} + \textbf{first } Z) \textbf{ fby } (\textbf{y} + \textbf{next } Z)$$

Thus we can rewrite the program as

$$\textbf{f where}$$
$$f = 1 \textbf{ fby } (1 \textbf{ fby } f + \textbf{next } f);$$
$$\textbf{end};$$

(because **0 + first f** is *1*). The parentheses are not really necessary—the precedence of **fby** is lower than that of **+**.

This program is not, however, another example of a variable being defined in terms of its own future. The operation **fby** introduces a 'delay' of one time unit, and two of them introduce a delay of two time units. In the expression **f + next f** on the right-hand side, occurrences of **f** refer to the value which that variable had two iterations previously, and so **next f** refers to the value on the previous iteration. Using two nested **fby**'s we can define a variable by specifying explicitly its first two values and giving an expression for the value of time $t + 2$ in terms of the values at times $t + 1$ and t. To give another example, the definition

$$\textbf{h} = 0 \textbf{ fby } (1 \textbf{ fby } 3 * (\textbf{next } \textbf{h}) - \textbf{h});$$

specifies that **h** will take on the values

$$0, 1, 3, 8, 21, 55, \ldots$$

In the same way three **fby**'s can be used to specify a variable in terms of its previous three values, four allow us to go back four instants in time and so on.

5. Continuously Operating Programs

Probably the most unconventional idea in Luswim is that computations do not terminate. A conventional program which runs forever given a particular input is usually considered to be in a failure mode (e.g., in an infinite loop) caused by errors in the program or in its data. In actual fact, however, the view that infinite or nonterminating computations are inherently undesirable is not very realistic. In most engineering applications a device (a bridge, a telephone circuit, a pump or a car) is considered to have failed when it *ceases* to perform the activity for which it was designed. The better the design and manufacture of a product, the longer its lifetime. The 'ideal' product would therefore last forever, i.e., it would be a continuously operating device. There are a few exceptions (e.g., explosive weapons), but in general engineers are concerned with building objects which operate indefinitely.

It is certainly true that some programs are meant to be used only once (say to compute the first million primes), but genuine 'one-off' efforts are very rare. Most supposedly finite programs (such as compilers) are intended to be run repeatedly (and indefinitely) on different sets of data. Sometimes a program is devoted to maintaining a single data structure, such as a master file, which slowly evolves over a period of time. Finally, there are more and more examples of "real time" systems (operating systems, process control systems, air traffic control systems) which must be continuously operating in a very literal sense. Some software engineers now advocate that even supposedly conventional programs are best thought of as running uninterruptedly.

Lucid's infinite histories are therefore not as unrealistic as they might seem. The input to a program which runs indefinitely is the infinite history of the values 'fed into' it, and the output is the infinite history of all the values produced. A Lucid program can therefore be thought of operationally as repeatedly reading in values of its input variables and producing values as its results (output need not be produced at the same rate that input is consumed). In Lucid this is the more natural approach, and continuously running programs are if anything easier to write than 'finite' ones. The following Lucid program, **m + n**, for example, can be thought of as a continuously operating program which repeatedly inputs pairs of numbers and outputs their sums. It corresponds roughly to the PASCAL program

```
program sum(input, output);
var m, n : integer;
begin
  while true do
  begin
    write('n?'); read(n);
    write('m?'); read(m);
    writeln(m + n)
  end
end.
```

In the same way the program

$$(-b + sqrt(d))/(2 * a)$$
where
$$d = b * b - 4 * a * c;$$
end

repeatedly reads in the coefficients of a quadratic and outputs the largest real root (the result is an error object if there is no real root).

Although Luswim programs are all *fomally* nonterminating, the input/output conventions of pLucid (and of its sublanguage pLuswim) allow us to write programs whose *actual* output is finite. To terminate a pLucid program, we simply 'output' the special end-of-data object denoted in the language by **eod**. When the output routine of the pLucid interpreter is asked to output this special object, it closes the output stream and terminates normally. For example, the program

3 fby 5 fby eod

will put **3** and **5** on the standard output, then terminate.

The pLucid interpreter applies an analogous convention to its input stream. When an end-of-file condition is encountered on the input stream, it automatically returns the end-of-data object whenever the evaluator demands later values of the input. The end-of-data value is propagated by the data operations and is treated almost like the error object. Terminating the input stream of most 'normal' programs (like the running sum program above) automatically causes the output stream to terminate as well, after which the interpreter will make a normal exit. (Notice that certain histories, such as those of the form $\langle 3, 2, 5, eod, 4, 7, eod, \ldots \rangle$, can not be input or output directly—the convention does not permit it.)

We should emphasise, though, that **eod** is not part of Lucid itself, not in the same way that **next** or **fby** are. This special object is provided by the algebra P. Other members of the Lucid family could be indexed with different algebras containing different special objects (such as array-index-out-of-bounds) and this would allow different input/output conventions on different interpreters. From the formal, mathematical point of view, input and output are always infinite sequences, even if all but a finite number of their components are the end-of-data value.

6. Programs with Memory

The two programs above both specify pointwise functions, i.e., the value of the output at time t depends on the values of the inputs at time t. By using the Lucid functions, however, we can write programs whose outputs vary with time, programs which can remember input values from one iteration to the next. The program

$$s$$

```
where
  s = 0 fby s + x;
end;
```

outputs a running total of all the values previously input. If the input (i.e., **x**) takes on the values

2, 0, 3, 5, 2, 8, ...

then the output will be

0, 2, 2, 5, 10, 12, 20, ...

This running total program corresponds to the PASCAL program

```
program tot(input, output);
var x, s : integer;
begin
  s := 0;
  while true do
  begin
    write('x?'); read(x);
    s := s + x;
    writeln(s)
  end
end.
```

(As in previous examples, the PASCAL version prints its own prompts.) Here is a modified version of the "total" program

$$t$$

```
where
  s = 0 fby t;
  t = if x ne 0 then s + x else 0 fi;
end;
```

which acts as before except that it interprets a "0" in the input as an instruction to reset the 'accumulator' **s** to 0. If **x** takes on the values

3, 5, 7, 0, 1, 6, 6, 4, 0, 2, 0, 3, 5, ...

then the output will be

3, 8, 15, 0, 1, 7, 13, 17, 0, 2, 0, 3, 8, ...

Another program which is not pointwise is

$$(\textbf{next next x}) - (2 * \textbf{next x}) + x$$

(the parentheses are not really necessary). This program computes the second difference of its input. If x takes on the values

$$2, 3, 7, 16, 32, 57, \ldots$$

the output will be

$$3, 5, 7, 9, \ldots$$

The program uses the Lucid operation **next** to look ahead two steps in the future of its input. This does not mean, however, that an implementation would require a clairvoyant keyboard; only that the output will lag the input by two times instants. In this program as in many others, we cannot interpret the time index as being real physical time. The semantics does not (as it might seem) imply the existence of a central co-ordinating clock.

These are just some of the many different effects which can be achieved with the Luswim functions **next** and **fby**. It cannot be emphasised too strongly that the comments in this section are not additions or extensions to Luswim. They are just that—comments on the formal semantics of Luswim, i.e., on the semantic of Iswim in general and the definition of $Lu(A)$.

7. Functions in Luswim

We have so far considered only "zero order" Luswim programs, i.e., programs in which the variables are all nullaries. This corresponds roughly to restricting ourselves to a subset of PASCAL without functions or procedures. One of the great advantages of Lucid's 'algebraic' approach to iteration is that functions come 'free of charge,' so to speak. $Luswim(A)$, i.e., $Iswim(Lu(A))$, already allows user defined functions, including recursive definitions (there are no procedures, of course, because there are no side effects). There are therefore no design decisions to be made as regards function definitions in Luswim. In this section, as in the previous one, we can (and must) restrict ourselves to investigating the *consequences* of the formal semantics of Luswim.

The $Luswim(A)$ programmer can include function definitions in his or her program (i.e., use variables as other than nullaries) but, since $Luswim(A)$ is $Iswim(Lu(A))$, they denote operations over the universe of $Lu(A)$. In other words, their denotations take histories as arguments and produce histories as results. They are not literally data operations, i.e., operations over the universe of A.

There is, however, a large class of history operations whose members are 'really' just data operations. These are the pointwise operations; an operation is pointwise if (informally speaking) the value of its result at a given point in time depends only on the value of its arguments at that point in time. More precisely, an *n*ary operation *f* over $Lu(A)$ is pointwise iff

$$f(A_0, A_1, \ldots, A_{n-1})_t = f(A_0', A_1', \ldots, A_{n-1}')_{t'}$$

whenever $(A_i)_t = (A_i')_{t'}$ for all i less than n.

Pointwise operations are, in a sense, data operations "in disguise": it is easy to show that an operation *f* is pointwise iff there is a data operation d (i.e., an operation d over the universe of A) such that the value of the result of *f* at time t is the result of applying d to the values of the arguments at time t. On the algebra $Lu(A)$, the ordinary symbols are assigned the disguised pointwise versions of the operation associated with them in A. If a $Luswim(A)$ programmer writes a definition which does not use any of the special Lucid operation symbols, the operation defined will be a pointwise version of the operation specified by the same definition considered as an $Iswim(A)$ definition. For example, if a $Luswim(Z)$ program contains the definition

f(x, y) = x * x + y * y;

(Z the algebra of integers), then the operation associated with **f** will be a pointwise history operation *f* such that

$$f(x, y) = \langle x_0^2 + y_0^2, x_1^2 + y_1^2, x_2^2 + y_2^2, \ldots \rangle$$

for any histories x and y. This pointwise interpretation principle applies even to recursive definitions; if

Fac(n) = if n < 1 then 1 else n * Fac(n − 1) fi;

then **Fac** will denote the history operation which, given a history, returns the history of factorials of the corresponding components of the argument.

Programmers can think operationally in terms of 'calling' and 'returning' provided their 'recursion time' is in a sense orthogonal to Lucid time. The above definition, for example, states that the value of **Fac(n)** at time t is the value of **n * Fac(n − 1)** at the same time t, if the value of **n** at that time is at least one. Recursive computations must be thought of as running to completion between the steps of the iteration.

The 'pointwise interpretation' principle extends to sets of mutually recursive definitions, and in fact to entire programs. If a *Luswim*(*A*) program uses none of the special Lucid functions, it acts as a continuously operating program which repeatedly accepts input and produces the output computed by its *Iswim*(*A*) version (i.e., by the same program considered as an *Iswim*(*A*) program).

In general, however, Luswim programmers use Lucid operations in their definitions. The operations defined are therefore not just pointwise versions of data operations. Instead, they can display the kind of dynamic properties possessed by the Lucid functions.

As a simple example, the definition

$$\textbf{diff(a)} \ = \ \textbf{next a} \ - \ \textbf{a};$$

specifies **diff** to be the difference operation on histories. If **x** takes on the values

$$0, \ 1, \ 4, \ 9, \ 16, \ 25, \ \dots$$

then **diff(x)** will take on the values

$$1, \ 3, \ 5, \ 7, \ 9, \ \dots$$

The "second difference" program, which appeared in the previous section, could therefore be rewritten

$$\begin{aligned}&\textbf{diff(diff(x))}\\&\quad\textbf{where}\\&\qquad\textbf{diff(a)} \ = \ \textbf{next a} \ - \ \textbf{a};\\&\quad\textbf{end}\end{aligned}$$

We could also define an operation **secondnext**, which takes us two steps into the future, and rewrite the program as

$$\begin{aligned}&\textbf{secondnext(a)} \ - \ \textbf{2} * \textbf{next a} \ + \ \textbf{a}\\&\quad\textbf{where}\\&\qquad\textbf{secondnext(a)} \ = \ \textbf{next next a};\\&\quad\textbf{end}\end{aligned}$$

Recursive definitions which use the Lucid functions can specify powerful 'dynamic' operations which produce unusual effects. For example, we can define a parameterized version of **next**:

$$\textbf{find(i, a)} \ = \ \textbf{if i eq 0 then a else find(i} \ - \ \textbf{1, next a) fi};$$

If **i** takes on the values

$$0, \ 1, \ 2, \ 0, \ 1, \ 2, \ \dots$$

and **a** the values

$$0, 1, 4, 9, 16, 25, 36, 49, \ldots$$

then **find(i, a)** will take on the values

$$0, 4, 16, 9, 25, 49, \ldots$$

We can rewrite our second difference program once again as

> **find(2, x)** − 2 ∗ **find(1, x)** + **find(0, x)**
> > **where**
> > > **find(i, a)** = **if i eq 0 then a else find(i** − 1, **next a) fi;**
> > **end**

We can also write the program as

> **df(2, x)**
> > **where**
> > > **df(i, a)** = **if i eq 0 then a else df(i** − 1, **next a** − **a) fi;**
> > **end**

In this program **df** denotes a parameterized differencing operator— **df(i, a)** is the ith difference of **a**. Finally, we can define a summation operator as follows

> **tot(x)** = **s**
> > **where**
> > > **s** = 0 **fby s** + **x;**
> > **end**

8. Continuously Operating Functions

The claims just made may well appear paradoxical, if not completely incredible, because there is no way in which the usual calling–stacking–returning operational view of recursion could possibly account for the behavior just described. Nevertheless, these claims can be verified by referring to the semantics of Iswim and the definition of $Lu(A)$. (They can also be validated by running the programs on the pLucid interpreter.)

The results of the programs appear somewhat less strange if one forgets (for the moment) about the operational interpretation of histories and thinks of them as static objects—in other words, if the programs are understood as Iswim programs over the algebra $Lu(A)$, and not Luswim programs over A. Earlier in the chapter, however, we explained at length that it was in general not advisable to think this way. Must we conclude that iteration is after all incompatible with recursion? That Lucid has, like many other languages before it, broken down with the introduction of "procedures"?

Fortunately, this is not the case, as we indicated in the introduction. There is a way to extend the operational, iterative view of Lucid programs to include those with nonpointwise user defined functions. To do this it is necessary to modify the operational notion of "function" in exactly the same way as the operational notion of program is modified to mean continuously operating program. What is needed is the notion of a *continuously operating function*; what we have already called a "filter".

The usual PASCAL calling–returning view of functions (and procedures) sees them as basically 'one-off' devices. They behave like PASCAL programs themselves; they accept a set of input, perform some computations, and produce the 'final' result. Of course these functions are, like programs, intended to be run over and over again, but there can be no connection between different calls (just as there can be no connection between different runs). This view of functions is unable to account for the activity of something like **tot**, defined earlier. Of course, we can imagine **tot** being given its input history all at once and then later producing the result history all at once, but then we lose sight of the operational significance of histories.

In order to understand **tot** we must imagine that it is a 'black box', a 'filter' which is repeatedly being given input values, which is repeatedly producing output values, but which maintains its identity between inputs. If we allow these devices to retain some internal memory from one input to the next, then it is easy to see that they can compute nonpointwise history functions. For example, the running total history function (the denotation of **tot**) can be computed by a filter capable of remembering one natural number—the total of the inputs accepted so far. For each input, the box accepts the argument, increases its memory by that amount, and emits, as the result, the new total.

The concept of a filter ('continuously operating function') is obviously closely related to the idea of coroutine [see Kahn and McQueen (1977)]. Coroutines are PASCAL-like functions which have persistent internal memory both explicitly, in that value of local variables are saved between calls, and implicitly, in that execution takes up where it left off after the last return. ALGOL, with its **own** variables, offers a similar if more restricted version of the coroutine facility. With **own** variables, ALGOL functions have explicit persistent memory, but not implicit (calling the function a second time, it starts again from the beginning, but with the **own** variables retaining their values from the previous call). Luswim filters can be thought of as working this way, but with one important difference.

In ALGOL every call to the function uses the same **own** variables, whereas in Luswim each function applied to a distinct history (or histories) (with distinct global histories), corresponds to a filter with its own persistent memory. Thus in

$$\textbf{tot(n} \ast\ast \textbf{2)} + \textbf{tot(n} \ast\ast \textbf{3)}$$

there are two filters, one keeping a running sum of the values of **n** $\ast\ast$ **2** and one keeping a running sum of the values **n** $\ast\ast$ **3**. Moreover, we have to imagine that filters are given inputs all the time, even though we might only need the value of the function at one particular time. (These spurious invocations of the filter are simply to update the values of the local variables; the values of the outputs are discarded.) For example, in the program

> **if p then a else tot(n** $\ast\ast$ **2)/tot(n** $\ast\ast$ **3) fi**
> **where**
>   **tot(b) = next s**
>   **where**
>   **s = 0 fby s + b;**
>   **end;**
>   **n = 1 fby n + 1;**
> **end**

we must imagine there are two filters as just described, but we must imagine them working for all values of **n** $\ast\ast$ **2** and **n** $\ast\ast$ **3**, even though we only need their values when **p** is false.

9. Filters and Recursion

The notion of coroutine or filter is not, however, quite general enough to give an operational meaning to all nonpointwise functions. The problem is that a coroutine is required to return a value every time it is called; and we have already seen (while discussing continuously operating programs) that the use of **next** applied to the input can cause the output to lag. If we drop the requirement that our black boxes (continuously operating filters) produce output for each input, we can think of any history function which can be defined in a Luswim program as being computed by some such device.

When a function is defined recursively, an arbitrary number of filters can be set up. For example, if **f** is defined as follows:

$$\textbf{f(x) = x fby f(x) + f(next x);}$$

and **f** is used with argument **x** which takes on the values $x_0, x_1, x_2, \ldots ,$ then a filter is set up for **f(x)**, one for **f(next x)**, another for **f(next next x)** and so on. The filter for **f(x)** outputs x_0 and sets up a filter for **f(next x)**, whose output is to be added to the output of **f(x)** itself, i.e., to x_0 followed by $\ldots$. The filter for **f(next x)** outputs x_1 and sets up a filter for **f(next next x)** whose output is to be added to that for **f(next x)** and so on.

A little study will show that the output values of **f(x)** are

$$d_0, d_1, d_2, \ldots$$

where

$$d_n = \sum_{i=0}^{n} \binom{n}{i} x_i$$

i.e., the values

$$x_0, \; x_0 + x_1, \; x_0 + 2x_1 + x_2, \; x_0 + 3x_1 + 3x_2 + x_3, \ldots$$

What actually happens, with this growing set of filters all working in parallel, is hard to imagine, to say the least, but we can easily verify that the indicated sequence is a solution to the equation defining **f**.

Fortunately, we can produce function definitions whose operational interpretation is more straightforward. One example is the function **first**, with the definition

> **first(x) = y**
> **where**
> **y = x fby y;**
> **end**

This function corresponds to a filter which outputs its first input value continually, independent of any later input values. This function is so useful that we will adopt it as a basic Lucid operation, along with **next** and **fby**.

Using **first** we can define a number of other useful functions. One particularly useful one is **whenever**, with the definition

> **whenever(a, b) = if first b**
> **then first a fby whenever(next a, next b)**
> **else whenever(next a, next b)**
> **fi;**

(The pLucid interpreter supplies **whenever** as a predefined infix operator.) It corresponds to a filter which inputs values for **a** and **b** at the same rate and outputs the value of **a** if the value of **b** is true (otherwise it just carries on inputting). Actually, if the value input for **b** is false, the value input for **a** is not even looked at; the filter is not "strict". The operational reality of nonstrict filters (i.e., filters which can 'skip' parts of their input) is questionable, but they are useful conceptually. (That is, the operational notion of 'filter' is useful in developing programs, but an actual implementation may have to work differently.)

The function **whenever** also is included as a basic Lucid operation (as the infix operator **whenever**), as is the following function **upon** (read it as "advanced upon"), with the following definition:

$$\begin{aligned}\textbf{upon(a, b)} &= \textbf{first a fby}\\&\quad \textbf{if first b}\\&\quad\quad \textbf{then upon(next a, next b)}\\&\quad\quad \textbf{else upon(a, next b)}\\&\quad \textbf{fi;}\end{aligned}$$

(The pLucid interpreter also supplies **upon** as an infix operator.) This corresponds to a (non-strict) filter which inputs values for **a** and **b** and outputs **a** and repeats it, while inputting values for **b** (not **a**), until the value input for **b** is true, at which point it inputs a value for **a**, and outputs that repeatedly, while inputting values for **b**, until **b** is true again and so on.

The operational interpretation of nonpointwise functions will be considered more closely in the chapter on Lucid as a programming language. Nonpointwise functions are the result of the constructive interaction of the two features, iteration and recursion. Lucid is able to form a synergistic union of these two features because in Lucid they both appear in an equational form; in Lucid both iteration and recursion are based on the notion of the least fixed point as a set of equations. In a language such as PASCAL or PL/I, iteration and recursion appear to clash, but the conflict is really between two very different points of view, namely, the imperative and the declarative. In Lucid this conflict has been resolved, and the various features are free to cooperate fruitfully.

Some of the ways in which the features work, in particular the usefulness of nonpointwise functions, were not foreseen by the authors. Our original intention was to develop Lucid as some sort of mathematically clear single-assignment language; we had no intention of complicating the task by adding a 'coroutine feature'. The ability to define nonpointwise functions was a serendipitous consequence of the *prescriptive* use of the denotational (history-function) semantics. It seems that nonprocedural languages in general tend to have extremely useful features not consciously introduced by the designers. We will see further examples of this phenomenon in Lucid in the later chapters.

10. Programs and Flow Graphs

One surprising fact about Luswim is that it does not really *look* like a dataflow language. It looks more like one of the functional, lambda-calculus languages—which is hardly surprising, considering that Luswim *is* a member of the Iswim family. Nevertheless, someone reading about a "dataflow language" would naturally expect to see dataflow networks. They might even expect that a dataflow language to be a graphical language. We gave a simple example of a dataflow network in Chapter I. So what has happened to them?

Luswim (and Lucid) are textual languages; a program is a one-dimensional sequence of characters, not a two-dimensional network of processors and communication lines. Nevertheless, the user can still think of the program as specifying a network and can still use network diagrams as a programming aid. Within certain limits, every Luswim program determines a network and every network determines a program. Text and dataflow diagrams are related in Lucid in much the same way that text and control flow diagrams are related in PASCAL. Text and diagrams are not different ways of expressing different things; they are different (complementary) ways of expressing the same things.

The relationship between flow graphs and sets of equations was first explicitly stated by Kahn (1974), though the idea is implicit in work in many other areas of engineering concerned with flow in networks. In Kahn's scheme the arcs (communication lines) in a network correspond to individual variables in a program, and processing nodes (filters) in a graph correspond to operations or functions in the program. The correspondence is simplest if filters are allowed only one output line each, and all duplicating of data is done by special copy nodes. In this case the translation of a network into equations is straightforward. Each variable V corresponds to the output of some filter f whose input lines correspond to the variables $X, Y, Z, \ldots$. Then the definition of V in the textual program is

$$V = f(X, Y, Z, \ldots)$$

Input arcs have no definitions in the textual program.

For example, the graph

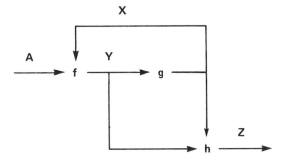

corresponds to the equations

$$Y = f(A, X);$$
$$X = g(Y);$$
$$Z = h(Y, X);$$

The copy nodes have not been drawn at all; instead, they are shown as T-junctions. Feedback loops in the graph correspond to recursively defined variables. In the above, for example, the values output by **f** are processed by **g** and are then fed back in to one of the inputs of **f**. As a result, in the textual program the variable **Y** is defined indirectly in terms of itself.

When Kahn first presented this correspondence, the equations were used to *describe* the activity of the network. Kahn stated the principle that this activity is, under certain circumstances, exactly described by the *least fixed point* of the program interpreted over a domain of histories. [Faustini (1982) gives a complete proof of this principle.] In Lucid, we have reversed the relationship between graphs and programs. It is the text which is the original version, and the network is understood as the description (or implementation) of the text. Nevertheless, the textual and graphical are still complementary representations of the same basic dataflow 'algorithm'.

It would be possible to give a precise specification of a graphical form of Luswim, and prove a version of the Kahn principle for the two forms. We could even produce a graphics-based implementation which would allow the user to draw graphs directly. This would eventually be worth the (rather large) effort involved but takes us far beyond the scope of this book. For the time being we will have to content ourselves with the informal use of dataflow diagrams as an aid to programming and documentation.

Our experience in using graphs this way has been very positive. However, for a long time we found it very difficult to draw diagrams of any size. They tended to be very large and rambling, and many drafts were required before the arcs lined up neatly. Finally we discovered a simple graph-drawing methodology which allows most graphs to be drawn quickly with a minimum of fuss.

The idea behind the methodology is the thesis that most filters 'basically' have one input and one output, and that most dataflow graphs are 'basically' simple pipelines. (In UNIX, pipelines are the only form of graph allowed by the shell language.) Of course this principle is not literally true, but we can use it to produce a first approximation. More general graphs are produced by imagining that some filters have extra 'auxiliary' inputs, and that some pipelines have 'auxiliary' feed-back and feed-forward lines leading into these auxiliary ports. Sometimes these extra ports are fed by whole auxiliary pipelines running in parallel.

Consider, for example, the following running average program.

$$\textbf{next s/n}$$
$$\textbf{where}$$
$$\textbf{s = 0 fby x + s;}$$
$$\textbf{n = 0 fby n + 1;}$$
$$\textbf{end}$$

The basic plan is that the input **x** is run first through an 'accumulating' filter, then through a dividing filter, then through **next**. The values of **n** are generated by an auxiliary pipeline. The resulting diagram is

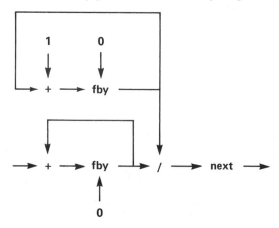

11. Implementing Luswim

Throughout this chapter (and in the first chapter) we have been talking about Lucid in terms of dataflow, but we have never made this concept very precise. This was deliberate since we were trying to convey a programming philosophy rather than a precise operational concept that describes the behavior of a particular machine configuration. In this section we will describe (briefly) how programs actually might run. This will not replace the concepts introduced earlier, even when they seem to be in conflict. The formal semantics of Lucid is denotational, not operational. The operational ideas discussed earlier can therefore be used as a *guide,* but do not have to be followed as a *specification.*

We have already seen (in earlier sections) that many Luswim programs are really very 'conventional' and correspond to ordinary iterative programs in a language like PASCAL. This suggests that such programs could be compiled into sequential code and run on a standard von Neumann machine. This is in fact possible. Farah (1977) defines a 'compilable' subset of Lucid which can be translated into an ALGOL-like imperative language.

There are, however, obvious limitations to the compiling approach. Although individual clauses can be understood as iterative algorithms, the same cannot usually be said of programs as a whole. A Luswim program is best understood as a network of filters processing streams of data. This form of computation cannot easily be described in terms of iteration, in which a number of 'global' values are repeatedly updated.

The problem is especially acute with Luswim programs which use nonpointwise user defined functions (such **tot** in Section 7). The concept of filter is completely missing from PASCAL. In PASCAL, functions can have no local memory which persists from one call to the next. In a sense, PASCAL allows only pointwise functions. It is possible to *simulate* filters in PASCAL, but it is very difficult and very complicated. Values retained between calls must be stored in variables global to the function definition. This is extremely inconvenient; it is also incorrect for filters which are being used in more than one place. There is no simple way to simulate the way in which different 'invocations' of a Luswim filter operate completely independently.

Recently, a number of new languages [such as OCCAM, described in INMOS (1982)] have appeared which attempt to remedy this defect. These languages are still imperative (based on the assignment statement) but nevertheless have moved away from the conventional concept of a single central store. In these languages a function definition is treated as a 'template' for a process with internal memory. The programmer is able to set up separate 'instances' of a template, each instance having its own identity and its own persistent internal memory. As the computation proceeds, processes (or "actors") can send messages to each other and even (though not in OCCAM) cause more actors to be created or destroyed dynamically.

These languages are not really dataflow languages (their model of computation is much more elaborate), but dataflow algorithms can be expressed in them. There is therefore some hope that Luswim (and Lucid) could be compiled into one of these 'message passing' languages. Pilgram (1983) describes a technique that works for a large number of Luswim programs. One great advantage of this approach is that the target languages are low level and basically still conventional. This means that the compiled code could be run on a system built from more or less conventional components.

The compilation process is not, however, as simple as it might appear, even when the target language allows actors as well as ordinary functions.

The first problem is that it is not always possible to compute the values of variables in strict 'chronological order'. It may well happen that the computation of (say) the time 2 value of x needs the result of the computation of the time 12 value. Programs with 'anachronistic' dependencies can arise whenever the operation **next** is used. Sometimes the anomalies are small (involve only one or two time instants) and can be smoothed out by a compiler. Sometimes, however, the time inversion can be very large. For example, the following program

> **first answer fby eod**
> **where**
>   **answer = if iseod n then [ ] else n :: next answer fi;**
> **end**

produces a list of all those objects read in (until an *eod* was encountered). This program works by defining **answer** in terms of its own future. The implementation must somehow remember all the values of **n** read in before the *eod* was reached, and these elements are then added on to the empty list in reverse order, using ::. This program could of course be written recursively, or it could be written iteratively using an ⟨⟩ to add successive elements of the current value of **n** to the end of a list which starts off as []. (This latter algorithm would involve a great deal of copying.) If the compiler were given the (reasonably efficient) definition above, it would have no choice: it would have to remember all the individual values of **n**. This is rather a lot for a mere compiler to discover. Instead, it would probably decide that the definition of **answer** violates the requirement of any compiling algorithm that the elements in a sequence be evaluated in the order in which they appear in the sequence. The compiler could then politely decline to accept the above program.

It could be argued that the program just given is stylistically bad or even pathological (it can hardly be understood in terms of pipeline dataflow). Unfortunately, there is another obstacle to compilation which arises in even apparently innocuous programs. The second problem (a far more serious one) arises because the filters in a Luswim program may not require all the values of their input. The needs of a filter may be *intermittent*: it might require (say) the values at times 0 and 1 but not those at times 2 and 3; then it may need those at time 5, 6 and 7, but not at times 8 and 9; and so on. Any attempt to compute these intermediate values (as is required by naive pipeline dataflow) will involve the implementation in unnecessary computations. These computations will certainly waste resources and may even cause deadlock (if the extra computations fail to terminate).

The program

```
diffac(n) whenever n < next n
  where
    diffac(n) = fac(next n − n);
    fac(n) = if n eq 1 then 1 else n * fac(n − 1) fi;
  end
```

produces the stream of factorials of positive differences of the numbers in its input stream. A naive implementation would try to generate the stream of all factorials of differences and then throw away those corresponding to negative differences. This naive approach would fail because the **diffac** 'blows up' (fails to terminate) whenever its input decreases from one value to the next. It is not even enough to 'prefilter' the input to **diffac**; the expression **diffac(n whenever n < next n)** would give completely different results.

One solution to this problem (adopted by many dataflow languages) is to define it out of existence by excluding nonstrict operations like **whenever**. We consider this far too drastic: for Lucid, it would mean dropping **first, next, fby** and even **if–then–else** as well. It would mean rewriting nearly every program in the book. It would no longer be possible to write filters which actually *filter*—which discard some of their input. Instead, we would have to trace the input stream back to its source and 'hack' its generator so that the unwanted values are never produced. This places an enormous burden on the programmer and is completely alien to the modular approach that dataflow ought to offer.

This second difficulty is truly unavoidable. We must therefore conclude that naive pipeline dataflow (whether simulated with actors or otherwise) is not suitable as a basis for a completely general Lucid implementation. We need some more general form of dataflow in which it is not required that all the values of a stream are actually computed, and in strict chronological order.

The simplest solution is to expand the model of dataflow slightly by allowing processes to send some control information upstream. For example, if a filter realises it does not need the next value due to appear, it can send a 'kill token' ("lethon") upstream, which cancels the computation of the value in question. Pilgrams's compiling algorithm works this way. In addition to lethons he has other tokens carrying other messages. His main problem is handling the case in which a single producer filter is supplying copies of its output to a number of consumers with different patterns of needs. Nevertheless Pilgram's approach is capable of compiling correctly a surprisingly large class of programs.

Unfortunately, there are still many programs that cannot be compiled correctly. The problem is that even with lethons there is still no sure way for a compiler to know which computations are necessary. A filter receiving a lethon cannot just suspend all internal computation. It may have to keep updating some internal values (such as counters) so that they will have the proper values when output must again be produced. Some input values may be needed to keep the internal memory 'ticking over', and this means that lethons cannot always be propagated upstream. Other difficulties arise with feedback loops. It seems that there is no entirely correct, completely reliable implementation which still tries to interpret the Lucid time parameter as in any sense corresponding to *real* time.

Fortunately, there is a relatively simple way of implementing Lucid, which is based on the idea of considering Lucid time as a formal property of a value, that has nothing to do with actual time. This is an implementation by means of a demand-driven interpreter. The idea is that the operating system demands the value of the program at different 'times' 0, 1, 2, 3, etc. To calculate these values the interpreter evaluates subterms at other times. The demand pattern for the program itself is entirely 'conventional' (in strict chronological order), but the demand patterns for subterms need not be.

Consider, for example, the program

$$\mathbf{y}$$
$$\textbf{where}$$
$$x = 1 \textbf{ fby } x + 1;$$
$$y = 1 \textbf{ fby } y + 2 * \dot{x} + 1;$$
$$\textbf{end}$$

(whose value is the stream of squares of the positive integers). The first demand would be for the value at time 0, which in turn would produce a demand for **y** at time 0, which, by definition of **y**, is 1. This then is the value of the program at time 0. Then there would be a demand for the value at time 1, and hence for the value of **y** at time 1. This results in a demand for the value of **y** + **2** * **x** + **1** at time 0, which in turn generates demands for **y** + **2** * **x** and 1 at time 0. The former demand results in demands for both **y** and **2** * **x** at time 0, and the latter of these results in demands for **2** and **x** at time 0. (There is thus a tree of demands, and the demands on distinct branches of the tree could be made and satisfied simultaneously if the interpreter were implemented in a multiprocessor environment.) The demands for **2** and **1** are met immediately, by the numbers 2 and 1, and the value of **y** at time 0 has already been found to be 1. (We assume that this value has not been thrown away.) The value of **x** at time 0 also is 1, by the definition of **x**. The value of **2** * **x** at time 0 is thus found to be 2, and the value of **y** + **2** * **x** at time 0 is 3. Finally, the value of **y** + **2** * **x** + **1** at time 0, which is also the value of **y** at time 1 and the value of the program at time 1, is 4.

This example has been very simple, and could in fact have been handled by a compiler quite easily, but the method of computation used by the interpreter is quite different from the one a compiler would use, and it can handle the intermittent and anachronistic patterns of needs that cause difficulties for a compiler.

The demand-driven scheme extends easily to handle programs with user-defined functions as well. We simply allow the values of variables to depend on a *place* as well as a time parameter. The place parameter is a finite sequence of integers which gives the calling sequence which led to the evaluation of the particular value in question. The place parameters can be very long, but a simple coding system can be devised so that demands themselves refer only to the simple (small integer) codes.

The demand-driven scheme just described is, however, completely impractical. The problem is that computed values are not saved. If these values are demanded again, they must be recomputed. As a result, even simple algorithms are ridiculously inefficient. Fortunately it is a relatively easy matter to add memory. Each time a value is computed, it is labelled (with the time and place parameters) and stored in a big 'warehouse'. Every time a value of a variable is requested, the interpreter first checks that the value is not already on hand. The warehouse must therefore act as an associative store, but this can be easily (and efficiently) simulated with hashing.

This describes the essential features of the Lucid interpreter, written by Calvin Ostrum when he was an undergraduate student at the University of Waterloo. Earlier, simpler interpreters along the same lines were written by T. Cargill, M. May and P. Gardin (all of whom were students at the time).

The main problem with this modified interpreter is that it never forgets anything. The available memory can get filled up quite rapidly. What is needed is some sort of garbage collection to get rid of the values of variables that are never going to be needed again. In the current pLucid interpreter, which is based on Ostrum's interpreter but has been extended by A. Faustini at the University of Warwick, this is taken care of by a "retirement age" garbage collection scheme. The value of a variable at a particular time reaches retirement age if it survives more than a certain number of garbage collections without being referred to. If this happens it will be retired (i.e., collected up) at the next garbage collection. The "certain number" is determined dynamically. The number is decremented after each garbage collection, so that it tends to be no larger than necessary. However, during evaluation it is incremented every time use is made of a value which would have been retired at the next collection. This keeps the age large enough so that useful values are kept around.

The retirement plan is remarkably effective, but it is still only a heuristic. There is no guarantee that useful variables will not be retired too soon, or that useless values will not be kept on too long. Fortunately, the consequences of early or late retirement are not serious. If the retirement ages are too high, it means only that space is wasted on values which are not needed. If the retirement ages are too low, it means only that *time* is wasted in recomputing values. One of the greatest advantages of the demand-driven scheme is the fact that the storage management strategy affects performance but not correctness.

The interpreter is complete (it can handle the whole language), but it is implemented on a conventional one-processor von Neumann machine (usually a VAX), so it is not very efficient. Lucid can only realise its full potential when it can be run on a dataflow machine. There are (as we mentioned in the introduction) a number of dataflow machines planned, and at least one actually operating (at the University of Manchester). T. Sargeant (1982), at Manchester, has produced a compiler that compiles Lucid into Manchester machine code, and many programs have been run.

Unfortunately the Manchester dataflow machine is based on *data*-driven, rather than *demand*-driven, dataflow. This means that the flow of demands as well as the memory management must be simulated (the latter can be quite difficult). The performance is therefore far less than what is possible in principle. We are now considering possible designs for a *demand*-driven machine similar to the Manchester machine but which would work like the interpreter. With a machine of this type the language (Lucid) and its implementation would finally be perfectly matched. We have good reason to be optimistic about such a combination.

IV LUCID: LUSWIM WITH NESTED ITERATION

The language Luswim has shown itself to be surprisingly well suited for specifying unconventional, dataflow or 'coroutine' forms of computation (surprising, that is, in view of its simplicity). The Luswim programmer soon finds out, however, that the language is also surprisingly *unsuited* for expressing more conventional iterative algorithms.

Suppose, for example, that we wanted to generalise the moment program in the preceding chapter to compute arbitrary moments (the nth moment of a series is the sum of the nth powers of its elements). To do this, we need to be able to compute arbitrarily high powers of the values in the input stream, and not just the squares. Of course, we can add a recursive definition of a function **pow**:

$$\textbf{pow(x, n)} = \textbf{if n eq 0 then 1 else x} * \textbf{pow(x, n} - \textbf{1) fi;}$$

so that in general the value of **pow(x, n)** is the value of **x** raised to the value of **n**. On the other hand, we might prefer to use an iterative algorithm to compute powers. After all, the whole point of Lucid is to allow iteration. In PASCAL, at least, an iterative version is very easy to write; we just add the following procedure:

```
function pow(x : real; n : integer) : real;
var k : integer;
    y : real;
begin
  y := 1;
  for k := 1 to n do
    y := y * x;
  pow := y
end;
```

If we try to formulate this algorithm in Luswim, however, we run into surprising difficulties. To understand the nature of these difficulties let us consider a very simplified form of the problem of computing powers, one which can be done in Luswim, and then try to generalise the solution.

The simplest form is one in which we need to compute the power for particular values of **x** and **n**—say 3 and 8, respectively. We need to write a program which computes 3^8. (Our Luswim program will actually produce this value over and over.)

This problem is particularly simple in PASCAL. We just use a **while** loop that accumulates products of 3 until it has 8 of them.

```
program pow(output);
var p : real;
    i : integer;
begin
  i := 0;
  p := 1;
  while i < 8 do begin
    i := i+1;
    p := p * 3
  end;
    write(p)
end.
```

The **while** loop in the program looks like some we have already considered, which we have translated into Luswim without any particular problem. There is, however, one crucial difference: the PASCAL loop will eventually *halt*. It is not in any sense meant to go on forever; it is not continuously operating.

The Luswim equations

$$i = 0 \text{ fby } i + 1;$$
$$p = 3 \text{ fby } 3 * p;$$

imitate the loop of the PASCAL program. But they specify an infinite, unending computation, whereas the PASCAL program specifies only eight values for **i** and **p**. Of course, we can use the pLucid *eod* object to limit the output of a program to only one value. But which value? The program **first p fby eod** outputs only the first value of **p**, and the program **first next p fby eod** outputs only the second. Obviously we could continue in this way and write a program which produces only the eighth (time 9) value of **p**, but it does not generalise very well. We need an operation which can 'extract' single values of a stream, values which may take arbitrarily long to produce.

1. The Operation asa

Luswim already has a way of selecting certain desired values from a
stream—the operation **whenever** (abbreviated **wvr**) introduced in the last
chapter. In general **y wvr q** is the sequence of all values of **y** for which the
corresponding value of **q** is *true*. In our particular case, **p wvr i eq 8** gives
us those values of **p** which correspond to a value of 8 for **i**. In general,
there may be infinitely many values of **y** corresponding to a value of *true*
for the 'test' **q**; and if not, **y wvr q** will eventually have ⊥ as its value. In
either case, if we are simulating a **while** loop whose halting condition is **q**,
we are interested only in the first of these values, i.e., the value which **y**
has when **q** is *first* true. This value, of course, is just **first(y wvr q)**; in the
example under discussion,

first(p wvr i eq 8).

Our complete program is therefore

first(p wvr i eq 8) fby eod
    where
      i = 0 fby i + 1;
      p = 1 fby 3 ∗ p;
    end

We can make the notation even more suggestive by introducing a new
infix operator **assoonas** (abbreviated as **asa**), with **y asa q** defined to be
first(y wvr q). Our program then becomes

(p asa i eq 8) fby eod
    where
      i = 0 fby i + 1;
      p = 1 fby 3 ∗ p;
    end

The value of **y asa q** is the value **y** has when **q** is true for the first time.
It should be clear that a 'simple' PASCAL **while** loop of the form

$V_0 :=$ ⋯
$V_1 :=$ ⋯
⋯
while C **do begin**
$V_0 :=$ ⋯
$V_1 :=$ ⋯
⋯
end

can be simulated with an expression of the form

> **... asa** *C* **fby eod**
> **where**
> $V_0 = \cdots$ **fby** $\cdots$;
> $V_1 = \cdots$ **fby** $\cdots$;
> **...**
> **end**

Our problems begin, however, when we try to generalize the program to give a continuously operating one with two input variables **x** and **n** and with output the **n**th power of **x**. This is easy enough in PASCAL:

```
program pow(output);
var x, p : real;
    n, i : integer;
begin
  while true do
  begin
    read(x, n);
    i := 0;
    p := 1;
    while i < n do
    begin
      i := i + 1;
      p := p * x
    end;
      write(p)
  end
end.
```

We might rush to the terminal and type

> **p asa i eq n**
> **where**
> p = 1 fby x * p;
> i = 0 fby i + 1;
> **end**

but the results will be unexpected, to say the least. (The program is intended to run continuously and therefore should not produce *eod*.) For example, if the first input values of **x** and **n** are 2 and 5, the program will not output anything (it will be waiting for more input)! If the next values are 3 and 8, still nothing is produced! Finally, if 7 and 2 are input, the program finally produces a number 6! The next output is also 6, regardless of the next input, as are all other outputs.

The cause of this confusing behavior is not hard to find. Our iterative power algorithm works only if **x** and **n** are constant (do not change with time). If **x** is constant the equation **p = 1 fby x * p** generates powers of **x**; but if **x** itself is changing, **p** accumulates the running product of the values of **x**. Similarly, if **n** is constant in time then **p asa i eq n** does yield the **n**th value of **p**; but if **n** itself is changing, it yields the value which **p** has when **n** and **i** first happen to coincide. The **asa** is chasing a moving target!

2. Nesting in HyperpIswim

We can perhaps understand the problem a little better if we consider the following program in HyperpIswim (where we can define infinite lists). In the program the iterative algorithm to compute the power is simulated with infinite lists.

```
Aux(x, n)
  where
    Aux(y, m) = Asa(p, c) :: Aux(tl(y), tl(m))
      where
        x = hd(y);
        n = hd(m);
        p = 1 :: prod(x, p);
        i = 0 :: add(1, i);
        c = equ(n, i);
      end
        where
          prod(k, l) = k * hd(l) :: prod(k, tl(l));
          add(k, l) = k + hd(l) :: add (k, tl(l));
          equ(k, l) = k eq hd(l) :: equ(k, tl(l));
        end;
    Asa(y, q) = if hd(q) then hd(y) else Asa(tl(y), tl(q)) fi;
  end
```

The inputs to this program, namely the values of the input variables **x** and **n**, are intended to be infinite lists—lists of all the individual numbers input. For example, if (as we have already supposed) the first three individual values of **x** are 2, 3 and 7, and those of **n** are 7, 2 and 8, then the input values of **x** and **n** are infinite lists of the form [2 3 7 ...] and [5 8 2 ...], respectively.

This program does in fact work; with input as indicated, its output is an infinite list of the form [32 6561 49 ...]. It works even though the body of the inner **while** is just a translation into the clumsy HyperpIswim notation of the Luswim program (the variable **c** corresponds to the expression **i eq n**). The difference between the two programs is nevertheless not hard to see. The HyperpIswim program uses the auxiliary function **Aux** to 'run' through the input. Each pair of numbers input is passed into the **where** clause and the desired result is extracted with the **Asa** function. Each of these pairs of numbers generates a different 'invocation' of the where body, and in each of these invocations the value of (say) **p** is a different infinite sequence. In other words, each of the infinitely many pairs of individual inputs determines an entire infinite sequence of values for **p**. The entire collection of individual values associated with **p** is *doubly* infinite. The Luswim version fails because its sequences are only singly infinite, i.e., they depend on only a single time parameter.

The two programs resemble each other because the second uses a little sleight of hand with variables. The variables **x** and **n** are used in two different ways, inside and outside the **where** clause. On the outside, **x** represents the entire list of all values for **x** ever input; in other words, the analog of a Luswim history. Inside, however, it represents (because it has been redefined) a single individual number—the analog of a Luswim constant. Different invocations of the while body will correspond to different individual values for the inner **x**. If we trace the definitions back, we see that the inner **x** is the head of **y**, which is in turn a parameter of **Aux**. As **Aux** 'runs through' the outer values of **x** and **n**, the different values of **y** correspond to the result of removing more and more items from the head of **x**. Thus the value of the expression **hd(y)** runs through the components of the list denoted by the outer **x**. In other words, the inner **x** 'runs through' the components of the outer **x** one at a time. In each invocation of the **where** body the pair of values of **x** and **n** represent a 'snapshot' of the activity recorded by the outer values—the result of 'freezing' the outer activity at a given point in time.

We can make this clearer by using different variables for the inner, 'frozen' values of **x** and **n**. If we use **X** and **N** for these values, the program becomes

```
Aux(x, n)
  where
    Aux(y, m) = Asa(p, c) :: Aux(tl(y), tl(m))
      where
        X = hd(y);
        N = hd(m);
        p = 1 :: prod(X, p);
```

```
        i = 0 :: add(1, i);
        c = equ(N, i);
    end
    where
        prod(k, l) = k * hd(l) :: prod(k, tl(l));
        add(k, l) = k + hd(l) :: add (k, tl(l));
        equ(k, l) = k eq hd(l) :: equ(k, tl(l));
    end;
    Asa(y, q) = if hd(q) then hd(y) else Asa(tl(y), tl(q)) fi;
end
```

Now a single, infinite value of **x** corresponds to infinitely many ordinary values of **X**—and N bears the same relation to **n**. The variables **X** and **N** therefore 'run through' the components of the corresponding lists. For each of these values, infinite lists **p**, **i** and **c** are created, and thus the effect of nested iteration is obtained.

Clearly what is missing from Luswim is nested iteration—the ability to define whole families of subcomputations, one for each step in the 'main' computation. HyperpIswim has it, but only in a crude and indirect form—indeed, the reader may be confused or skeptical about our operational interpretation outlined above. Luswim has nesting (with its **where** clause) but it is nesting of scope only. We cannot imitate the HyperpIswim program in Luswim—in Luswim everything is a sequence, and there are no 'scalars'.

The definitions of a **where** clause define single sequences, not families of histories, one for each 'timepoint' in the outer computation. In operational terms, we saw that the body of a Luswim **where** clause defines a single iterative computation which proceeds in parallel with the computations on the 'outside'—not a family of subcomputations, each of which runs to completion while the main computation is held in a state of suspended animation. In the imperative languages, nested iteration is supplied almost automatically. The values of variables remain unchanged unless they are forced to change by the execution of an assignment statement. Therefore, to get the nesting effect it is enough simply to stop doing things to the variables in the main computation while the subcomputation is being performed. In Luswim, on the other hand, the values of variables are normally in the process of changing, not of remaining constant. The different computations which produce the values of the variables proceed simultaneously and (except for data dependencies) independently, without the intervention of some central control.

3. Nesting with whenever and upon

There is in fact one way to achieve nesting in Luswim. We can use **upon** to achieve a temporary suspension of the activities of the main computation, and then use **whenever** to extract the results of subcomputations which proceed during the suspension of the main computation. Here is the power program using **whenever** and **upon** in this way.

```
p whenever c
   where
     N = n upon c;
     X = x upon c;
     p = 1 fby if c then 1 else X * p fi;
     i = 0 fby if c then 0 else i + 1 fi;
     c = i eq N;
   end
```

The variable **p** accumulates powers of the current suspended value **X** of **x**, and is reset back to 1 each time the required power is obtained. The operation **whenever** is used to extract these desired final values of **p**.

This approach is not, however, really suitable. For one thing, it is very inconvenient: the condition must be mentioned several times, and new 'inner' names must be devised for global variables. For another, the different subcomputations are not really independent. If one of the iterations 'blows up'—i.e., the halt condition never becomes true—then succeeding subcomputations never get done. This is true even if the particular subcomputation is computing a value which in the end is not needed. Finally, this method works only if the subcomputations are producing a finite object—and so take only a finite number of steps.

4. Going beyond Luswim

In a sense, the **whenever/upon** approach is only a particular *implementation* of a certain, limited kind of nesting. Nesting is important enough that it should be available in as general a form as possible, and in an abstract (implementation independent) a form as possible. It does not seem to be possible to solve all these problems conveniently and remain within the Iswim family. It is necessary to extend Luswim to a new language, Lucid (i.e., full Lucid), which is not simply a member of the Iswim family.

One way to do this is to extend the notion of sequence to allow the values of a sequence to depend on more than one time parameter. This was the approach which was originally adopted, as in Ashcroft and Wadge (1977). Fortunately, there is a much simpler way to extend

Luswim, more in accord with the operational view of suspending a main computation while a subcomputation proceeds.

Consider again the problem with the attempted Luswim power program. The program works, provided that the values of the globals of the clause (**x** and **n**) are constant (in time). Given nonconstant values for **x** and **n**, the value which we would like the clause to have at time t is z where $\langle z, z, z, \ldots \rangle$ is the value the clause would have if **x** and **n** had the values

$$\langle x_t, x_t, x_t, \ldots \rangle \quad \text{and} \quad \langle n_t, n_t, n_t, \ldots \rangle$$

with x and n being the values of **x** and **n**, respectively). For example, suppose again that x and n are of the form

$$\langle 2, 3, 7, \ldots \rangle \quad \text{and} \quad \langle 5, 2, 2, \ldots \rangle$$

respectively. If **x** and **n** had the values $\langle 2, 2, 2, \ldots \rangle$ and $\langle 5, 5, 5, \ldots \rangle$, then the clause would have the value $\langle 32, 32, 32, \ldots \rangle$; if **x** and **n** had the values $\langle 3, 3, 3, \ldots \rangle$ and $\langle 2, 2, 2, \ldots \rangle$, then the clause would have the value $\langle 9, 9, 9, \ldots \rangle$; and if **x** and **n** had the values $\langle 7, 7, 7, \ldots \rangle$ and $\langle 2, 2, 2, \ldots \rangle$, then the clause would have the value $\langle 49, 49, 49, \ldots \rangle$. When we put together the results of these 'hypothetical' subcomputations, the resulting value for the clause is $\langle 39, 9, 49, \ldots \rangle$. This is in fact the value we really want: 32 is 2^5, 9 is 3^2, and 49 is 7^2. Of course, this is not the value that the clause has as a Luswim program—we have already seen that its Luswim value is the sequence $\langle 6, 6, 6, \ldots \rangle$.

It would not be hard to change the semantics of Luswim so that clauses would give us the desired nesting effect. At present the value of the clause

$$
\begin{aligned}
&S \\
&\quad \textbf{where} \\
&\qquad V_0 = E_0; \\
&\qquad V_1 = E_0; \\
&\qquad \cdots \\
&\quad \textbf{end}
\end{aligned}
$$

(let us assume for the sake of simplicity that all variables are nullaries) in an interpretation I is the value of S in the interpretation I', which is the least satisfying the definitions in the body and agreeing with I except possibly for the values of some of the locals. As a first step, notice that we can reword this definition so that it gives an 'instant by instant' specification of the value of the clause, as follows:

> The value of the clause at time t is the value of S at time t in the interpretation I'_t, which is the least satisfying the body and differing from I at most in the values assigned to the locals.

The new form of the definition is equivalent to the standard one, but comes closer to expressing the idea that there should be an entire subcomputation (and an entire inner interpretation) for each step in the main computation. There is, of course, no nesting obtained, and the reason is clear: the 'inner' interpretations I_i' are all the same.

It is not hard, however, to see how the reformulated definition can be changed to yield a nesting effect. We simply require that the globals of the clause be given constant values in each inner interpretation; in particular, that the value of a global V in the inner interpretation I_i' be the constant sequence $\langle v_t, v_t, v_t, ... \rangle$, where $\langle v_0, v_1, v_2, ... \rangle$ is the value of V in the 'main' interpretation I. It should be apparent from what has been said earlier that this will in fact give the effect of the subcomputations being run while the main computation is 'suspended'. In particular, our exponential program will now work.

The change in the semantics of Luswim does indeed give us a language in which nesting can be expressed. The modifications have the effect of forcing the value of a clause to be a pointwise function of the values of its globals. This modified Luswim, however, would no longer be a member of the Iswim family, because we tampered with the 'generic' semantics of Iswim's **where** clause. In particular, some definitions of globals (such as **H = next G**) true outside a clause are no longer true inside—occurrences of a variable *inside* denote difference things than occurrences outside. This modified Luswim would be much closer to a language like PASCAL, where nesting is almost automatic, with the restriction that inside a block no assignments to globals are allowed.

There is, however, one glaring flaw with this solution to the nesting problem—we lose most of Luswim's dataflow capabilities. In modified Luswim, user defined functions can still be thought of as filters, but only as filters without memory (because the functions are guaranteed to be pointwise). Our running average program, for example, would no longer work: the value of the clause

> **next(s/n)**
> **where**
> **n = 0 fby n + 1;**
> **s = 0 fby s + a;**
> **end**

is that of the variable **a**. In each subcomputation specified by the body, the value of **a** will be 'suspended' at its outer value. This means that the value of **s** inside the clause is that of **a** $*$ **n**, and so the value of **next(s/n)** inside the clause is that of **a** itself.

It should be apparent, then, that the two different semantics for **where** clauses are incompatible. In Luswim the 'main' computations proceed in parallel with the computation specified by the body, while in the new language the main computation is suspended. We obviously cannot have it both ways at once; nevertheless, it is hard to choose between these two notions of 'subcomputation'. From the few examples we have seen already, it seems that both notions can, in different circumstances, be appropriate and useful. We could always produce two separate languages, one for the 'plumbing' style of programming and one for the more conventional approach. But what would we do when faced with a problem in which both forms of subcomputation were suggested? The example given at the beginning of the book is a case in point. In computing a running root-mean-square of a stream of numbers, we used one filter (with memory) which accumulated averages, and another pointwise filter which extracted square roots using a nested subcomputation.

Our (i.e., Lucid's) solution to the problem of mixing the two notions of subcomputation has evolved considerably. The first approach was to provide two different versions of **where** clause in the same language. One of these was the **where** of modified Luswim in which the values of globals are 'frozen', while the other one was the ordinary **where** which imports its values 'fresh'. Later, we divided the collection of program variables into two sets (boldface and lightface). In this second approach there was only one **where** clause, but lightface variables were always frozen and boldface were always fresh. This proved simple in theory but confusing and unworkable in practice.

In Ostrum's (1981) Luthid interpreter, the programmer gave declarations of those variables to be imported fresh (**nglobal**) and frozen (**eglobal**). This was a great improvement, but still not completely satisfactory (even though the **nglobal** list is easily dispensed with). Programmers found it very confusing that a variable could mean one thing inside and another outside a clause. It is not in the spirit of functional programming; it corresponds to the situation in an imperative language; where globals retain their initial values if no assignments are made to them.

5. The is current Declaration

In this book we present our most recent solution, one which we hope resolves these difficulties. The Lucid clause in its latest form allows the programmer to give new names to the frozen values of chosen variables (or, more generally, expressions). The new names are used inside the clause to refer to the value of the specified expression at the suspended global time; in other words, to the current 'outer' value of the expression. Any variable can be used to denote the frozen value, even the same variable whose frozen value is being named. Often we will use a variable in upper case (such as **N**) to remind us of the fact that the value being denoted is 'really' just a datum (actually a constant stream) and not an arbitrary stream.

In general the value of the clause

$$H \textbf{ where}$$
$$V_0 \textbf{ is current } E_0$$
$$V_1 \textbf{ is current } E_1$$
$$\cdots$$
$$\cdots$$
$$L_0 = D_0$$
$$L_1 = D_1$$
$$\cdots$$
$$\textbf{end}$$

at time t is h_t, where h is the value of H in interpretation I_t''; and I_t'' embodies the least solution of the equations in the body, which differs from the interpretation I_t' at most in the values assigned to the locals of the clause; and I_t' differs from I only in that the value of V_i in I_t' is $\langle v_t, v_t, v_t, \ldots \rangle$, v being the value of V in I.

Here is the power program in Lucid:

```
p asa i eq N
   where
      N is current n;
      X is current x;
      i = 0 fby i + 1;
      p = 1 fby X * p;
   end
```

The programmer can imagine that the clause is evaluated over and over, each evaluation giving rise to a separate subcomputation specified by the equations in the body. At each time t the inner computation is started from scratch—the values of **i** and **p** are generated by induction from the initial values 0 and 1. The values of **X** and **N** remain constant during the course of a given subcomputation, but may change from one subcomputation to the next. During the subcomputation that takes place at outer time t (or rather between outer times t and $t + 1$), **X** and **N** have the 'outer' values of **x** and **n**, respectively; i.e., the values of **x** and **n** at time t. The programmer can imagine that each inner computation proceeds until the desired value is extracted, and that all the intermediate results are then discarded; so that all trace of the activity is removed. The next 'invocation' of the clause can be thought of as starting again from scratch. If there were no freezing, there would be no point in repeatedly abandoning one subcomputation and restarting the next from scratch. Without freezing, all the different subcomputations would be identical, and so nothing would be gained by restarting new ones at the beginning.

Of course the subcomputation specified by a clause with **is current** declarations is not restricted to be a Lucid version of a simple while loop. The subcomputation in the body could itself use filters, defined with clauses not containing **is current** declarations. For example, we can re-write the above program as

```
prod(if odd(k) then p else 1 fi) asa k eq 0
    where
    N is current n;
    X is current x;
    p = X fby p * p;
    k = N fby k div 2;
    prod(c) = y where
                y = 1 fby y * c;
              end;
    odd(i) = i mod 2 eq 1;
    end
```

(This program computes powers by the more efficient method of repeated squaring.) The filter **prod** accumulates running products. In each computation we can imagine a **prod** filter being set up, values being fed into it and their product being accumulated. Once the required value is obtained, however, the filter is discarded. The filters in a nested computation like the above are not required to run forever; the whole dataflow network is dismantled after each subcomputation and is rebuilt anew when the next subcomputation begins.

Naturally, what we have described is only an imaginary 'virtual' implementation. It is a convenient way of thinking about computation but not necessarily a sensible way for an actual machine to carry them out. A real implementation, even one based on pipeline dataflow, might handle nesting very differently. It might, for example, keep the network specified by the body of the clause intact from one subcomputation to the next. Before the start of a new subcomputation it would clean up all the datons left sitting on arcs and reinitialise the internal states of all the filters. The pLucid interpreter uses yet another approach. It does not even try to simulate the nesting effect. Instead, it tags demands and results with a whole sequence of time parameters. One parameter keeps track of 'local' time, another time in the enclosing loop, a third time in the next enclosing loop and so on.

Obviously, a clause specifying a subcomputation can itself contain clauses which specify subcomputations. In such cases it is not hard to see that the effect is roughly what happens in imperative languages: on entering the subsubcomputation both the subcomputation and the enclosing main computation are essentially suspended. When the value computed by the subsubcomputation is obtained, the subsubcomputation is 'exited' and the subcomputation reactivated. Here, for example, is a program which computes the base ten logarithm of the components of an input stream of rational numbers between 1 and 10.

```
midlog asa abs(mid − X) < 0.0001
   where
   X is current x;
      low = 1 fby if X < mid then low else mid fi;
      hi = 10 fby if X < mid then mid else hi fi;
      mid = a asa err < 0.0001
         where
         S is current low * hi;
         a = S/2 fby(a + S/a)/2;
         err = abs(S − a * a);
      end;
      lowlog = 0 fby if X < mid then lowlog else midlog fi;
      hilog = 1 fby if X < mid then midlog else hilog fi;
      midlog = (lowlog + hilog)/2;
   end
```

In the subcomputation (performed once for every input value) a sequence of upper and lower bounds (**hilog** and **lowlog**) to the logarithm of the current value **X** of **x** is generated, together with corresponding lower and upper bounds **low** and **hi** on **X**. On each step of the subcomputation, **X** is compared with the geometric mean mid of **hi** and **low** (i.e., the square root of their product) to determine in which of the subintervals **[low, mid]** or **[mid, hi]** it lies. The new bounding interval is either **[low, mid]** (if **X** < **mid**) or else **[mid, hi]**. At the same time, the logarithm **midlog** of **mid** is computed, and the new pair of logarithms corresponding to the new values of **low** and **hi** is either **lowlog** and **midlog** or **midlog** and **hilog**, as appropriate. Since **mid** is the geometric mean of **low** and **hi**, the logarithm of **mid** must be the the the arithmetic mean (i.e., the average) of the logarithms of **low** and **hi**.

The square root of **low** * **hi** is computed, by the nested subsubcomputation, using our naive form of Newton's method.

Each input value of **x**, i.e., each of the values taken on by **X**, gives rise, in the nested subcomputation, to a whole series of values for **hi**, **low**,

mid, **hilog**, **lowlog** and **midlog**. If the particular value of **X** is 8, for example, then the the pair (**low**, **hi**) of bounds will take on the values

$$(1, 10), (3.162, 10), (3.162, 5.623), \ldots$$

mid will take on the values

$$3.162, 5.623, 4.217, \ldots$$

and **midlog** will take on the values 0.5, 0.75, 0.625, ...

Now on each step of this nested subcomputation we have an entire nested subsubcomputation which proceeds by generating better and better approximations to the the square root of the current value of **low** $*$ **hi** (this value is called **S** in the subsubloop). On the third step of the nested subcomputation (for example) the variable **A**, which is defined 'two levels deep' (so to speak), will take on the sequence of values 8.891, 5.446, 4.356, 4.219, ... as it approaches the square root of 17.783, the product of the current values (3.162 and 5.623) of **low** and **hi**. When this approximation becomes accurate enough, the value is extracted and the whole nested subsubcomputation is 'aborted'.

Of course on the next step of the subcomputation another invocation of the subsubcomputation is started again from scratch until it, too, has supplied its value and been scrapped. This process continues until the value of **mid** is close enough to that of **X**; then the entire subcomputation is discontinued, with the desired value of **midlog** being saved from the wreckage. At this point we 'surface' to the main computation with the approximation to the log of the current value of **x**. Once this has been handed over (as the current output), we take the next value of **x** and start up another invocation of the subcomputation. On each step of this new subcomputation we start up a subsubcomputation, run it until the desired value is obtained, and so on.

If we wanted to comprehend the entire history of the computation as a whole, we could proceed as follows. The history of a variable on the outside is determined by outer time alone, and so is represented by a sequence in the usual way. A variable defined one level deep, however, varies with both outer and inner time and its history is therefore essentially a doubly infinite matrix. In the same way, the entire history of a variable defined three levels deep would be a triply infinite cube (a three-dimensional array of values).

We do not, however, recommend this mode of thinking. Clearly nesting can proceed to any desired depth, and can be arbitrarily mixed up with nonnested (parallel, coroutine style) subcomputations. The resulting computation can become very elaborate. It is much better to think locally and modularly, concentrating on only one level at a time. The computations in the enclosing level are thought of as suspended while the 'current' subcomputation proceeds, and subsubcomputations are thought of as taking place 'instantaneously'. The denotational semantics of Lucid does not involve higher dimensional histories and reflects this modular approach to nesting.

6. Mixed Clauses

We see, then, that there are two radically different notions of subcomputation: that of parallel subcomputation (a 'coroutine' or filter) and that of nested subcomputation. It is only natural to speculate that these two are only two extremes ('yin' and 'yang', so to speak), and that there may be other concepts of subcomputation intermediate between the two. This is in fact the case. There is an apparently endless variety of forms of subcomputation, and some of these will be examined in a later chapter. Even in Lucid itself a restricted mixture of the two extremes can be made available, simply by allowing some values to be imported 'frozen' while others are imported 'fresh'. In Lucid there is no requirement that the globals of a clause be treated uniformly, i.e., that they all be frozen or that they all be fresh.

Here is an example of a 'mixed' clause; the body of the clause uses both the frozen value of **n** and the fresh value of **p**. If we assume that **p** is the stream of all prime numbers, the value of

> **i asa p > N/2**
> > **where**
> > **N is current n;**
> > **isdiv = (N mod p) eq 0;**
> > **i = 0 fby if isdiv then i + 1 else i fi;**
> > **end**

at time t will be the number of prime divisors of the value of **n** at time t.

The denotational semantics is simple enough but the operational significance of 'mixed' freezing is not readily apparent. If 'nesting' and 'parallel' are the two opposite modes of subcomputations, how can they be reconciled?

There are in fact two complementary ways of viewing such mixed clauses, depending on whether the subcomputations they define are 'basically' nested or 'basically' running in parallel.

The first point of view is to regard such clauses as being primarily nested subcomputations in which certain variables (those not defined by an **is current** declaration) are restarted from the beginning at the commencement of each new subcomputation.

The example given above is best understood in this way. We imagine that on each step of the main computation we take the current value of **n** (which we call **N**), enter the subcomputation, and start generating the values of **p** (i.e., the primes) from the beginning. For each of the values of **p** so obtained we test whether or not the value divides **N**. If it does, the local variable **i** is incremented by 1, otherwise left unchanged. The value extracted from the subcomputation is the value **i** has when the **p** is first greater than **N/2**.

The clause is intended to be used in a context in which the value of the global **p** is the stream $\langle 2, 3, 5, 7, 9, 11, \ldots \rangle$ of all the primes. In these circumstances the clause is calculating the number of distinct primes which divide the current value of **n**; in other words, the value of the clause at time t is the number of distinct prime divisors of the value of **n** at time t. If, for example, the value of **n** is

$$\langle 12,8,15,60,17, \ldots \rangle$$

then that of the clause must be

$$\langle 2,1,2,3,1, \ldots \rangle$$

In the example clause above the 'halting condition' (**p > N/2**) was given explicitly, as the second argument of the **asa**. In the semantics of clauses with freezing, however, there is a 'built in' halting condition—namely, the time at which the inner time has 'caught up' with the outer time. The value of the clause is the value which the subject expression has at this time. This means that the values can be extracted from a subcomputation without using the operation **asa**. This is appropriate when the algorithm uses exactly all values of the restarted expressions up to the current time. This is often what is desired.

Here, for example, is a program which computes the second moment of the values of **i** and **i**'s next value; in other words, the value of the clause at time t is the root mean square of the difference between the next value of **i** and the earlier ones.

```
sqrt(next(s/n))
  where
    J is current next i;
    s = 0 fby s + (i − J) * (i − J);
    n = 0 fby n + 1;
  end
```

If the value of **i** is of the form $\langle 3, 5, 7, 4, \ldots \rangle$, then that of the clause is of the form

$$\langle 2, 3.162, 1.915, \ldots \rangle$$

The value at time 2 (1.915) is $\sqrt{(3-4)^2 + (5-4)^2 + (7-4)^2/3}$.

We can understand this clause operationally as 'basically' a nested subcomputation inside which the values of **i** are regenerated from the beginning each time. As these values are generated, the sum of the squares of the differences between the regenerated earlier values and the frozen outer value (**J**) is accumulated. The loop 'halts' when inner time coincides with outer time and the required average is extracted.

The other way of viewing a mixed clause is to consider it as a family of Luswim clauses, with the parameters of the family being the values of the variables which are specified as current values of expressions. The following clause, for example,

```
next s/n
where
  K is current k;
  n = 0 fby n + 1;
  s = 0 fby s + pow(p, K);
end
```

has as its value at time t the (**k** at time t)th moment of the values of **x** up to time t. We can think of the variable **k** as denoting the parameter, and each individual numeric value of **k** determines a conventional Luswim clause. If **k** has been defined (outside the clause) to be constantly 3, then the clause itself is equivalent the ordinary Luswim clause

```
next s/n
where
  n = 0 fby n + 1;
  s = 0 fby s + x ** 3;
end
```

which computes the running third moment. Similarly, in an environment in which **k** is constantly 2, the clause in question is equivalent to the Luswim clause

```
next s/n
where
  n = 0 fby n + 1;
  s = 0 fby s + x ** 2;
end
```

which computes the running second moment of **x**. In an environment in which the value of **n** changes irregularly with time between 2 and 3, the clause can be interpreted as sampling the appropriate outputs of two different simultaneously running 'coroutines' defined by the two clauses above, one computing the second moment and the other the third. On each time step the mixed clause effectively yields the corresponding output of one of the two 'coroutines' and discards the output of the other.

The same interpretation can, of course, also be applied to user defined functions which are defined using clauses with mixed nesting. For example, given the definition

mom2(x, m) = next s/n
      where
        M is current m;
        s = 0 fby s + (x − M) ∗ (x − M);
        n = 0 fby n + 1;
      end;

then the value of **mom2(a, i)** at time t is the second moment of the first $t + 1$ values of **a** about the value of **i** at time t. We can regard **mom2** as 'basically' an ordinary Luswim function, i.e., a filter, but with a parameter **m**. Thus **mom2(x, 0)** is the result of running **x** through a running sum-of-squares filter. If **i** is varying in time with values in the range 1 to 4, for example, we can think of **mom2(a, i)** as a filter formed by running four simple moment filters in parallel and, at each time step, selecting (according to the value of **i**) which of the individual outputs to pass on and which to discard.

It is possible, of course, to apply sometimes the one operational view and sometimes the other to the same object. The above Lucid function, for example, could also be understood as defining a nested subcomputation in which the first parameter is restarted. From this point of view the evaluation of **mom2(a, i)** at time t involves taking the value of **i** at time t and then entering the nested subcomputation, regenerating the values of **a**, then exiting with the required moment. We could think of **mom2** as basically a conventional pointwise function which takes 'all of' **a** as its first argument. This view is probably more appropriate when understanding an expression like **mom2(a, avg(a))**, which produces a running variance of **a**.

We would certainly sympathise with the reader who feels that mixed freezing is obscure and complicated, and who is skeptical of its usefulness. Earlier versions of Lucid did not allow mixed freezing, and even when it was made possible we felt for a long time that mixed loops were bizarre constructs not worth the trouble of outlawing. Experience, however, seems to indicate that it is less strange and more useful than would appear at first sight. Mixed clauses can appear spontaneously in supposedly ordinary programs, usually when the programmer wants to pass a whole stream of values (such as the primes) to a subloop. Mixed nesting may prove to be a powerful programming technique; mixing will also be discussed in a later chapter.

V PROGRAMMING IN LUCID

In the preceding chapters we have presented the basic 'tools' in the Lucid programmer's kit. The reader should now have some knowledge of these basic techniques and concepts—filters, nesting and so on. The knowledge presented so far, however, is in a sense 'tactical.' The reader may be wondering about strategy—how does one plan out a Lucid program in the first place? In other words, what *methodology* should the Lucid programmer use?

Of course, we could adopt a sort of nonprocedural Cowboy attitude. We could claim that Lucid is such a good language, that its tools are so powerful, that you do not need strategy. This attitude is not completely unfounded. Programs in Lucid (and in nonprocedural languages in general) tend to noticeably simpler, more elegant, and above all shorter than corresponding programs in the competing imperative languages.

We cannot stop programmers from using the language in any way they want, but as for ourselves we think that programming strategy is all-important—no amount of cleverness or powerful tools can compensate for a bad strategy. It is true, though, that a powerful language can reduce the size of problems so that the Cowboys can take on bigger tasks than ever before, while relying only on their wits. Nevertheless, even the toughest Cowboy will eventually be 'Dry Gulched' by a really nasty problem, and having powerful tools only postpones the day of reckoning.

The most important strategy in any language is modularity: 'encapsulating' parts of a program that perform certain tasks, then using these parts as 'black boxes'. In using this approach each 'module' should have a relatively simple function or role which can be understood from the outside—knowing *what* it does but not *how*. The modular approach allows a programmer to break a large problem down in to smaller ones. In Lucid (as in Iswim and most other functional languages) the module is the function. The user defines a function in terms of a body (the expression on the right-hand side of the definition) but can use it without reference to this body.

In Lucid (as in Iswim but not in LISP) functions can be written in terms of other functions, with the definitions of the subfunctions 'hidden' within the main definition (inside a **where** clause). This allows the programmer to structure the program in a hierarchy (or tree) of modules; the main program being a small module using a few submodules, each of these in turn are simple modules using other subsub modules. Finally, at the bottom of the tree are found modules which use only presupplied data and operations. The modular or hierarchical approach allows the programmer to simplify the design problem by reducing the solution of a large problem to that of solving a large number of small problems.

There is general agreement that the hierarchical approach is very effective. There is, however, some debate as to whether modules should be developed top down ('fleshing out a skeleton') or bottom up (building up more and more powerful tools). The best approach is to use the bottom-up method (tool building) as a long-range strategy, but to use the top-down approach in constructing one particular program. Lucid is not particularly committed to either the top-down or bottom-up approach. However, in a dataflow language it is much easier to fit together modules developed bottom up because of the narrowness of the interface between modules.

The modularity principle does not, however, by itself constitute a methodology. Since it can be used in almost any high-level language, including imperative ones like PASCAL, the advice to "be modular" says nothing about how Lucid differs from imperative languages. The real question is how to use effectively the tools peculiar to Lucid. Modularity breaks a problem into small subproblems; but how are each of these to be solved? How are modules broken down into submodules, and how do they interact with each other? These are the crucial questions.

The real difference between Lucid and imperative languages is the *way* in which the problem and its solution (the program) are broken up into modules. In imperative languages the basic concepts are "storage" and "command". Modules therefore represent commands to change the store, and the hierarchical approach means expressing complicated commands in terms of simpler ones. In Lucid, the basic concepts are those of "stream" and "filter". A module in Lucid is therefore a filter, and the hierarchical approach involves building up complicated filters by 'plumbing together' simpler ones.

The languages Lucid and PASCAL are, therefore, not just different ways of saying the same thing; they are different ways of saying different things. Lucid and PASCAL are based on different forms of computation, i.e., on different notions of what constitutes an algorithm. There is, of course, some overlap. Conventional iteration can (as we saw) be expressed in Lucid; and dataflow can be expressed in PASCAL (although ironically FORTRAN, with its COMMON blocks, is better suited). Nevertheless PASCAL and Lucid programs normally represent two very different solutions to the same problem.

The difference can be summarised as follows: the PASCAL programmer's algorithm could be 'drawn' as a *control* flow chart, while the Lucid programmer's algorithm could be drawn as a *data* flow chart.

The best way to convey the programming methodology appropriate for Lucid is to present a few example problems and their solutions (in pLucid).

1. Hamming's Problem, a Simple Dataflow Example

The first problem which we will consider is that of producing the stream of all numbers of the form $2^I 3^J 5^K$ in increasing order, and without repetitions. This stream should therefore begin

$$1, 2, 3, 4, 6, 8, 9, 10, 12, 15, 16, 18, \ldots$$

[this problem is discussed in Dijkstra (1976), where he attributes it to R. Hamming]. The problem is easy enough to state, but for the imperative programmer it is not at all obvious how to proceed. In fact, the program as stated is extremely difficult to do in PASCAL because we have demanded *all* the numbers. But even if we simplify it and demand (say) only the first thousand, there is still no self-evident solution. The average undergraduate would probably use three nested loops to generate an array filled with the 'Hamming numbers', but unordered and with numbers outside the required range. The naive program would then sort this array and print it out without duplications. Of course, an experienced programmer could do much better, but a good program is difficult to write (sizes of arrays have to be worked out) and can be quite complex.

The Lucid programmer could always 'transcribe' the PASCAL solutions, but in this case (as in many others) it would be a bad mistake. There is a very easy dataflow solution to the problem, and the solution can be expressed naturally and elegantly in Lucid.

The dataflow solution (which we learned from Gilles Kahn) is based on the following observation: if h is the desired stream, then the streams $2 * h$, $3 * h$ and $5 * h$ (the streams formed by multiplying the components of h by 2, 3 and 5, respectively) are substreams of h. Furthermore, any of the values of h other than 1 are values of at least one of the three substreams. In other words, the values of the stream h are 1 followed by the result of *merging* the streams $2 * h$, $3 * h$ and $5 * h$. In Lucid we can express this fact with the equation

h = 1 fby merge(merge(2 * h,3 * h),5 * h);

with **merge** a filter (to be defined) which produces the ordered merge of its two arguments. The dataflow graph looks like this:

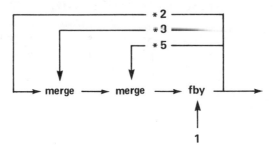

It is not hard to see that it actually works. The **fby** node 'primes the pump' with the number 1. This number is sent on as the first output, but a copy is also sent up and back through the three 'multiplying' nodes. As a result datons representing 2 and 3 arrive at the first (leftmost) **merge** node, and the 2 is sent on to the second **merge** node. At the other input of this second merge node, a 5 is waiting; the 2 is sent on, one copy proceeds as the second number output, while the other passes through the feed-back loops and appears as a 4, a 6 and a 15, which queue up at the input arcs of the **merge** nodes.

To complete our program, all we have to do is find a definition for **merge**. The following recursive definition is the one that comes first to mind, especially for programmers who are used to recursive, LISP-style programming.

merge(x, y) = if first x < first y
then first x fby merge(next x, y)
elseif first y < first x
then first y fby merge(x, next y)
else first y fby merge(next x, next y)
fi;

(notice that when **first x** and **first y** are equal, only one is 'sent on'; this is to avoid duplications in the merged result).

The above definition is correct, but is not really satisfactory. It is not really in the spirit of Lucid and of dataflow. Lucid certainly allows such definitions, and they do have a dataflow interpretation, but this interpretation involves a dynamic, expanding dataflow net (with more and more **merge** nodes being generated 'at run time'). A programmer who writes a definition like that has slipped into the mistake of viewing streams as static objects, like infinite lists. This is a very bad habit, one which people experienced in 'functional programming' can find hard to shake. The whole point of Lucid is to make it easy and natural to express iteration and dataflow directly, when appropriate. Recursive definitions, when they are not appropriate, can be cumbersome and hard to understand. They can also be inefficient on some kinds of dataflow machines and even on conventional machines. The pLucid interpreter in particular often performs much better with iterative programs.

There is in fact a straightforward iterative way to merge two streams, one which is familiar to every applications programmer. To merge **x** and **y** you take the values of **x** until they exceed the next available value of **y**; then the values of **y** until they exceed the next available value of **x**; then the values of **x**, and so on. While the values of one stream are being taken (and passed on as output), the values of the other are 'held up'.

It is not hard to express this iterative algorithm in Lucid. We simply use the function **upon** to 'slow down' the two streams. Recall that the values of **x upon p** are those of **x**, except that the new values are 'held up' (and the previous one is repeated) as long as the corresponding value of **p** is false. (**x upon p** is the stream **x** with new values appearing *upon* the truth of **p**). If we let **xx** and **yy** be the 'slowed down' versions of **x** and **y**, respectively, the desired output is (at any given time) the least of the corresponding values of **xx** and **yy**. When this least value is **xx**, a new value of **x** must be brought in; when it is **yy**, a new value of **y** is required. Our program definition of **merge** is therefore

> **merge(x, y) = if xx <= yy then xx else yy fi**
> **where**
>   **xx = x upon xx <= yy;**
>   **yy = y upon yy <= xx;**
> **end;**

(if **xx** and **yy** are equal, both input streams are 'advanced'; thus duplications in the output are avoided).

Our complete Hamming program is therefore

> **h**
>   **where**
>   **h = 1 fby merge(merge(2 ∗ h, 3 ∗ h), 5 ∗ h);**
>   **merge(x, y) = if xx <= yy then xx else yy fi**
>   **where**
>   **xx = x upon xx <= yy;**
>   **yy = y upon yy <= xx;**
>   **end;**
>   **end**

2. Using Dataflow to Enumerate the Primes

The next problem which we consider is that of generating the stream of all primes. From the dataflow point of view, the strategy is obvious: generate the stream of natural numbers greater than 1 and pass it through a filter which discards those numbers which are not prime. The filtering is accomplished using the operator **whenever**. Our program is therefore of the form

> **n whenever isprime(n)**
> **where**
> **n = 2 fby n + 1;**
> **isprime(n) = ⋯;**
> **end**

and its dataflow graph looks like

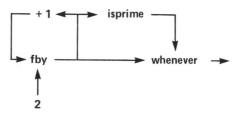

To complete our 'proto-program' we need only fill in the definition of **isprime**. The simplest way to test if a number is prime is to run through all numbers greater than 2, whose squares are less than the one in question, looking for a divisor. This is a simple, conventional nested iteration which can be easily written in Lucid:

> **isprime(n) = not(div(i, N)) asa div(i, N) or i * i < N**
> **where**
> **N is current n;**
> **i = 2 fby i + 1;**
> **div(x, a) = a mod x eq 0;**
> **end;**

(**div(a, b)** is true if **a** divides **b**). We could make a modest improvement by having an extra inner loop variable which accumulates the square of **i**:

> **isprime(n) = not(div(i, N)) asa div(i, N) or j > N**
> **where**
> **N is current n;**
> **i = 2 fby i + 1;**

```
    j = 4 fby j + i + i + 1;
    div(x, a) = a mod x eq 0;
end;
```

However, with or without this minor improvement, the simple definition of **isprime** does far too much work. There is no point, for example, in testing to see if 4 is a divisor if you already know that 2 is not. The most efficient way to proceed is to test only for *prime* divisors (whose squares are no greater than the number in question). But we have the stream of primes 'on tap': namely, the output of the main program. We need only give a name to these values and use them in the body of **isprime**. This actually works, provided we 'prime the pump' by using **fby** to specify explicitly the fact that 2 is the first prime. The resulting program is

```
prime
   where
      prime = 2 fby (n whenever isprime(n));
      n = 3 fby n + 2;
      isprime(n) = not(divs) asa divs or prime * prime > N
            where
               N is current n;
               divs = N mod prime eq 0;
            end;
   end
```

(notice that the resulting program has a loop with 'mixed freezing'; in the inner **where** clause n is available only in the frozen form **N**, but **prime** is used 'fresh').

For the sake of variety, let us now try a completely different strategy. A number is prime if it is not composite; this suggests that we generate the stream of all composite numbers and take its complement (with respect to the natural numbers greater than 1). The proto-program looks like

```
complement(composite)
   where
      composite = ···;
      complement(x) = ···;
   end
```

Our first subproblem is that of defining the **complement** filter. In general, it is not possible to compute the complement of an arbitrary stream, because it is impossible to know for sure that a given number will *never* show up. However, if the stream is already sorted (and is infinite so that it never 'runs dry'), then there is no problem: a number **N** is in the complement of the stream if the values in the stream go past **N** without ever actually equaling **N**. This observation leads immediately to the following definition of complement:

```
complement(x) = i whenever iskipped
    where
    i = 2 fby i + 1;
    iskipped = I < x asa I le X
        where
            I current is i;
        end;
end;
```

This first attempt is not really very good, though, because the testing of each value of **i** requires restarting the stream **x** from the beginning. What we need is an algorithm that gradually transforms the stream **x** into its complement.

Such an algorithm is not hard to find. Consider, for example, the following possible values for **x**:

$$5, 7, 8, 12, ...$$

The desired values of the complement are

$$3, 4, 6, 9, 10, 11, ...$$

and these values can be classified as follows: those between 1 and 5 (2, 3 and 4), those between 5 and 7 (6), those between 7 and 8 (none), those between 8 and 12 (9, 10 and 11) and so on. This suggests that we generate the stream of 'intervals'—lists of numbers lying between successive values of **x**. These intervals can then be strung together to produce the desired stream of complements.

This is not at all hard to do. There are three stages in the transformation: (i) produce the stream **e** of pairlists of endpoints of these intervals; (ii) produce the stream **l** of intervals (each value of **l** is a list of numbers); then (iii) 'read off' the values of **l** one by one to produce the stream **c** of complements. Here is the new definition:

```
complements(x) = c
    where
    e = [%1, first x%] fby [%next x, next next x%];
    l = interior(e) whenever interior(e) ne [ ];
    c = element(l);
    interior(e) = m asa I eq k − 1
        where
```

```
        I is current hd(e);
        J is current hd(tl(e));
        k = J fby k − 1;
        m = [] fby k − 1 :: m;
      end;
   element(l) = hd(r)
      where
        L = l upon r eq [];
        r = first L fby if r ne [] then tl(r) else next L fi;
      end;
  end
```

For example, if **x** takes on the values given above, **e** takes on the values

$$[1\ 5],\ [5\ 7],\ [7\ 8],\ [8\ 12],\ ...$$

l takes on the values

$$[2\ 4],\ [6],\ [9\ 10\ 11\ 12],\ ...$$

and therefore **c** takes on the values

$$2, 3, 4, 6, 9, 10, 11, 12, ...$$

Note how, in the definition of **element**, we use **upon** to slow down l while its elements are being 'read off'. We filtered out the empty values of l to make this definition easier to write.

The above definition is satisfactory and illustrates well the way in which Lucid allows dataflow to be mixed with more conventional forms of iteration (e.g., in the definition of the pointwise function **interior**).

In actual fact, though, there is a much simpler way to define complement; it can be done in three lines, using **upon**. We simply slow down the stream **x**, repeating each value until a counter catches up with it. Then we just select those values of the counter which are not equal to the corresponding value of the slowed down **x**.

```
        complement(x) = i whenever i ne xx
           where
             xx = x upon i eq xx;
             i = 2 fby i + 1;
           end
```

(The value at a given time of **xx** is the least value of **x** not less than the corresponding value of **i**).

For example, with the values of **x** given earlier, the following values of **X** and **i ne xx** will be produced

i	xx	i ne xx
1	*2*	*true*
2	*2*	*false*
3	*5*	*true*
4	*5*	*true*
5	*5*	*false*
6	*7*	*true*
7	*7*	*false*
8	*11*	*true*
9	*11*	*true*
⋮	⋮	⋮

and it is easy to see that the required values of **i** are selected.

Now that we have solved the first subproblem, we can move on to the second, that of producing the stream of composites. A number is a composite if it is a proper multiple of some number greater than 2. This suggests defining a filter that yields the stream of proper multiples of values of its input stream. This is not hard to do, providing we are allowed to assume that the input stream is increasing.

```
pm(x) = (2 * first x) fby merge(i * first x, pm(next x))
   where
   i = 3 fby i + 1;
end;
```

The definition is fairly easy to understand. The proper multiples of the values of **x** are twice **first x**; or **first x** multiplied by numbers greater than 3; or proper multiples of values of **next x**.

The composite numbers are then just the result of applying **pm** to a variable which takes on the values 2, 3, 4, ... Fitting all the definitions together, we have the following prime generating program:

```
complement(composite)
   where
   composite = pm(n)
         where
         pm(x) = (2 * first x) fby merge(i * first x, pm(next x))
            where i = 3 fby i + 1; end;
         n = 2 fby n + 1;
      end;
   complement(x) = i whenever i ne X
         where
         X = x upon i eq X;
```

```
          i = 2 fby i + 1;
       end;
 merge(x,y) = if xx < = yy then xx else yy fi
          where
              xx = x upon xx < = yy;
              yy = y upon yy < = xx;
          end;
end
```

There remains one very important improvement which can be made in this program. The definition given for **pm** is rather inefficient in that it produces far too many values in the substreams which are merged to give the stream of composites (recall that **merge** eliminates these duplications). The class of composites is indeed the class of all proper multiples of numbers greater than two; but it is enough to take only *prime* multiples thereof. Since the program is generating the primes, they are at hand, and we can rewrite the program as

```
prime
   where
      prime = complement(composite);
      composite = pm(2 fby next prime)
             where
                 pm(x) = (2 * first x) fby merge(i * first x, pm(next x))
                     where i = next prime; end;
                 n = 2 fby n + 1;
             end;
      complement(x) = i whenever i ne X
             where
                 X = x upon i eq X;
                 i = 2 fby i + 1;
             end;
      merge(x,y) = if xx < = yy then xx else yy fi
             where
                 xx = x upon xx < = yy;
                 yy = y upon yy < = xx;
             end;
   end
```

Of course, this introduces a feedback loop into the program: the stream of primes is being used to generate the stream of primes. As we have already seen, this is not necessarily a mistake; as long as the computation of a given prime involves only primes already computed, there is no danger of the feedback loop drying up and the program going into deadlock. In this case we must 'prime the pump' by applying **pm** to **2 fby next prime**, rather than to **prime** itself.

Sometimes it is very easy to see that deadlock is impossible, and many programs pass a simple syntactic test [the "cyclesum test" of Wadge (1981)] that ensures their robustness. For other programs, however, like the one above, it is not so obvious, and often the lack of deadlocks is a result of particular properties of the algorithm and the data it manipulates. In the above program, for example, a little analysis will verify that deadlock is avoided only because there is always a prime between n and $2n$ ($n > 1$).

With some more complicated definitions, especially ones involving recursively defined nonpointwise filters, it is in fact quite possible to make a mistake. For example, if we had defined **pm** in the original program by the following equation,

$$\textbf{pm(x)} = \textbf{merge(i} * \textbf{first x,pm(next x))}$$
$$\textbf{where}$$
$$\textbf{i} = \textbf{2 fby i} + \textbf{1;}$$
$$\textbf{end;}$$

nothing ever comes out of the filter so defined (because we never 'prime the pump' with an **fby**). The equation above is a true statement about the desired stream function, but that stream function is not the *least* solution (this example, in a slightly different form, is due originally to David Park).

3. Processing Text as Streams of Characters

For a change of pace we will now look at a more practical, down to earth example: text formatting. We will write a program which accepts a text (in English) in which sentences (but not words) are spread over lines in an arbitrary manner. The output is required to be the same text, formatted so each line is as close to 72 characters long as possible, without exceeding this length. We will assume that a sentence is terminated by a period. The only other punctuation allowed will be the comma. Each punctuation symbol must appear on the same line as the word preceding it. Words in the source can be separated by arbitrary numbers of blanks. The input is the stream of source characters (a character being a string of length 1); the output will be a stream of strings terminated by newline characters, each of these strings being a line of output.

Our strategy, as usual, is to send the input through a series of filters that gradually transform it into the output. The first stage replaces newlines by blanks; the second compresses blanks, so that each word is separated from the following one by exactly one blank. Next, we accumulate sequences of nonblank characters into words (and discard the blanks), giving a stream of words. Finally, the last filter accumulates the words into lines which are produced each time they have grown big enough.

Our proto-program, therefore, looks like

formline(formword(cblank(rmnewline(S))))
  where
    formline(z) = ⋯;
    formword(y) = ⋯;
    cblank(x) = ⋯;
    rmnewline(x) = ⋯;
  end

The separate filters are relatively easy to define.

The simplest, **rmnewline**, can be done with **if–then–else**:

rmnewline(x) = **if** x **eq** '\n' **then** ' ' **else** x **fi;**

The filter **cblank** involves a simple application of **whenever**:

cblank(x) = x **whenever** x **ne** ' ' **or** next x **ne** ' ';

For **formword**, we again use **whenever** to select ripe, fully formed words from the stream of partially formed words:

formword(y) = w **whenever ready**
  where
    w = **first** y **fby if** next y **ne** ' ' **then** w ˆ next y **else** ' ' **fi;**
  ready = next y **eq** ' ';
  end

Here, for example, are sample values of **y**, **w** and **ready**

y	w	ready
'T'	'T'	false
'h'	'Th'	false
'e'	'The'	true
' '	' '	false
'b'	'b'	false
'o'	'bo'	false
'o'	'boo'	false
'k'	'book'	true
' '	' '	false
⋮	⋮	⋮

The final filter, **formline**, works on the same principle. It builds up partial lines word by word and selects 'ripe' ones using **whenever**.

```
formline(w) = line whenever lineready
   where
      line = w fby if not lineready then line ^ ' ' ^ next w
                                    else next w;
      lineready = length(line) + length(next w) + 1 > 72;
   end;
```

The whole program is therefore

```
formline(formword(cblank(rmnewline(S))))
   where
      formline(w) = line whenever lineready
         where
            line = w fby if not lineready then line ^ ' ' ^ next w
                                          else next w fi;
            lineready = length(line) + length(next w) + 1 > 22;
         end;
      formword(y) = w whenever ready
         where
            w = first y fby if next y ne ' ' then w ^ next y else ' ' fi;
            ready = next y eq ' ';
         end;
      cblank(x) = x whenever x ne ' ' or next x ne ' ';
      rmnewline(x) = if x eq '\n' then ' ' else x fi;
   end
```

Clearly, a more elaborate version, which right justifies as well, could be organised on roughly the same lines. It could produces an intermediate stream of 'prelines', a preline being a list of words of roughly the right length. The prelines could then be fed into a 'spacing' filter which would produce actual lines padded out with spaces. The more elaborate formatter could also detect the end of the input stream and 'flush' the last line without attempting to justify it.

4. A Data Processing Example

For our next 'down to earth' example, we present a simple (and very simplified) example of 'data processing'. The program generates a stream of messages to members of a library. The messages warn the reader that they have books which are overdue, or which were returned late and so incurred a fine. There are two inputs to the program: a stream of records of the library's holdings and a stream of records of books returned during the day. Each record of a holding identifies its title (which we assume is unique), the current borrower (or "none" if there is none), and the current date due (again "none" if it is not on loan). Both streams are assumed to be already sorted according to title.

Records will be represented as pairlists with the first component in each pair describing the nature of the data in the second, e.g.,

```
[[title 'War and Peace']
 [borrower 'N. Bonaparte']
 [due [[year 1814]
   [month 7]
   [day 12]
   ]
  ]
 ]
```

Of course the data types of pLucid are not quite the best for this particular example; it would be better to use a member of the Lucid family with 'records' much as in PASCAL or COBOL. However, records are easily simulated with pairlists, as above.

```
message
  where
    message = 'Dear' ^ borrower ^ ':\n' ^
      case status of
        "overdue": 'The book' ^ title ^ 'is overdue, please return it';
        "late": 'Please pay a fine on the book' ^ title ^
          'which was returned late';
        default: '';
      end;
    status = if precedes(today, datedue) then "OK"
             elseif returned then "late"
                     else "overdue" fi;
    return = contents('returns');
    holding = contents('holdings');
    returned = titleof(t) eq title
          where
              t = return upon titleof(return) eq title;
          end;
    title = titleof(holding);
    datedue = comp(holding, "due");
    borrower = comp(holding, "borrower");
```

```
titleof(r) = comp(r, "title");
precedes(date1, date2) =
  year1 < year2 or
  (year1 eq year2 and month1 < month2) or
  (year1 eq year2 and month1 eq month2 and day1 < day2)
    where
      year1 = comp(date1, "year");
           year2 = comp(date2, "year");
    month1 = comp(date1, "month");
      month2 = comp(date2, "month");
        day1 = comp(date1, "day"); day2 = comp(date2, "day");
    end;
comp(l,w) = hd(tl(c)) asa W eq hd(c)
    where
      W is current w;
      L is current l;
        m = L fby tl(m);
        c = hd(m);
    end;
contents(s) = filter('cat' ^ s, 0, 'i');
end
```

The heart of the program is the definition of **returned**; this variable is true of the corresponding value of **holding**, which refers to a book which has just been returned. The definition uses **upon** to slow down the stream of returns, each return being held up until its corresponding holdings record appears. The function **contents**, which is defined using the system inter-face pseudo function **filter**, yields the stream of objects in the file named by its argument.

The rest of the program is fairly conventional. For example, the func-tion **comp** is a pair–list lookup function. If **w** is a word and **l** is a pairlist, **comp(l, w)** is the second component of the pair in **l** whose first component is **w**. If **l** is the pairlist given in the paragraph above, **comp(l, "due")** is

[[year 1814] [month 7] [day 12]]

The function **comp** therefore simulates the "." operation of PASCAL: **comp(l, "due")** corresponds to the PASCAL expression **l.due**.

This function is computed in a simple subloop. The current values **W** and **L** of **w** and **l** are 'frozen', then the program simply runs down the list **L** until a pair with head **W** is found.

5. Swap Sorting in Lucid

Modern computing machines still spend a large part of their total operating time sorting: putting sequences of data into some predetermined order. In the past quarter century many different sorting algorithms have been defined and countless imperative sorting programs have been written. It is only natural, then, to ask how one would write a sorting program in Lucid. In this section and the next we will study a number of sorting algorithms and compare the dataflow approach to the imperative one. Sorting may seem like a somewhat 'boring' topic, but it is a very important one; and our study of sorting algorithms will illustrate very clearly the difference between Lucid and imperative programming and the underlying contrast between dataflow and control flow. For simplicity, we will restrict ourselves to sorting sequences of integers only.

The imperative approach is based on the idea of processing data *at rest*. The imperative programmer naturally tends to think of sorting as a problem of sorting data stored in memory—what is usually called sorting "in place". Also, since imperative programming is inherently sequential, the tendency is to concentrate on algorithms which do one small piece of reordering at a time. The 'unit' of reordering is the exchange or 'swap' (of the contents of two storage locations). From the imperative point of view, a sorting algorithm is seen as an algorithm for generating an appropriate sequence of swaps which puts the stored data in the desired order.

Simplest of all these swap-sorting algorithms is probably the selection sort: find the biggest number in the sequence, swap it with the last element, find the next biggest, swap it with the next to last element, and so on. Here is a PASCAL procedure which does an exchange sort on a vector of 10 numbers (we assume that the type **vector** has been defined to be **array[0..9] of integer**).

```
procedure ssort(a : vector);
var i, j, Imax : integer;
procedure swap(var a : vector; i, j : integer);
var Temp : integer;
begin
  Temp := a[i];
  a[i] := a[j];
  a[j] := Temp
end;
begin
  for i := 0 to 9 do read(a[i]);
```

```
for j := 0 to 8 do begin
   Imax := 0;
   for i := 1 to 9-j do if a[Imax] < a[i] then Imax := i;
   swap(a, j, Imax)
end
end;
```

Can we write a sort-in-place algorithm like this in Lucid? The answer is "yes"—provided the underlying algebra has the right data structures and operations. We need arrays—sequences of data objects which can be accessed randomly, i.e., which can be indexed (since only one dimension of indexing is required, it would be better to call them "vectors"). We need a binary subscripting operation which takes a vector **a** and an index **i** and returns the value of the **i**th component—in PASCAL notation, **a[i]**. We also need a ternary operation **swap** such that **swap(a, i, j)** is the vector which results when **i**th and **j**th components of **a** are swapped. The selection sort algorithm might look like this in an appropriate member of the Lucid family:

```
ssort(a) = a asa k eq 0
   where
   A is current a;
   k = length(A) − 1 fby k − 1;
   a = A fby swap(a, imax, k);
   imax = imax asa j eq K + 1
      where
      K is current k;
      A is current a;
      j = 1 fby j + 1;
      imax = 0 fby if A[j] > A[imax]
                  then j else imax fi;
      end;
   end;
```

(We have reused the identifiers **a** and **imax** in an attempt to imitate the style of the PASCAL program.) In Lucid, **ssort** is a function: if **a** is a vector, the value of **ssort(a)** is the sorted version of **a**. The body of the **where** clause describes a purely conventional iterative algorithm with a nested subloop for finding the largest of the remaining unsorted elements. The variables are used in much the same way as they are in the PASCAL program. There are two loop variables in the main loop, **a** and **k**. As the computation proceeds, **a** is always going to be a permutation of the 'outer' original **a**, and **k** counts down from 9. At each step in the iteration the last 9-**k** values of **a** are already in sorted order, i.e., **a[k + 1..9]** consists of the 9-**k** largest elements in ascending order.

It is not hard to imagine that 'conventional' programs like the one above could be compiled into an imperative language and run on a von Neumann machine. Even a semi-intelligent compiler could be expected to notice that the loop variable **a** is updated purely by swapping and therefore store all the values in one place and actually perform the swaps.

It should also be apparent that the other various iterative in-place/swapping algorithms can be translated into Lucid. Here is a Lucid form of the next simplest sorting method, the 'bubble' sort.

```
bsort(a) = a asa k eq 0
  where
    A is current a;
    N is current length (a);
    k = N − 1 fby k − 1;
    a = A fby
      (a asa j eq K
        where
          A is current a;
          K is current k;
          j = 0 fby j + 1;
          a = A fby if a[j] > a[j + 1]
                    then swap(a,j,j + 1)
                    else a fi;
      end);
  end;
```

Neither of these two definitions can be used in programs in pLucid— pLucid does not have vectors. It does, however, have lists, and vectors can easily be simulated with lists. We need only define two functions, **swap** (as above) and **component** (with **component(a, i)** being the **i**th component of **a**; in PASCAL notation, **a[i]**). Adequate definitions are easy to find:

```
component(a, i) = hd(l) asa j eq I
  where
    I is current i;
    A is current a;
    j = 0 fby j + 1;
    l = A fby tl(l);
  end;
swap(a, i, j) = b asa next l eq nil
```

```
            where
              A is current a;
              I is current i;
              J is current j;
              n = 0 fby n + 1;
              l = A fby tl(l);
              AI = hd(l) asa n eq I;
              AJ = hd(l) asa n eq J;
              c = case n of
                I : AJ;
                J : AI;
                default: hd(l);
              end;
              b = [%c%] fby b <> [%next c%];
            end;
```

Naturally, we would not expect the resulting pLucid versions of selection or bubble sort to be particularly efficient. They are using a data type (lists) designed for *sequential* access to simulate other objects (vectors) designed for *random* access.

6. Dataflow Sorting in Lucid

The two examples just given are examples of Lucid programming but not of dataflow programming—the algorithms are iterative algorithms, not dataflow algorithms. The programmer, whether using PASCAL or Lucid, still thinks of the data as being processed while at rest. As long as Lucid is used this way, it is basically a form of rigorously structured programming in which (i) globals cannot be altered in nested loops; and (ii) loop variables are all initialised and updated together. Lucid used in this way is therefore essentially a *single assignment* language (like ID or VAL). These are sometimes called dataflow languages but single assignment by itself still means processing data which is *at rest*.

Therefore, instead of working our way through the interchange sorting algorithms, coding them up in Lucid, let us see if we cannot approach the sorting problem from the dataflow point of view. In fact we can already apply the dataflow approach to the lowly Bubble Sort. The Bubble Sort algorithm can be viewed as involving going over the vector from beginning to end repeatedly until the array is in order. Bubble sorting is a kind of 'combing' operation: the comb is dragged across the vector over and over until it is finally 'smooth' (sorted). Normally, one imagines the procedure being carried out with only one comb, so that the second pass cannot begin until the first pass is ended. This assumption, however, is just a reflection the strictly sequential, one-operation-at-a-time outlook characteristic of the imperative languages. In reality, there is no reason not to use more than one comb and *start the second pass before the first has finished.* The second 'comb' could follow close behind the first.

Now imagine that the two combs (processors) are at rest and that the data is in motion. The stream of data is passing through two *filters,* each of which performs a bubblepass—we now have a dataflow algorithm. Of course, there is no reason to restrict ourselves to only two bubblepass filters; we can use as many as we like. A stream of *N* numbers will be completely sorted once it has passed through *N* such filters.

Each bubble filter works by remembering one datum, namely the largest it has seen so far in its input (with *eod* considered as infinite). Every time it receives a new input, it compares the new input with its current maximum, keeps the larger of the two as the new maximum and sends the smaller on as output.

This is not hard to formalise in Lucid; and there is no need for any 'storage' (except of single values in the bubble filters). A simple minded translation of bubble sort looks like this:

```
bsort(a) = bubbles(a, slength(a))
  where
    bubbles(a, n) = if n eq 0
                    then a
                    else bubbles(bubble(a), n − 1) fi;
    bubble(a) = smaller(max, next a)
      where
        max = first a fby larger(max, next a);
        larger(x, y) = if iseod(y) then y elseif x < y then y else x fi;
        smaller(x, y) = if iseod(y) then x elseif x < y then x else y fi;
      end
    slength(x) = index asa iseod x;
  end;
```

Unfortunately, this version is a little bit too simple minded. For one thing, it needs to know the length of **a**, which means using **slength** to go all the way to the 'end' of **a** (i.e., until *eod* is encountered) before any processing begins. Also, each bubble filter passes over the whole stream when we know that the input to the *n*th filter has its first *N* − 1 components already in order. Here is a better version that does not need length and that strips off the last output of each filter before passing it on to succeeding ones.

```
bsort(a) = if iseod(first a) then a else
              follow(bsort(allbutlast(b)), last(b)) fi
    where
      b = bubble(a);
      bubble(a) = ··· {as before};
      follow(x,y) = if xdone then y upon xdone else x fi
                 where xdone = iseod x fby xdone or iseod x; end
      last(x) = (x asa iseod next x) fby eod;
      allbutlast(x) = if not iseod(next x) then x else eod fi;
    end
```

and the dataflow diagram looks like

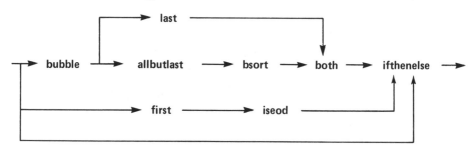

[There is one unusual feature of this dataflow diagram, namely the **if–then–else** 'node'. In ordinary pipeline dataflow this would not work. The point of **if–then–else** is to avoid computation; but how can a node affect activity upstream? In reality, a Lucid implementation would use demand-driven computation. For this reason the **if–then–else** node does work, because it prevents demands going upstream to start unneeded computation. However, we still encourage programmers to think in terms of data-driven computation when designing their algorithms. One way of reconciling the two points of view is to imagine that the **if–then–else** node works as follows: the test races ahead to the node, and then the node sends messengers up the arc not selected to 'call off' any computations which may have been started. The use of 'kill tokens' (or "lethons") in an actual implementation might not be practical; but there is no harm in the programmer imagining their use, because the complications can be ignored.]

We can try to make our program even smarter by checking if the first bubble pass was successful in completely ordering the stream, and so avoid later computation. This 'clever' version is as follows:

```
bsort(a) = if iseod(a) then a
     elseif in order(b) then b else
        follow(bsort(allbutlast(b)), last (b)) fi
   where
     b = bubble(a);
     bubble(a) = ⋯ {as before};
     inorder(b) = inordersofar asa iseod(next b)
        where
             inordersofar = true fby inordersofar and b < next b;
        end;
     follow(x,y) = {as before};
     allbutlast(x) = ⋯ {as before};
     last(x) = ⋯ {as before};
   end;
```

Actually, this new version is not quite as clever as we might think. The outcome of the test **inorder(b)** is not available until all the values of **b** have been produced. If we want to avoid sending the stream on to **bsort** before we are sure that it is not already sorted, these values must queue up somewhere while we wait to see what to do with them. We could avoid queuing and send them along anyway, with the idea that when and if we finally discover that no further sorting is required, we will abandon the computations generated by the unnecessary passes. In this case, though, there is no guarantee that all or even any of the unnecessary computations will actually be avoided. It seems that as a general rule the computational complexity of parallel algorithms is not easy to determine, at least when an implementation is allowed to try and get a 'head start' by beginning computations which may later prove to be unnecessary. (The demand-driven Lucid interpreter performs only those computations which are required; it is not allowed to 'speculate' about the usefulness of particular results.)

The bubble and selection sort are in a sense 'iterative': the stream passes through a *series* of filters in a straight line: there is no branching in the flow. There is also a whole family of dataflow sorts which are 'hierarchical' or 'recursive' in the sense that they divide the input into two parts, sort the parts, then recombine them.

The first of these recursive ones is 'merge' sort: the input stream is divided (by taking alternative items) into two streams, each of these is sent to be sorted, and the result is then merged. Here is the network.

msort(a) = if iseod(first next a) then a
     else merge(msort(b0), msort(b1)) fi
where
    p = false fby not p;
    b0 = a whenever p;
    b1 = a whenever not p;
    just(a) = ja where ja = a fby if iseod ja then eod
        else next a fi; end;
    merge(x,y) = if takexx then xx else yy fi
      where
        xx = (x) upon takexx;
        yy = (y) upon not takexx;
        takexx = if iseod(yy) then true elseif
            iseod(xx) then false else xx < yy fi;
      end;
end;

Here is the dataflow diagram:

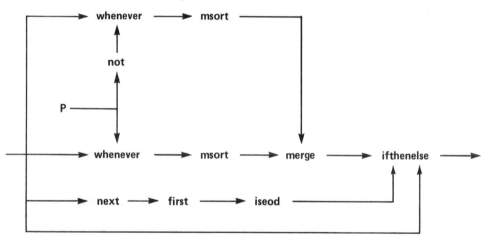

The **merge** function here is a revised version of the definition used earlier; it has been revised to handle pseudo-finite streams, i.e., streams in which *eod* appears.

Many applications programmers will find merge sort very familiar. There is in fact a whole family of more or less elaborate sorting methods (the "external" sorts) based on this same principle. The external sorts are very important in data processing software. They are written in imperative languages like COBOL but are not exchange sorts; they are used to sort data sets, stored on tape, which are too big to fit into memory. The

COBOL routines simulate the action of the merge function above, reading data, item by item, from one or the other of two tape drives and writing the merged result on a third. The external sort programs represent true dataflow algorithms (although they are usually not recursive). Programmers often think of the tapes as storing a stream of records. The programs are not really being run on a von Neumann machine: the machine is involved, but most of the data is stored outside the von Neumann memory. Tape storage is different in character from von Neumann storage: you do not update a tape by performing a sequence of assignments to various 'locations' on the tape. The data on a tape can only be processed by putting it in motion, i.e., by reading through the tape.

Finally, we give another 'recursive' dataflow sort, which works as follows: the input stream is divided again into two, but not at random; the first half consists of those *less than* the first element in the stream, and the second half of those *greater than or equal to* the first datum. By dividing the stream this way, we save ourselves a merge; we just output all of the sorted first half and then all of the sorted second half. Here's the program:

qsort(a) = if eof(first a) then a else follow(qsort(b0), qsort(b1)) fi
  where
    p = first a < a;
    b0 = a whenever p;
    b1 = a whenever not p;
    follow(x,y) = ⋯ {*as before*};
  end

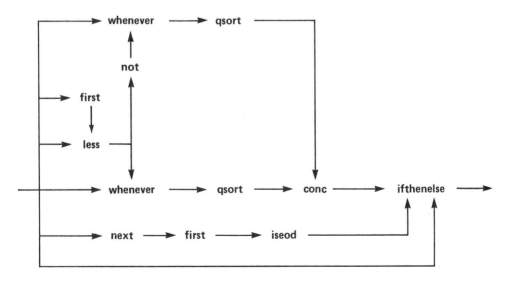

Which of these is better? The recursive ones perform a total of order N log N comparisons compared to the repetitive ones, which may do order N^2. On the other hand, **bsort** is good for lists which are almost sorted. It is difficult to say anything more definite about complexity without a more precise operational semantics. A great deal depends on the implementation; on whether the program is compiled into an imperative language, or evaluated by a demand-driven interpreter, or [as in Sargeant (1982)] run on a dataflow machine.

Even though the examples given in this chapter are still relatively small, it should be clear that the dataflow approach is applicable to (and well suited for) a large class of problems. It should also be apparent that Lucid can express these algorithms quite naturally (especially since conventional iteration is still available—programmers are not forced to forget everything they ever learned). The examples just given have, of course, revealed a few deficiencies in the language—such as the lack of arrays, records, and other data types, or the lack of 'filters' with more than one output. In a later chapter of the book we will consider these limitations in more detail and show that at least some of them can be solved quite easily without violating Lucid's basic principles.

Nevertheless, it is remarkable how much can be done in what is after all a very simple language. It is especially surprising that arrays (randomly accessible data at rest) were not needed in any of these problems; iterative algorithms with array loop variables do not arise naturally even though the solutions of these same problems in (say) PASCAL would make heavy use of arrays. It seems that *random access* storage is not as important as one might think. Many programs in imperative languages use arrays with a pointer to simulate streams; in other words, to simulate serial access.

7. Input/Output in Lucid

One common misconception about nonprocedural languages is that they are unsuitable for applications involving complicated input and output. Input and output operations are supposedly so dynamic that they cannot possibly be described by static mathematics. This belief is apparently confirmed by experience with some nonprocedural languages, in particular with LISP and PROLOG. In both these languages the pure subsets do not allow I/O, and the programmer is forced to use 'dirty' features whose invocation causes input or output to occur as a side effect.

This belief is nevertheless a misconception. It is the result of an unwarranted generalisation based on experience with languages which in some ways are very limited. We have already seen, in Chapter III, that I/O does not *have* to be one of the skeletons in the nonprocedural cupboard. We have already seen examples of programs which (say) read numbers in as input and write numbers out as output. All that is needed is the right mathematical objects (infinite lists or streams) together with an appropriate I/O convention.

Of course the programs seen up to now have been based on a very simple-minded form of input/output. These programs all acted as filters, transforming one or more input streams of data objects into an output stream of data objects. What about printers, plotters, VDUs and typesetters? What about terminals, transducers, card readers and lightpens? Surely *real world* I/O needs *commands* to move a cursor around the screen or to lift the pen off the paper.

In actual fact streams of data objects are adequate for almost every form of I/O, no matter how 'dirty' the application may seem. Those who insist that there must be more to input and output are confusing software and hardware, and are confusing data and machinery. Consider a typical VDU terminal connected to a computer. The interface between the terminal and the computer is very narrow, both physically and logically. Physically, the interface is a single wire capable of carrying signals in both directions. Logically, the interface consists of two streams of *characters,* one stream flowing from the terminal to the computer, the other flowing from the computer to the terminal. Of course, the terminal interprets some of these characters (such as ordinary letters of the alphabet) as data items. These represent information to be displayed on the screen. Others (such as control characters) are treated as commands. They may cause the position of the cursor to change, or cause the screen to be erased. However, the distinction between 'data' and 'command' (which is not necessarily a sharp one) is made by the device and not by the program feeding the device. The purpose of the program is to generate the required stream of characters. The program produces a stream of *information,* and nothing more. Only hardware can produce *activity.*

Imperative languages often obscure the fact that data and commands are really just two different forms of information. For example, in PASCAL the data sent to the outside world appears as arguments of the various I/O commands. However, the control information is treated very differently. If the programmer wants the printer to start a new line, he or she must cause a **writeln** command to be executed (instead of sending a **newline** character). Similarly, to detect the end of input the programmer has to evaluate a predicate, rather than test the last character input to see if it was a special end-of-file character. It is hardly surprising, then, that imperative programmers think of I/O as involving two completely different aspects, data and control. They naturally assume that nonprocedural languages, which manipulate data only, are incapable of performing I/O.

In actual fact programs intended to drive an output device do not involve any special techniques not required by other forms of information processing. The goal is to generate a particular stream (of characters), the only difference being that some of these may be nonprinting characters. This causes no difficulty in pLucid; quoted strings allow an escape convention similar to that of C. Thus **'hello world\n'** is a string of length 12 whose last character is a newline character. The pLucid interpreter normally prints strings as character constants—enclosed in quotes—using the escape conventions, separated by blanks. On input, it expects strings to be represented in the same way (the output of one running pLucid program can therefore be sent as input to another). There are, however, options which cause input to be read character by character, and output strings to be produced without quotes, with escapes 'expanded', and without separating blanks. Output from a program being interpreted under these options can be sent directly to a device. The result will be flashing lights, whirring tape drives, strange beeping noises and any other activity the programmer might desire.

The information-stream view of input/output is inadequate in only one respect: it does not allow the programmer to specify the *rate* at which output is produced and input consumed. It does not even allow the programmer to specify the way in which input and output interleave. You can write programs that run interactively in pLucid, but the interactive property is a result of the way the interpreter works. It is not specified by the program. This is a genuine weakness of Lucid, though not of dataflow in general. The problem can be solved by using a more elaborate notion of stream, one in which "pause objects" (or "time outs") can occur. Alternatively, we can allow datons to carry 'time stamps' indicating when they were produced. These ideas will be discussed briefly in Section 10.

The basic principles discussed are illustrated by the following simple program. It inputs a character stream **c** (in which it expects only blanks and digits). It interprets sequences of digits as numerals and extracts the corresponding stream of integers. The positive numbers in this stream are filtered out and reconverted into a character stream, each number being printed on a new line.

```
d
    where
        k = 0 fby if c eq ' ' then 0 else 10 * k + val(c) fi;
        n = k whenever c eq ' ';
        pn = n whenever n > 0;
        num = (s asa i eq 0)^'\n'
            where
                N is current pn;
```

```
              s = ' ' fby dig(i mod 10)^s;
              i = N fby i div 10;
           end;
      d = substr(m, 1, 1)
         where
           ln = length(m);
           m = nnum fby if ln > 1 then substr(m, 2, ln)
                 else next nnum fi;
           nnum = num upon ln eq 1;
         end;
      val(z) = case z of '0' : 0; '1' : 1; '2' : 2; '3' : 3; '4' : 4;
                 '5' : 5; '6' : 6' '7' : 7; '8' : 8; '9' : 9;
                 default: 0;
         end;
      dig(z) = if z eq 0 then '0' else substr('123456789', z, z) fi;
   end
```

In this program **k** is the stream of partial values accumulated as a numeral is being scanned. The stream **n** of completed numbers is extracted from **k** with a simple **whenever**. The output processing begins when **pn** (the positive numbers to be output) is converted into the stream **num** of corresponding numerals, each value of which is a string of the appropriate digits terminated by a newline character. Then this stream of strings is broken down into the corresponding stream of individual characters (this last step is not really necessary; the pLucid interpreter will do it automatically).

The above program illustrates a problem that appears very often in programs doing I/O-related processing, but is encountered elsewhere as well. Nearly every one of the filters described above has the property that the input and output rates are different. For example, several values of **c** will be consumed for each value of **n** produced (because each number is represented by several digits). On the other hand, each value of **pn** produces several values of **d**, for the same reason.

In imperative programs this kind of interface is often the result of "reading and writing" inside a loop. In Lucid, loops have no side effects. Even nested loops (using **is current**) can produce only one value per step of the outer computation. The usual imperative programs are impossible to imitate directly, and so many people conclude that Lucid is hopelessly limited in this respect. These sort of programs are not, in fact, hard to write in Lucid. In those cases in which many input values are required for each output, the operation **whenever** can be used to obtain the 'speed up' effect. Conversely, the operation **upon** can be used to 'slow down' a stream being consumed.

The programmer can write special-purpose expressions using **when-ever** and **upon** as required, just as in the above program. There is, however, a more systematic technique: to use 'bundling' and 'unbundling' filters. A bundling filter gathers up individual items in its input and passes on 'bundles' (strings or lists) from time to time. An unbundling filter does the opposite, accepting a stream of bundles and producing (at a much faster rate) a stream of individual items. (The function **element** used in one of the prime generating programs given earlier is a list unbundler.)

We can easily abstract the definition of a string unbundler from the definition of **d** in the above program.

> **unb(b) = substr(m, 1, 1)**
>   **where**
>   **ln = length(m);**
>   **m = B fby if ln > 1 then substr(m, 2, ln) else next B fi;**
>   **B = (b whenever b ne '') upon ln eq 1;**
>   **end;**

(notice that empty values of **b** are filtered out; this was not necessary in the example program). For example, if the first few values of **b** were

> '*The*', '*quick*', '*brown*', ...

then the first few values of **unb(b)** would be

> '*T*', '*h*', '*e*', '*q*', '*u*', '*i*', '*c*', '*k*', '*b*', ...

Here is the definition of a character bundling operation.

> **bun(x, p) = y whenever next p**
>   **where**
>   **y = x fby if p then ' ' else y ^ x fi;**
>   **end;**

In general, the values of **bun(x, p)** are those obtained by concatenating values of **x** up to but not including the points at which **p** is true. For example, if the first few values of **x** are

> '*H*', '*o*', '*w*', ' ', '*n*', '*o*', '*w*', '\n', '*b*', ...

then the first few values of **bun(x,x eq ' ' or x eq '\n')** are

> '*How*', '*now*', ...

Bundling could have been used in the program above. First, we would use **whenever** to compress blanks and remove leading blanks, as in the formatting example (call the resulting stream **a**). Then we would bundle the values of **a** using the expression **bun(a,a eq ' ')**. Then the resulting stream of numerals could be converted to a stream of numbers by means of a *pointwise* conversion function.

8. Debugging Lucid Programs

Propagandists for the nonprocedural approach often emphasise the fact (or the claim) that programs in these languages tend to contain far fewer bugs. There is, of course, some reason to expect that this is true; many of the most error-prone features (**goto** statements, side effects, pointer variables) have been completely eliminated. Programs are also much shorter, so that remaining bugs have less room to hide.

On the other hand, new features have been added and very complicated data types can be constructed. Also, backtracking and 'lazy' evaluation can be operationally very complicated, so complicated that the programmer finds it impossible to understand what the program is actually doing. Execution traces are therefore usually worthless. Also, the program is often 'preprocessed' by the implementation into an unintelligible form before being passed on to the actual interpreter. Run-time error messages often refer to the transformed version and so are of little help.

Experience has shown that programmers using Lucid are still not quite infallible. Errors still occur, and can result in total rubbish being produced as output. What should the Lucid programmer do in a 'bug situation'?

The most important piece of advice to the bug victim is still DON'T PANIC. Help is at hand, though not always in the form in which it is available to the imperative programmer. (Sorry, no core dumps.)

The safety net provided by the pLucid interpreter is the run-time error system. Every time an operation (such as addition) receives operands (such as strings) which it cannot handle, a report is sent on the standard message output. The pLucid preprocessor passes the source program through several stages of message; but it passes parts of the original source on as well. When the interpreter delivers an error message, it is able to display the source line containing the relevant occurrence of the operation symbol in question, and even points it out to remove all doubt. The report states the exact nature of the error and displays the 'culprit' (the unexpected value). This feature allows the programmer to catch and exterminate most simple, local bugs.

Some bugs, however, manage to produce global rubbish without local errors, or produce inexplicable local errors. What should the programmer do then?

The pLucid interpreter does have a demand trace facility, but this is intended for research purposes and is unlikely to be of any help in debugging. The problem is that the interpreter computes values of variables in a very mixed-up order. Also, the time/place tagging system is very hard to understand. The second rule of debugging is therefore DON'T TRACE.

Fortunately, there is a third rule of debugging, one which is more helpful: BE SYSTEMATIC. Try to narrow down the search for the bug until it is confined to a single line or expression and cannot escape being seen. This rule is true in all programming languages but is especially useful on dataflow programs. In a Lucid dataflow program there are no side effects, and the interface between modules (filters) is very narrow. If a buggy program consists of three filters in series, then at least one of these filters must be malfunctioning. Therefore, test them, one at a time, by examining the values of the intermediate streams. This sort of testing needs a proper programming environment for it to be carried out in the most convenient way (Boffins, please note). However, even with just the pLucid interpreter and an editor a reasonable procedure is available.

For example, suppose that a formatting program like the one given earlier is acting up. The program is a big **where** clause of the form

```
formline(formword(cblank(rmnewline(S))))
    where
        formline(x) = ···
        formword(x) = ···
        cblank(x) = ···
        rmnewline(x) = ···
        ···
    end
```

Testing begins by running the program with the subject replaced by **rmnewline(S)**. If that is successful, the next test is the same program with **cblank(rmnewline(S))**—and so on for the other filters. Once the faulty filter is found, its subfilters can be systematically tested until the bug is finally located.

The real first principle of debugging, though, is not to create bugs in the first place. For help in these matters please consult a local Preacher or Wizard. The greatest help the Wizards could provide would be a sophisticated type checker which could detect, at compile time, at least some of the mistakes which at present are not caught until the operations are attempted. Chapter VII contains a further discussion of this issue. As for the Preachers, their most valuable piece of advice is probably "test as you write". In other words, test the **rmnewline** filter as soon as it is written, before the filters downstream are constructed (or else write simple versions of all the filters and test the whole pipeline).

9. Interfacing with UNIX, or Lucid Goes Cowboy

Yes, this is the section that many of you have been waiting for. You have patiently read pages and pages of self-righteous preaching about the "purity" of Lucid and the evils of languages with "impure" features. Now, it seems, we are forced to admit that even Lucid has its own version of LISP's notorious PROG feature. You knew we would have to give in sooner or later. It just proves once again that you cannot do *real* computing without commands.

If this is what you are expecting from this section, then we fear you will be somewhat disappointed. The pLucid interpreter does in fact provide an interface to the 'real world'; and this feature could be used to evil ends. But it is not inherently dirty, and can be used in a manner consistent with the immaculately pure and functional Lucid semantics.

Why, some of you might ask, do you need a feature like this at all? Why not do everything in Lucid? Why open the door to temptation? Surely you do not want Lucid programs demeaning themselves by cooperating with programs written in PASCAL, C or even (ugh!) BASIC!

We can sympathise with this point of view but must reject it as unrealistic. We have never claimed that Lucid is a universal programming language adequate for all applications. Furthermore, the existing pLucid interpreter is far from adequate (in terms of performance) even for applications for which the language itself is suitable. If we try to force people to choose between doing all of a program in Lucid, or doing none of it in Lucid, they will usually be forced to choose the latter. However, if the language has a 'loophole' so that some of the work can be done in other languages, then users can enjoy at least *some* of the benefits of definitional dataflow programming.

Suppose, for example, that the programmer wanted to implement some sort of database system—a record library or something similar. It would be completely unreasonable to try to do it all in pLucid. The interpreter is far too wasteful of space and time, and the language was not intended for database applications in the first place. At the same time, the actual user interface might be much easier to write in Lucid (or PROLOG, or LISP) than in a lower level language. Is it really such a bad idea to write the interface in Lucid and the actual data management part in C? Is this not a better solution than writing it all in C?

The interface with a particular operating system depends on the system itself. With the old-fashioned, JCL-type operating systems this could be quite difficult. These systems are all based on commands which update files. UNIX, however, is very different. In UNIX there are still commands, of course, but the system has a very large 'pure' subset. This pure subset is based, like Lucid, on the notion of a filter. The interpreter itself is designed so that Lucid programs can be used as filters and appear in pipelines. This, in a sense, is UNIX's interface with Lucid. The pLucid interpreter simply reverses the idea, and allows the pLucid programmers to use UNIX filters in their own pLucid 'pipelines'.

The interface is syntactically very simple. The interpreter provides a pseudo-operation **filter** which takes three arguments, the first of which should be a string. The interpreter evaluates this expression (**filter** applied to its arguments) as the stream of values which results when the values of the second argument are fed into the standard input of the UNIX filter denoted by the first argument. (The third argument is used to specify various options). For example, the output of the pLucid program

$$\textbf{filter('sed s/1/11/g', i} \ast\ast \textbf{2, ' ')}$$
$$\textbf{where}$$
$$\textbf{i = 3 fby 1 fby 9 fby eod;}$$
$$\textbf{end;}$$

is 9, 11, 811. (each occurrence of the digit **1** has been replaced by **11**). UNIX filters expect streams of *characters;* the characters transmitted are those which make up the representation of pLucid data as constants. Different elements in the stream are separated by newlines.

The interface function **filter** can also be used inside nested loops and function definitions; different invocations of the specified process will be spawned as needed. Suppose, for example, that **tot** is a filter which produces a running total of the numbers it reads in. The pLucid program

$$\textbf{avg(a} \ast\ast \textbf{2)} - \textbf{avg(a)} \ast\ast \textbf{2}$$
$$\textbf{where}$$
$$\textbf{avg(x) = next s/n}$$
$$\textbf{where}$$
$$\textbf{s = filter('tot', x, ' ');}$$
$$\textbf{n = 1 fby n + 1;}$$
$$\textbf{end;}$$
$$\textbf{end;}$$

produces a running standard variance of its input stream **a**. There is only one textual reference to the 'external' function **tot**, but when the program is interpreted (or rather, *evaluated*) the pLucid evaluator will correctly set up two versions of **tot**. One of the **tot** processes will be fed the values of **a**, and the other will be fed the values of **a** $\ast\ast$ **2**.

The interface is not quite as simple as it appears to the user. In UNIX, pipelines are data driven and values are produced in order. However, the pLucid interpreter works on a demand-driven basis, and demands are not necessarily generated in chronological order. Also, there are severe limits on the number of pipes and processes a user can set up. In spite of these difficulties the pLucid interface is good enough to be useful and shows what is possible in principle.

Of course there is no guarantee that the UNIX process named as the first argument of **filter** is a pure filter. It could be a command which causes a side effect. Using **filter** in this way is genuine dirty Lucid programming. There are, however, situations in which side effects are excusable. An equation like

$$y = \text{filter('tee xvals', x, ' ');}$$

is equivalent (as far as the output of the program is concerned) to the equation **y** = **x**. There is no side effect on the pLucid program itself. But running the program does have a side effect—it causes the values of **x** to be dumped on the file **xvals**. Of course, this would be very useful for debugging: it allows the programmer to 'spy' on selected parts of the program without altering the program or its output.

There is even another naughty but nice use of side effects. Suppose that **term** is a filter that sends its standard input straight to a terminal, and sends any input from the terminal to its standard output. When a program containing the equation

$$y = \text{filter('term', x, ' ');}$$

is run, the person sitting at the terminal will be able to act as a 'human filter'. Values of **x** will be sent one by one to the terminal, and values of **y** will be read from the keyboard. This could be useful in debugging. It could also be useful in top-down testing: you can test a program even though some crucial filter is not yet written. The equation above allows the programmer to 'stand in' for the unwritten filter, and do its work by hand.

The pLucid/UNIX filter works well because pLucid and UNIX are well matched: programs in both systems are organised on roughly the same principle, namely as dataflow. In this situation the distinction between programming language and operating system language begins to blur. Once you have devised a dataflow solution to a problem, you have a choice about how to proceed. You can write the program as 'basically' a shell pipeline, in which pLucid programs can appear (thanks to the interpreter). On the other hand, you can write it as 'basically' a pLucid program in which UNIX filters appear (thanks to the **filter** interface).

In the first situation pLucid is being used as a programming language along with (say) PASCAL or C. In the second case, however, pLucid is being used as a kind of high-level equational operating system language (LUNIX?). Of course the pLucid interpreter is too inefficient to make the second approach as useful as it could be; but the pattern is clear. Perhaps in the not too distant future, when the nonprocedural millennium has arrived, the development will reach its logical conclusion. This conclusion is the complete abolition of the distinction between a system language and a programming language. This would also mean the abolition of the distinction between "programming in the small" and "programming in the large".

10. Interactive and Real-Time Programming

What? Writing programs that interact with their users—in real time! Surely this is impossible (and undesirable) in a nonprocedural language. Have they no shame? Is nothing sacred? (Or rather, is nothing profane?)

The above paragraph characterises the possible reactions of some of our readers on seeing the title of this section. Those of Mystical tendencies will be shocked to see us demean ourselves even further by taking on dynamic (and, therefore, supposedly nonmathematical) concepts such as "interaction" and "real time". As if ordinary input/output was not bad enough. Other readers, of the Western (Cowboy) persuasion will also be shocked—and in a state of total disbelief. They have always assumed that nonprocedural languages are fine for abstract, mathematical, ivory-tower activities (infinite lists of primes and such) but useless for real world computation. The Mystics and the Cowboys are on most questions totally opposed, but they do agree on one thing. They both assume that nonprocedural languages are not really "of this world"—that they are incapable of specifying genuine activity.

The Mystics think this is a good thing. They look down on concepts such as interaction as "low level" and "operational". They believe programmers should turn their backs on all this confusing talk about things happening, data being input and output and systems changing their state. Their languages deal with abstract, eternal, unchanging pure and clean mathematical values. The concept of some particular thing happening at some particular *time* is alien to their whole way of thinking. They leave it to the lower orders (implementers) to worry about such trivial, distracting and menial details.

The Cowboys, not surprisingly, have a different view of the matter. They see the Mystics as being hopeless snobs who refuse to soil their hands doing a little work. They consider it to be sheer insanity to pretend that the correctness of a program can be discussed in purely static terms.

For once, it must be admitted that there is something to the Western point of view. For example, consider a simple stack-based desk calculator. The input (of a complete session) is a finite sequence of commands (to stack a given number, to add the top two stack elements, etc.). The output is also a finite sequence (of numbers computed). But a program that produces nothing until the user signs off could hardly be considered correct! An even better example is a screen editing program. Imagine a user invoking a screen editor. Nothing appears on the screen. Then the user tries to move the cursor around on the screen. No effect. Even the commands to enter and delete text seem to be completely ignored. Finally, the user types the quit command in anger and frustration—only to see the screen come to life, the cursor bounce around, and pieces of text appear and disappear. The performance turns out to be an "instant replay" of the editing session that seemed to have failed. The editor has indeed produced the correct output. Of course the output appeared too late to be of any use—but we must learn to think abstractly about these things!

Needless to say, nobody really believes that time is unimportant, not even the most ethereal of the Mystics. There are in fact many implementations of nonprocedural languages which allow the user to interact with programs. Interactive programs are especially easy to write in Lucid, because input and output are already treated as streams of values. Here, for example, is a program implementing a simple desk calculator like the one mentioned above.

```
hd(stack) whenever cmd eq "w"
  where
    stack = [] fby
          if isnumber(cmd) then cmd :: stack
          elseif cmd eq "+" then hd(stack) +
            hd(tl(stack)) :: tl(tl(stack))
          elseif cmd eq "*" then hd(stack) * hd(tl(stack)) :: tl(tl(stack))
          elseif cmd eq "w" then tl(stack)
          else stack fi;
  end
```

When this program is evaluated, the evaluator will ask for the first value of **cmd**. The user might type in **35** (which the program interprets as a command to push 35 on its internal stack). No output will be produced, but the second value of **cmd** will be requested. If **73** is typed in, there will again be no output from the program, only a request for the third value of **cmd**. If this third value is + (meaning add the last two numbers), still no output will appear. However, if the next value of **cmd** entered is w (meaning write the top of the stack), the output **108** will finally be produced. If the program is run with the evaluator's prompts turned off, it will behave just like a program written in PASCAL with **read** and **write** commands.

The behaviour just described is an immediate consequence of the "laziness" of the demand-driven interpreter. The interpreter does not begin by trying to read anything in; it begins by trying to compute the first value of its output. The demand for this value 'propagates' through the program and generates demands for other values at other times. It asks for an input value only when it actually needs it—if it needs any at all. As soon as the time 0 value of the output has been computed and printed, the interpreter begins working on the time 1 value, and again asks for input only as required. It continues this way with the values at time 2, 3, 4 and so on forever, or until one of these values is *eod*.

The resulting behaviour is almost always satisfactory. For example, the program **A** * **A**, which gives repeated squares of the numbers in its input stream, will ask for a number, print its square, ask for another number, print its square and so on. The desk calculator program above will behave according to the naive view that it is obeying the commands typed in. And the screen editor (which appears in the pLucid manual) will behave like a normal screen editor written in a conventional command language. The convention that output be produced as soon as enough input is available to calculate it is nearly always what is required.

The interpreter avoids a number of I/O anomalies by always asking for input values in the correct order (time 0, 1, 2, 3, ...) even if it might need (say) the value at time 3 before it needs the value at time 2. It also is careful never to throw away input values. It does not want to find itself having to ask the user, "say, what was the 23rd number you typed in again?" As a result a program running on the evaluator appears to be operating in a 'pipeline' mode. This makes interaction with users much more natural and also allows a program running on the evaluator to be used in a UNIX pipe (UNIX is based on pipeline dataflow).

Nevertheless, the situation regarding interaction is not quite satisfactory. The behaviour described above is only a *side effect* of the design of a particular evaluator—it is not part of the semantics of the language itself. The semantics of Lucid specify that the output of the square program, given input ⟨3, 6, 1, 5, ...⟩, must be ⟨9, 36, 1, 25, ...⟩. The pLucid I/O convention specifies that these numbers will be read in and printed out in that order. But neither the semantics nor the I/O convention require that these inputs and outputs will be interleaved as desired.

It happens that a correct pLucid interpreter running the square program *must* behave as desired. On the one hand, it cannot produce the square of a number until it actually knows the number. This means that the output corresponding to a particular input must be produced after the input. On the other hand, if the interpreter has read in a number (say 6) it cannot wait forever before producing the corresponding output (36). The reason it cannot wait is that the following input may never arrive—the pLucid I/O convention allows finite 'nonterminating' input. For example, if a user types **3**, then **5**, then **6**, then drops dead (before he has a chance to close the input stream), the input is deemed to be $\langle 3, 5, 6, \perp, \perp, \perp, ... \rangle$. The formal semantics specify that the corresponding output must be $\langle 9, 25, 36, \perp, \perp, \perp, ... \rangle$. This means that the interpreter *must* eventually produce the output (36) corresponding to the user's last input. The interpreter *cannot* spend eternity waiting for the next input item.

Unfortunately, this argument applies only to certain programs. In general, the Lucid time parameter cannot be understood as counting the ticks of some global clock. The pLucid user who has succeeded in producing an interactive program is, in a sense, just lucky.

Problems can, therefore, arise when the user's luck runs out. Suppose we want to write a program which reads in two numbers and outputs the sum of their squares. The program x * x + y * y works fine. But suppose that we do not want to use the interpreter's own prompting system. Suppose instead we want to supply our own. We might naively expect

> **'the number x please\n' fby**
> **'the number y please\n' fby**
> **'the sum of their squares is\n' fby**
> **x ** 2 + y ** 2 fby eod**

to work, but we are in for a surprise. When run (without the interpreter's prompts) it will immediately output

> **the number x please**
> **the number y please**
> **the sum of their squares is**

and then apparently hang up. It is waiting for us to type in **x** and **y**! Since the values of the prompts do not depend on the input, they were produced immediately. Only when it attempts to produce the fourth output item does it finally have to read any input.

This program can be patched up. The expression

> **if x eq x**
> **then 'the number y please\n'**
> **else ' '**
> **fi**

now depends on the value of **x** and the evaluator will be forced to read (and store) the value of **x** before the second prompt appears. Nevertheless, this solution looks very dirty—far too dirty for a supposedly "clean" nonprocedural language. What if more complicated forms of interaction were required? Would these artificially induced dependencies become unmanageable? And what if we needed *assurance* that a given interaction pattern would always result. Since the behaviour is not part of the semantics, there is no hope for a formal proof. On the contrary: our transformation rules allow us to transform a program with artificial dependencies into the original one. After all, they have the same meaning.

The problem becomes more acute when we try to write programs whose *real-time* behaviour is important. By this we mean programs in which the *absolute* rate of input or output is important, not just the rate of input and output relative to each other. Here, even the interpreter falls down. The evaluator, being lazy, postpones all computations as long as possible. As a result it often finds itself in a situation in which it has accumulated a large debt of postponed computation which now must be cleared. At that point the performance suddenly (though temporarily) deteriorates. For example, the desk calculator program will not do any actual calculations until a **w** command is entered; then it must clear up its backlog. To the user it seems that addition and multiplication are very simple operations which are performed immediately, but that output is for some reason more time consuming. This kind of counter-intuitive behaviour can be avoided with artificial dependencies, but this solution is even less satisfactory than in the case of simple interaction.

The Mystics will argue that genuine "time" is an implementation concept and has no place in the semantics of a language, which must be "abstract". This is true as long as timing is part of *performance* and not part of *correctness*. Nevertheless, it cannot be denied that there are many applications in which timing (relative or absolute) is part of the specification itself. For these problems, timing refers to ends as well as means, and reference to genuine time in the program is still abstract.

At first sight, it might seem that Lucid could be adapted for real-time applications. We could tighten up the Lucid I/O convention and require that a correct implementation receive its input and produce its output in step with a global clock. With this convention real time would actually be part of the semantics. This proposal is not, however, very practical. It would mean abandoning operations like **whenever**, which do not respect the central-clock interpretation of the time parameter. It would mean complicated restrictions on user defined functions. It would probably mean abandoning nested iteration. There would not be much 'normal' Lucid left. For real-time problems Lucid really is *inherently* unsuitable.

This does not, however, mean that the Cowboys are right after all. Lucid may be unsuitable, but that does not mean that *all* nonprocedural languages are unsuitable. In fact, there is a simple way to generalise the Lucid notion of history to handle genuine time. We introduce a new data object which we use to 'pad out' ordinary Lucid histories to make Lucid time correspond to real time. This object (called a "hiaton", from "hiatus", a pause) can be thought of as the 'output' of a process which at a particular point in time has no 'genuine' data to send on. Using hiatonic streams, operations like **whenever** can be made to work in real time again. For example, the value of **n whenever isprime(n)** might be

$$\langle *, 2, 3, *, 5, *, 7, *, *, *, 11, ... \rangle$$

(with an asterisk representing the hiaton).

We cannot simply add the hiaton to the pLucid algebra in the same way the *eod* object was added. Hiatons are not normally combined with data objects. For example, the addition operation applied to the streams $\langle *, 5, *, *, 3, ... \rangle$ and $\langle 1, *, *, 2, 8, ... \rangle$ yields $\langle *, 6, *, *, 5, ... \rangle$. (The hiatons make clear the way in which an addition filter 'waits' for both summands before it produces their sum.)

Hiatonics seems to offer some hope of a nonprocedural dataflow approach to real time. In particular, the output of a first-come first-served merge node is now a *function* of its input. This node can in turn play a vital role in applications such as resource allocation. At present, however, a hiaton-based dataflow language has not even been specified, let alone implemented. It remains to be seen if the hiaton will fulfill its promise and take its place beside ⊥ and *eod*.

VI PROGRAM TRANSFORMATION

A program transformation rule is a rule which allows one to make changes in a program (usually, small changes) which preserve the *meaning* of the program. The 'meaning' of a program is the role which it performs when considered as a 'black box'. It is the transformation which the program applies to its input. In other words, the meaning of a program is its *input–output function*. If T is a program to which a transformation is to be applied and T' is the modified program which results, then T and T' produce the same output when given the same input. The two programs are said to be *equivalent*. Of course, by 'input' and 'output' we mean the (histories of) the input and output streams. Equivalent programs are, as 'black box' filters, interchangeable. It is possible, of course, that equivalent programs may *perform* differently—one may do its work more quickly, the other might require more resources. As far as the end results, however, equivalent programs are (from the 'outside') indistinguishable.

Every programmer uses the notion of input/output equivalence, at least informally. Programs are continually being modified, often solely to improve their performance. Any modifications to a working program would be expected not to alter the results; the modifications should be equivalence-preserving transformations. Often, programmers will write code they know to be inefficient, and expect to spend some time later improving the performance. Their strategy (a common and effective one) is to first produce a 'draft' program which may be extremely slow but is *simple* and *obviously correct*. Once the 'quick and dirty' version is running, it can always be gradually transformed into a more efficient but still equivalent program. The alternate strategy, of course, is to spend a great deal of time writing an efficient but incorrect program. Then the programmer spends even more time debugging—making it more correct but maintaining the performance. The first method has much to recommend it.

Naturally enough, even the best strategies are capable of producing programs with errors in them. Correcting these errors involves making changes which are *intended* to change the meaning of the program. Any program equivalent to an incorrect program is still incorrect! Nevertheless, even while correcting errors, it is usually necessary to ensure that *most* of the output remains unaltered. The concept of a 'meaning-preserving' change is certainly an extremely important one.

Most imperative programmers use only a very informal approach to the problem of program modification. There are a few precise transformation rules which can be applied (for example, renaming the dummy parameters of a procedure definition) but they are very rare. The existence of side effects, pointers and aliasing (among other things) make it very difficult to isolate the effects of even a very small change. For example, in PASCAL we cannot in general replace the integer expression $i + m(8)$ by $m(8) + i$ because the function m may affect the value of i. Nor can we reverse the order of the two apparently unrelated commands

$$x := a;$$
$$y := b;$$

because x may be another name for b!

In Lucid, however (as in Iswim and most nonprocedural languages) the situation is much different. There are no side effects, pointers or aliasing. The expressions $i + m(8)$ and $m(8) + i$ always yield the same value, and any two definitions in the body of a clause may be interchanged. The reason, of course, is that Lucid is based on the notation of ordinary mathematics, the arithmetic and other data operations are referentially transparent and the statements in a clause really are equations. In Lucid it is possible to formulate a number of reasonably simple yet extremely powerful transformation rules which take advantage of the situation. The rules allow us (for example) to perform symbolic calculations on data, expand function calls, eliminate unnecessary definitions and even collapse whole clauses to a single expression. These rules are even powerful enough to allow us to symbolically 'evaluate' entire programs, by transforming them to expressions consisting of a single constant. Most of these rules have their origins in the reduction rules of the Lambda Calculus. Darlington and Burstall (1973) used similar rules as the basis of their program transformation system, and others have extended this work.

The transformation rules are especially effective when used in conjunction with induction principles (one example of which will be given in a later section). They make it possible to transform one program into a totally different one, which computes its results by a completely different method.

One especially attractive feature of transformation rules in general is that they require no knowledge of any formal system other than the programming language itself. There is no need for the programmer to learn a second, more complicated assertional 'metalanguage' for stating properties of programs. Some of the rules require carefully stated restrictions concerning the scope of variables, but scope is something a programmer must understand anyway.

1. The Basis Rule

We begin by considering the following simple program

$$2 + 2$$

to add two and two. There is, of course, an even simpler program to which the above is equivalent; namely the program

$$4$$

It ought to be possible to transform the first into the second. The rule which allows us to carry out this transformation is the *basis rule*.

Let A be an algebra, T be a *Lucid(A)* program and $R = L$ be a 'conventional' equation in which the terms R and L have no where clauses, and no variables used as functions. If the equation is true in $Lu(A)$ (in the sense of ordinary equational algebra), then any occurrence of R in T can be replaced by L, provided the replacement does not introduce any new input (i.e., free) variables in T.

Since the equation $2 + 2 = 4$ is true in $Lu(P)$, we are allowed to transform the pLucid [i.e., *Lucid(P)*] program $2 + 2$ into the pLucid program 4.

The equation referred to in the basis rule may involve terms with occurrences of variables. Such an equation is true in an algebra if (and this is the convention of universal algebra) the two sides have the same value for all values of the variables in question. For example, since the equation

$$f * (i + 1) = (i + 1) * f$$

is true in P, the Basis Rule allows us to transform the program

```
f asa i eq N
   where
   N is current n;
   i = 1 fby i + 1;
   f = 1 fby f * (i + 1);
   end
```

into the program

f asa i eq N
   where
     N is current n;
     i = 1 fby i + 1;
     f = 1 fby(i + 1) ∗ f;
   end

In the same way the equations

if true then x else y fi = x
if false then x else y fi = y

can be used to 'evaluate' boolean expressions.

The question which immediately arises, of course, is how do we know that a given equation is true of $Lu(P)$? There are a small number of important equations such as

first(x fby y) = first x
next(x fby y) = y
first x fby next x = x
next(x + y) = next x + next y

that are true in $Lu(A)$ for all A. These can be verified 'in the metalanguage', by directly referring to the definition of $Lu(A)$.

The truth of a much larger collection of equations follows from the Extension Principle: If an equation has no occurrences of Lucid operators and is true in A, then it is also true in $Lu(A)$. The principle still leaves us with the problem of discovering equations true in A. This last problem, however, has nothing to do with Lucid or with programming per se; the question is rather one of formal reasoning about data types. We will not discuss this subject here except to point out that equations true in A could be derived from an equational specification of A.

There is also an important generalisation of the Extension Principle which gives us many useful equations. The generalised Extension Principle guarantees the truth of any equation obtainable from an equation true in $Lu(A)$ by substituting arbitrary terms for variables. For example, the equation

p + q = q + p

is true in $Lu(P)$ (because it is true in P). By substituting the term **x** for **p**, and the term **f(x − 1)** for **q**, we obtain the equation

x ∗ f(x − 1) = f(x − 1) ∗ x

Using this equation we can transform the program

> **f(N)**
> **where**
> **N is current n;**
> **f(x) = if x < 1 then 1 else x ∗ f(x − 1) fi;**
> **end**

into the program

> **f(N)**
> **where**
> **N is current n;**
> **f(x) = if x < 1 then 1 else f(x − 1) ∗ x fi;**
> **end**

The equation in question cannot be derived directly using the Extension Principle because it uses the variable **f** as a function; it is not an equation in the language of ordinary equational algebra.

There is, unfortunately, one serious limitation to the use of the Basis Rule: the equations true in the underlying algebra are not always those expected. For example, consider the *Lucid(Z)* program

> **f(i)**
> **where**
> **f(x) = f(x) − f(x);**
> **end**

with Z being the algebra (described earlier) based on the integers. We might be tempted to use the 'obviously' true equation

$$p − p = 0$$

derive

$$f(x) − f(x) = 0.$$

and transform our program to

> **f(i)**
> **where**
> **f(x) = 0;**
> **end**

which outputs a stream of 0s. The transformation is incorrect; the original program does not output anything at all. The flaw in the reasoning is assuming the correctness of the equation

$$p - p = 0$$

This equation is not true in Z, because it fails when $\mathbf{p}$ has the value $\bot$. In general, the presence of the extra partial objects in a continuous algebra can invalidate many supposedly natural equations (especially those involving two or more occurrences of the same variable on one side).

2. The Substitution Rule

The Basis Rule discussed above is based on the principle that expressions in Lucid are referentially transparent; it says that expressions having the same value can be interchanged. The Substitution Rule is also based on this principle, and on the fact that the statements in a **where** clause really are equations. The Substitution Rule says that (roughly speaking) occurrences of a variable can be replaced by the relevant definition.

Consider, for example, the following simple program

$$\mathbf{x + y \ where \ x = 2; \ y = 2; \ end}$$

using a **where** clause. The subject of the **where** clause is the expression $\mathbf{x + y}$, but it is obvious that in this context both $\mathbf{x}$ and $\mathbf{y}$ have the value 2. We would expect, then, that the program above is equivalent to

$$\mathbf{2 + 2 \ where \ x = 2; \ y = 2; \ end}$$

(and our later rules will allow us to convert this, in turn, to $\mathbf{2 + 2}$).
The Substitution Rule allows us to do this.

The Substitution Rule: Let W be a **where** clause containing a definition of the form

$$V = E$$

with V a variable and E an expression. Then E may replace any free occurrence of V in the subject of W, or in the right-hand side of a definition in the body of W, provided no name clashes result.

This statement refers to two concepts, namely those of "free occurrences" and "name clash", that need to be explained.

A *free occurrence* of a variable in a term is one which is not

(i)   in the right-hand side of a definition in a **where** clause which has the variable as one of its locals; or
(ii)   in the right-hand side of a definition which has the variable as one of its formal parameters.

In other words, a free occurrence is one where the variable has its 'outer' meaning. For example, in the term

> **f(next x + Y)**
> **where**
> **Y is current y − 1;**
> **s = f(Y upon x > 0)**
> **where**
> **f(a) = a ∗ x + b;**
> **end;**
> **x = a ∗ w − s;**
> **w = a/b**
> **where**
> **b = 5 + x;**
> **x = 5;**
> **end;**
> **end**

the occurrences of **a** on the line

$$f(a) = a * x + b$$

are not free (i.e., they are *bound*) because here **a** is being used as a formal parameter. The other two occurrences of **a** in the program, however, are free. The occurrence of **b** on the line just cited is free; but its occurrence later in the expression

$$a/b$$

is not because **b** is a local of the clause of which this expression is the subject.

In the expression

$$f(next\ x\ +\ Y)$$

which is the subject of the main clause, the occurrences of **x** and **Y** are not free. Both of these variables are locals; **x** is defined in the body and **Y** is the subject (left-hand side) of an **is current** declaration. The occurrence of **f**, however, is free. There is a definition of **f** inside the clause but it is not 'relevant' to the above occurrence. The definitions in the body of a clause are relevant only to occurrences of variables *inside* the clause. The occurrence of **f** in the expression

$$f(Y\ upon\ x\ >\ 0)$$

is therefore bound; here the definition

$$f(a) = a * x + b;$$

is relevant. Finally, the occurrence of the variable **y** in the **is current** declaration is free; no occurrence of a variable on the right-hand side of such a declaration is ever bound. The free variable of this expression are therefore **a**, **b**, **f** and **y**.

The Substitution Rule allows us to replace free occurrences of a given variable by a given expression. In these positions, the variable being replaced had its 'outer' meaning; we would therefore expect that the new expression have its 'outer' meaning as well. Sometimes, however, the new expression will be substituted into a context in which some of its free values become bound. As a result, the expression as a whole no longer has its outer value. In this situation we say that there is a *clash* of variables. There is a confusion between two different meanings of the same symbol.

The body of the example term above contains the definition

$$x = a * w - s;$$

We can therefore use the Substitution Rule to replace relevant occurrences of **x** by **a** ∗ **w** + **s**. One relevant occurrence is that in the subject of the main clause. If we perform the substitution, the result is

```
f(next (a * w - s) + Y)
  where
    Y is current y - 1;
    s = f(Y upon x > 0)
      where
        f(a) = a * x + b;
      end;
    x = a * w - s;
    w = a/b
      where
        b = 5 + x;
        x = 5;
      end;
  end
```

None of the variables in **a** ∗ **w** + **s** are bound in the new context, and no clash of variables results. This substitution is allowed.

The Substitution Rule would also allow us to substitute for the second relevant occurrence of **x**, in the expression

$$f(Y \text{ upon } x > 0)$$

There is one more relevant occurrence of **x**, namely, that in the definition

$$f(a) = a * x + b,$$

but the Substitution Rule does not allow the substitution to be performed. The problem is that a name clash involving the variable **a** results. If we ignored the restrictions and substituted anyway, the result would be the definition

$$f(a) = a * (a * w - s) \mid b;$$

This new definition, however, has a different meaning from the old one. The second occurrence of **a** in the definition now refers to the argument of **f**, and not the 'outer' value of **a**. There is no reason to expect that the transformed program will have the same meaning as the original.

There is, of course, one more occurrence of **x** in a subexpression, namely, that in the definition

$$b = 5 + x;$$

but this occurrence is not relevant to the definition

$$x = a * w - s;.$$

It occurs inside a clause whose body contains a different definition of **x** (namely, **x = 5;**), and innermost definitions always take precedence. We could, however, use the Substitution Rule with this inner, relevant definition and replace the occurrence of **x** by **5**. The resulting expression would be

$$
\begin{aligned}
&f(\text{next } (a * w - s) + Y) \\
&\textbf{where} \\
&\quad Y \text{ is current } y - 1; \\
&\quad s = f(Y \text{ upon } x > 0) \\
&\quad\quad \textbf{where} \\
&\quad\quad\quad f(a) = a * x + b; \\
&\quad\quad \textbf{end}; \\
&\quad x = a * w - s; \\
&\quad w = a/b \\
&\quad\quad \textbf{where} \\
&\quad\quad\quad b = 5 + 5; \\
&\quad\quad\quad x = 5; \\
&\quad\quad \textbf{end}; \\
&\textbf{end}.
\end{aligned}
$$

There is also a version of the substitution rule which can be applied to **is current** declarations.

The Declaration Substitution Rule: Let *W* be a where clause whose body contains a declaration of the form

V is current *E*;

Any occurrence of *V* in the subject of *W* can be replaced by *E*, provided there are no clashes of variables, and provided *E* occurs in a *synchronic* context.

The crucial concept here is that of a *synchronic* occurrence of a variable in a term. An occurrence of a variable *V* in a term *T* is synchronic if it is not within the scope of one of the special Lucid operations (such as **first** or **whenever**), or within the scope of a function variable defined directly or indirectly using the Lucid operations.

The fact that an occurrence of *V* in *T* is synchronic means that the value of *T* at any time *t* depends on the value of *V* at the *same* time *t*, and not on the value of *V* at any other time. Synchronic contexts are therefore 'transparent' contexts, out of the range of any of the Lucid 'time bending' operations.

For example, in the term

**(p asa i > N) + 3 ∗ M
where
N is current next n;
M is current m;
i = 1 fby i + 1;
p = M fby p ∗ M;
end**

the occurrence of **M** in the subject is in a synchronic context, but that of **N** is not. We are therefore allowed to replace **M** by **m**, yielding

**(p asa i > N) + 3 ∗ m
where
N is current next n
M is current m;
i = 1 fby i + 1;
p = M fby p ∗ M;
end**

but may not replace **N** by **next n**.

Name clashes can occur with the Declaration Substitution Rule when a local of the clause occurs free in *E*. For example, if the declaration of *M* were instead

M is current m + p;

then the substitution could not be performed. The problem is that the occurrence of **p** on the right-hand side of the above declaration refers to the 'outer' value of **p**; but any occurrence of **p** in the subject refers to its 'inner' value.

3. The Calling Rule

The Substitution Rule allows us to 'apply' the definition of an individual variable. There is a similar rule (actually, a generalisation), which allows us to do the same for definitions of function variables. Consider, for example, the program

> **sum(2, 3)**
> **where**
> **sum(x, y) = x + y;**
> **end;**

It seems perfectly obvious that the definition of **sum** implies that the expression **sum(2, 3)** has the same value as **2 + 3**. We would reason as follows: the first argument of **sum**, which is called **x** in the definition, is 'actually' **2**, and the second argument, which is called **y**, is 'actually' **3**. The value of **sum(2, 3)** should therefore be that of the expression **x + y**, when **2** is substituted for **x** and **3** is substituted for **y**. This reasoning is correct, and is formalised by the calling rule.

The Calling Rule: Let W be a clause containing a definition of the form

$$F(P_0, P_1, ..., P_{n-1}) = E;$$

(F, a variable, $P_0, P_1, P_2, ..., P_{n-1}$ the formal parameters, E an expression). Then, any relevant occurrence in the clause of an expression of the form

$$F(A_0, A_1, ..., A_{n-1})$$

can be replaced by E', where E' is the result of substituting (simultaneously) A_0 for all occurrences of P_0 in E, A_1 for all free occurrences of P_1 in E, ..., and A_{n-1} for all free occurrences of P_{n-1} in E. As before, these substitutions and the final replacement must not give rise to any clashes of variables.

An expression of the form

$$F(A_0, A_1, ..., A_{n-1})$$

can be thought of as a 'call' of the function F (hence the name of the rule) with actual parameters $A_0, A_1, ..., A_{n-1}$. The rule says that such a 'call' to F can be replaced by the 'body' of the definition of F, with the actual parameters substituted for the formal parameters. In the simple example given above, the Calling Rule allows us to replace the occurrence of **sum(2, 3)** by the result of substituting **2** for **x** and **3** for **y** in **x** + **y**; in other words, it allows us to replace **sum(2, 3)** by **2** + **3**, as desired.

The notion of a 'relevant' call is defined in almost the same way as with the Substitution Rule given earlier. The calls relevant to a definition are those appearing in the subject or in the right-hand side of a definition in the body, provided there is no 'intervening' definition in some subclause. For example, in the expression

$$h(x) + f(y)$$
$$\textbf{where}$$
$$x = y * g + 5$$
$$\textbf{where}$$
$$g = p - f(q * a + y);$$
$$q = k(3, z);$$
$$k(a, b) = a * a + f(b * b);$$
$$\textbf{end};$$
$$y = f(u) - u$$
$$\textbf{where}$$
$$f(d) = d * d - 5;$$
$$u = 135;$$
$$\textbf{end};$$
$$f(t) = (t - a) * (t + y);$$
$$\textbf{end}$$

the 'calls' **f(y)**, **f(q * a + y)** and **f(b * b)** are all relevant to the definition

$$f(t) = (t - a) * (t + y);$$

but the call **f(u)** is not. The definition relevant to this last call is

$$f(d) = d * d - 5;$$

because (as before) the innermost definition has precedence.

The Calling Rule allows us to 'expand' the first two calls, so that the resulting term will be

$$h(x) + (y - a) * (y + y)$$
$$\textbf{where}$$
$$x = y * g + 5$$
$$\textbf{where}$$
$$g = p - ((q * a + y) - a) * ((q * a + y) + y);$$

$$q = k(3, z);$$
$$k(a, b) = a * a + f(b * b);$$
end;
$$y = f(u) - u$$
where
$$f(d) = d * d - 5;$$
$$u = 135;$$
end;
$$f(t) = (t - a) * (t + y);$$
end

Any attempt to expand the third call (**f(b** * **b)**), however, will result in a clash of variables. The definition

$$k(a, b) = a * a + f(b * b)$$

would become

$$k(a, b) = a * a + ((b * b) - a) * ((b * b) + y);$$

and now the meaning has been changed. The variable **a** which occurs as a 'global' of the definition of **f** has been introduced into a context in which it is also being used as a formal parameter. The proper, 'outer' value is no longer available.

Individual examples of the 'clash of variables' are usually easy to understand—once they have been pointed out. It is much harder for the unaided programmer to detect clashes in a moderately complicated program. Fortunately, it is not too difficult to formulate the precise regulations regarding permissible substitutions, and these rules can be easily implemented as a checking program. A programmer using the transformation rules would indicate to the program which call is to be expanded. The transformation program would check that no clashes would occur, perform the expansion if it passed the check, otherwise it would tell the programmer exactly where the clash takes place. Programmers could therefore have absolute confidence in the correctness of their transformations, even if they themselves do not have a perfect grasp of the subtleties involved in the various restrictions on the transformation rules. (On the other hand, the people who implement the checking/transforming package must have a very good understanding of the rules. They would need a more detailed specification than that provided here.)

4. The Renaming Rules

The formal parameters of a function definition are sometimes called 'dummy' variables. The reason for this is that the choice of which variable to use is (almost) of no importance. These variables are just 'dummies' which stand in for the actual parameters of a call. The use of a variable like x as a formal parameter does not involve any reference to any value which x may have in the context of the definition. The following rule captures this idea by permitting us to change these variables.

The Formal Parameter Renaming Rule: Let

$$F(V_0, V_1, ..., V_{n-1}) = E;$$

be a definition appearing in the body of a where clause and let $U_0, U_1, ...,$ U_{n-1} be a new sequence of distinct variables. Then the above definition can be replaced by

$$F(U_0, U_1, ..., U_{n-1}) = E';$$

where E' is the result of (simultaneously) replacing each free occurrence in E of any V_i with the corresponding U_i, provided no clashes of variables result.

With this rule, clashes could arise if one of the Us is substituted into a context in which it is bound.

This rule could, for example, be used on the term given earlier to transform the definition

$$\mathbf{k(a, b) = a * a + f(b * b);}$$

into the definition

$$\mathbf{k(n, m) = n * n + f(m * m);}$$

and this change would allow us to apply the Calling Rule to the call of **f**.

There is a similar rule, the Local Variable Renaming Rule, for changing the local variables (those which are defined or declared) in a **where** clause.

5. The Addition and Elimination Rules

It should be apparent that repeated use of the Substitution and Calling Rules may sometimes result in the complete elimination of relevant occurrences of the variable in question. In such a case the definition which was used becomes 'redundant'. The Elimination Rule allows us to eliminate such redundant definitions.

The Definition Elimination Rule: Let W be a where clause and D a definition or declaration in the body of W which defines or declares a variable V. If V does not occur free in the subject of W or in any definition in the body of W, then W may be replaced by the clause W' formed by removing D from the body of W.

We have already seen that using the renaming rules allowed us to expand all three calls of **f** in the term given earlier, yielding

$$\begin{aligned}
&\textbf{h(x) + (y - a) * (y + y)} \\
&\quad \textbf{where} \\
&\quad\quad \textbf{x = y * g + 5} \\
&\quad\quad\quad \textbf{where} \\
&\quad\quad\quad\quad \textbf{g = p - ((q * a + y) - a) * ((q * a + y) + y);} \\
&\quad\quad\quad\quad \textbf{q = k(3, z);} \\
&\quad\quad\quad\quad \textbf{k(m, n) = m * m + ((n * n) - a) * ((n * n) + z);} \\
&\quad\quad\quad \textbf{end;} \\
&\quad\quad \textbf{y = f(u) - u} \\
&\quad\quad\quad \textbf{where} \\
&\quad\quad\quad\quad \textbf{f(d) = d * d - 5;} \\
&\quad\quad\quad\quad \textbf{u = 135;} \\
&\quad\quad\quad \textbf{end;} \\
&\quad\quad \textbf{f(t) = (t - a) * (t + z);} \\
&\quad \textbf{end}
\end{aligned}$$

The Elimination Rule allows us to eliminate the (now useless) definition

$$\textbf{f(t) = (t - a) * (t + z);}$$

and transform the above into

$$\begin{aligned}
&\textbf{h(x) + (y - a) * (y + y)} \\
&\quad \textbf{where} \\
&\quad\quad \textbf{x = y * g + 5} \\
&\quad\quad\quad \textbf{where} \\
&\quad\quad\quad\quad \textbf{g = p - ((q * a + y) - a) * ((q * a + y) + y);} \\
&\quad\quad\quad\quad \textbf{q = k(3, z);} \\
&\quad\quad\quad\quad \textbf{k(m, n) = m * m + ((n * n) - a) * ((n * n) + z);} \\
&\quad\quad\quad \textbf{end;} \\
&\quad\quad \textbf{y = f(u) - u} \\
&\quad\quad\quad \textbf{where} \\
&\quad\quad\quad\quad \textbf{f(d) = d * d - 5;} \\
&\quad\quad\quad\quad \textbf{u = 135;} \\
&\quad\quad\quad \textbf{end;} \\
&\quad \textbf{end}
\end{aligned}$$

It should be apparent that a function definition can be expanded out of a program in this way only if it is nonrecursive, i.e., only if the function is not defined in terms of itself either directly or indirectly. If a program has no recursive function definitions, then all function definitions can eventually be removed. Among other things, this means that an implementation of Lucid without functions can be converted into an implementation of a slightly extended language in which at least nonrecursive definitions are allowed. We just add a front-end to the existing implementation. The new front-end expands all the calls to the functions, then hands the resulting program over to the existing implementation.

The Elimination Rule, like all of the transformation rules, can be applied in reverse. The inverse rule (which we will call the Addition Rule) says that any definition can be added to the body of the clause, provided there are (in the subject or the other definitions) no relevant occurrences of the variable being defined, and provided the variable is not already a local of the clause. Once the definition is added, we can use the Calling Rule in reverse and introduce some calls to the function. This process could be thought of as increasing the 'modularity' of the program. Suppose, for example, that a clause contains the expressions $x ** 2 + b * x + c$, $(x + 1) ** 2 + b * (x + 1) + c$, and $(y - z) ** 2 + b * (y - z) + c$. We could introduce the function definition

$$f(v) = v ** 2 + b * v + c;$$

and replace the three expressions by $f(x)$, $f(x + 1)$ and $f(x - y)$. The restrictions on the Calling Rule (which still must hold when the rule is used in reverse) ensure that b and c have the same meanings in the three expressions as they do in the new definition.

6. The Amalgamation Rule

The determined use of the elimination rules can very often produce where clauses with empty bodies. As a simple example, the expression

$$\text{sum}(3, 5)$$
$$\textbf{where}$$
$$\text{sum}(x, y) = x + y;$$
$$\textbf{end}$$

can be transformed to

$$3 + 5$$
$$\textbf{where}$$
$$\text{sum}(x, y) = x + y;$$
$$\textbf{end}$$

using the calling rule, and then to

$$3 + 5$$
$$\textbf{where}$$
$$\textbf{end}$$

with the Elimination Rule. It seems only natural that we should be able to discard the useless **where** and **end**. This is in fact the case, and it follows as a special instance of a far more general rule which allows us to combine separate **where** clauses.

The Amalgamation Rule: Let $E(W, W', W'', ...)$ be an expression in which occur the **where** clauses $W, W', W'', ...$ with subjects $S, S', S'', ...$ and bodies $B, B', B'', ...$. Then $E(W, W', W'', ...)$ can be replaced by the clause

$$E(S, S', S'', ...)$$
where
$$B$$
$$B'$$
$$B''$$
$$...$$
end

(i.e., the result of replacing each of the **where** clauses by its subject, and making the resulting expression the subject of a **where** clause whose body is the result of merging the bodies of the separate **where** clauses).

As usual, restrictions on this rule are required to prevent name clashes. With the Amalgamation Rule it is necessary to ensure that the bodies of the various clauses are compatible (no variable is a local of more than one clause) and that no local of any of the clauses appears free in $E(W, W', W'', ...)$.

The Amalgamation Rule could, for example, be used to transform

$$\textbf{(g(a) } * \textbf{ x where g(u) = u } * \textbf{ 5; x = p } - \textbf{ q; end) } +$$
$$\textbf{f(b } * \textbf{ Z where Z is current z; b = p } + \textbf{ q; end)}$$

to

$$\textbf{g(a) } * \textbf{ x } +$$
$$\textbf{f(b } * \textbf{ Z)}$$
where
$$\textbf{Z is current z;}$$
$$\textbf{g(u) = u } * \textbf{ 5;}$$
$$\textbf{x = p } - \textbf{ q;}$$
$$\textbf{b = p } + \textbf{ q;}$$
end.

This transformation would not, however, be possible if in the first **where** clause x was renamed to **Z** (the clauses would then share a local) or if **g** was renamed to **f** (**f** appears free in the original expression as a whole).

The rule which allows us to change

$$E \text{ where end}$$

into E is a special case of the reverse of the Amalgamation Rule, one in which the list of **where** clauses is empty.

7. The Import and Export Rules

The block structuring of Iswim (and Lucid) allows a certain amount of 'information hiding'. Definitions of variables or functions which are used only in a certain expression can be placed in the body of a **where** clause whose subject is the expression in question. They do not have to be included at the 'main' level.

For example, in the following program to reverse lists

```
rev(L)
  where
    rev(x) = if x eq []
         then []
         else app(hd(x), rev(tl(x))) fi
           where
             app(a,m) = if m eq []
                   then [%a%]
                   else hd(m) :: app(a, tl(m)) fi;
         end;
  end
```

the definition of **app** does not have to be included in the body of the main **where** clause on the same level as the definition of **rev**. (In the LISP analog of this program, no such hiding is possible—in LISP all definitions appear on the same level.)

However, the program might well have been written in LISP style as

```
rev(L)
  where
    rev(x) = if x eq []
         then []
         else app(hd(x), rev(tl(x))) fi;
    app(a,m) = if m eq []
          then [%a%]
          else hd(m) :: app(a, tl(m)) fi;
  end
```

and it is not hard to see that the two programs are equivalent. To be able to transform the one into the other, however, we need a rule which allows us to 'import' and 'export' definitions across a clause boundary.

The Definition Import Rule: Any definition in the body of a **where** clause can be added to the body of any subclause appearing in the subject or in the right-hand side of any definition in its body, provided no clash of variables results.

To avoid clashes with this rule we must check that the variable defined is not already a local of the subclause, that free variables of the definition do not become bound in the subclause and that all free occurrences of this variable in the subclause are relevant to the original definition. In other words, the subclause must not appear in a context in which the variable defined is bound (unless it is bound by the original definition, i.e., the subclause is within the original definition).

In the example given above, we can take the second form of the program and use the Amalgamation Rule in reverse on the right-hand side of the definition of **rev** to get

```
rev(L)
  where
    rev(x) = if x eq [] then [] else app(hd(x), rev(tl(x))) fi
      where
      end;
    app(a,m) = if m eq [] then [%a%] else hd(m) :: app(a, tl(m)) fi;
  end
```

Then we use the Import Rule to add a 'copy' of the definition of **app** to the empty **where** body. Finally, since **app** no longer occurs free in the definition of **rev** or in the subject of the main clause, we can use the Elimination Rule to remove the definition of **app** from the body of the main clause.

In the following simple expression

```
a * x + b
  where
    a = p + q;
    b = p - w;
    c = j + k;
    x = f(z)
      where
        f(b, q) = b + q
          where
            q = z + c;
```

$$c = 3;$$
$$\text{end};$$
$$\text{end};$$
$$\text{end}$$

the definitions of **a**, **b** and **c** cannot be moved into the innermost **where** clause. That of **a** cannot be moved because **q** is redefined in the inner clause; that of **b** cannot, because **b** is bound (as a formal parameter) in the inner clause; and that of **c** cannot be moved because **c** is a local of the inner clause.

There is also a comparable rule for importing and exporting declarations.

8. The Parameter Insertion and Deletion Rules

The reader has probably noticed something slightly strange about the definition

> **app(a,m) = if m eq [ ]**
> **then [%a%]**
> **else hd(m) :: app(a, tl(m)) fi;**

for the function **app**. The strange thing is the way in which the function 'calls' itself: in the recursive subcall, the first argument is the same as in the original call. This first parameter is actually being used to 'drag around' a particular value from one call to the next.

This phenomenon ('baggage' parameters) is very common in languages like LISP and PROLOG, which have no scope structure and do not allow nested function definitions. The same problem arises in Iswim and Lucid if we write in the style of LISP, with all our function definitions on the same level. However, if we use Lucid's (i.e., Iswim's) facility for nested definitions, these values can appear as globals of the function definition and do not have to be passed around in parameter lists. We can rewrite the reversing program as

> **rev(L)**
> **where**
> **rev(x) = if x eq [ ] then [ ] else app(rev(tl(x))) fi**
> **where**
> **app(m) = if m eq [ ]**
> **then [%hd(x)%]**
> **else hd(m) :: app(tl(m)) fi;**
> **end;**
> **end**

Now the expression **hd(x)**, which before was being passed around as a parameter, appears in the definition of **app**. The variable **x** is a global (free) variable of this definition, but is at the same time a formal parameter of an enclosing definition. Variables used in this way are called *dynamic free variables*. Both PASCAL and Lucid allow dynamic free variables, but some languages (such as C) rule them out because they cause implementation difficulties.

There are no semantic difficulties with such variables in Lucid, and they can be very useful in helping the programmer avoid long parameter lists. Using the transformation rules given so far, however, it is not possible to perform the transformation described above which eliminates the extra parameters. We need two more rules designed for this purpose.

The first rule can be thought of as a 'backwards' form of the calling rule, in which an actual parameter is introduced into the definition of a function.

The Actual Substitution Rule: Let W be a **where** clause containing a definition of the form

$$F(P_0, P_1, ..., P_{n-1}) = E;$$

Suppose that in every relevant call to F, the actual parameter corresponding to the formal parameter P_i is the expression A or (inside E) the same formal parameter itself. Then the expression E can be replaced by the expression E' which results when all free occurrences of P_i are replaced by A.

As always, there are restrictions necessary to avoid errors connected with the binding of variables. With this rule it is necessary to ensure that (i) the substitution does not result in variable clashes, and that (ii) the free variables of A have the same bindings in their different occurrences as actuals.

For example, applying this rule in the original reverse program, we see that **hd(x)** is the only expression appearing as a first actual parameter of **app** other than **a** itself. Furthermore, the expression **hd(x)** has the same meaning (**x** is bound the same way) inside and outside the definition. Therefore, we can rewrite the definition of **app** as

app(a, m) = if m eq [ ] then [%hd(x)%]
else hd(m) :: app(hd(x), tl(m)) fi;

The formal parameter **a** is now useless, and our second rule allows us to eliminate it.

The Parameter Deletion Rule: Let W be a clause which contains a definition of the form

$$F(P_0, P_1, P_2, \ldots) = E;$$

Suppose that the formal parameter P_i does not occur free in E. Then this parameter can be deleted from the formal parameter list in the definition list and the corresponding actual parameters can be deleted from all relevant calls to F.

For once there are no restrictions regarding bindings of variables.

This rule can now be used to eliminate the first parameter in the definition of **app** above and give us the desired simplified program.

It should be apparent that there are a number of other rules which could be formulated (say, for permuting the order of parameters) and that some of the rules could be formulated differently (we could have combined the last two). Others could be either restricted or generalised. The reader may well be a little worried by the large number of rules and by the difficulty in formulating them precisely with a complete set of restrictions. After all, these restrictions are apparently too complicated to be presented in full even in a full-length book devoted to Lucid!

Fortunately, the situation is not as bleak as it may seem. It is in fact true that average programmers, even ones with training in logic, would find it almost impossible to keep in their heads a precise formulation of the rules with all the restrictions. It is also true, however, that there is no need for them to do so. The rules and all the algorithms for checking of bindings can be implemented in a 'verifier's assistant' program. The verifiers themselves need only have a more informal understanding of the kinds of changes that are possible. To transform one program into another, the human verifier would break the transformation down into a series of small, plausible steps, and ask the 'assistant' to check that the steps can be done. The assistant would try to select an appropriate rule from its database, then check that (say) no clashes of variables result, then report to its human master that everything is all right. Of course the assistant will sometimes report that a transformation is disallowed because of such-and-such a clash of bindings. It will sometimes even be forced to report to its master that it can find no way to check out a given step—in which case the human must try something simpler. In any case there is no need for the human to have a complete, detailed, and precise knowledge of dozens of rules with complicated restrictions. It is enough to understand the rules at roughly the informal level at which they have been presented in this section.

9. Symbolic Evaluation

The rules given above fall far short of being complete in the sense that they enable us to transform any two equivalent programs into each other. There are (as we shall in the next section) very simple examples of equivalent programs which perform their computations in very different ways and cannot be transformed into each other by the rules given above.

Thoro is, howevor, a weaker but still important sense in which the rules are "complete"—at least for some members of the Iswim and Lucid families. The transformation rules given are powerful enough to allow us to 'compute' the output of a given program, by reducing it to simple expressions whose value is 'known'.

This notion of completeness is easiest to state in the case of *Iswim(A)* with *A* an algebra which (like *P*) has a constant for every element of its universe (other than $\perp$), and which has only one partial object, namely $\perp$ itself. In this case any *Iswim(A)* program which terminates (does not have $\perp$ as its value) can be reduced, using the transformation rules given, to an equivalent program consisting of a constant. For these members of the Iswim family (at least), the transformation rules completely specify the semantics.

It is not hard at all to see why this must be true. To 'evaluate' a program using the transformation rules we repeatedly use the Calling Rule to expand function computations. The various renaming rules are used to allow the Calling Rule to be applied in situations where a clash of variables would otherwise result. The Basis Rule is used to perform the actual computations (e.g., replacing **2 + 2** by **4**), and the Elimination Rules are used to discard definitions and clauses which are no longer needed. If the output (value) of a program (involving integers) is, say, 3, then there will exist a strategy for transforming the original program into the program **3.**

We must emphasise that we are not proposing symbolic evaluation as a *practical* technique for implementing programs. The pLucid interpreter is based on entirely different principles. After the 'compiling' phase is finished, the actual evaluation proceeds without making *any* changes to the program being evaluated. In this section we want to show only that *in principle* the transformation rules can be used to obtain the value of any program. It is very important to know that this is possible, if only in principle, because it means that these rules by themselves determine the semantics of the language.

Consider, for example, the pIswim [i.e., *Iswim(P)*] program

rev([1 2])
where

rev(x) = if x eq [ ] then [ ] else app(rev(tl(x))) fi
   where
     app(m) = if m eq [ ] then [%hd(x)%]
         else hd(m) :: app(tl(m)) fi;
   end;
end

We begin the evaluation by applying the Calling Rule to the call of **rev** in the subject; this gives the expression

if [1 2] eq [ ] then [ ] else app(rev(tl([1 2]))) fi
   where
     app(m) = if m eq [ ] then [%hd([1 2])%]
         else hd(m) :: app(tl(m)) fi;
   end
     where
       rev(x) = if x eq [ ] then [ ] else app(rev(tl(x))) fi
         where
           app(m) = if m eq [ ] then [%hd(x)%]
              else hd(m) :: app(tl(m)) fi;
         end;
     end

The Basis Rule allows us to replace **[1 2] eq [ ]** by **false** and therefore also the whole top **if–then–else** by its 'false' alternative. We can use the Basis Rule some more to 'clean up' expressions such as **[%hd([1 2])%]**, and this gives us the expression

app(rev([2]))
   where
     app(m) = if m eq [ ] then [1] else hd(m) :: app(tl(m)) fi;
   end
   where
     rev(x) = if x eq [ ] then [ ] else app(rev(tl(x))) fi
       where
         app(m) = if m eq [ ] then [%hd(x)%]
            else hd(m) :: app(tl(m)) fi;
       end;
   end

Next, we apply the Calling Rule to the call **rev([2])** at the top, and, after some similar applications of the Basis Rule, the whole expression is

app(
   app(rev([ ]))

    where
      app(m) = if m eq [ ] then [2] else hd(m) :: app(tl(m)) fi;
    end
)
  where
    app(m) = if me eq [ ] then [1] else hd(m) :: app(tl(m)) fi;
  end
    where
      rev(x) = if x eq [ ] then [ ] else app(rev(tl(x))) fi
        where
          app(m) = if m eq [ ] then [%hd(x)%]
             else hd(m) :; app(tl(m)) fi;
        end;
    end

The expression **rev([ ])** now gets our attention. Using the Calling Rule it expands to

  if [ ] eq [ ] then [ ] else app(rev(tl([ ]))) fi
    where
      app(m) = if m eq [ ] then [%hd(x)%] else hd(m) :: app(tl(m)) fi;
    end

but the Basis Rule allows us to reduce this immediately to

  [ ]
    where
      app(m) = if m eq [ ] then [%hd(x)%] else hd(m) :: app(tl(m)) fi;
    end

The Definition Elimination Rule allows us to transform this expression into

                [ ]
              where
              end

and using the Amalgamation Rule in reverse we obtain [ ].
    The main expression has now become

  app(
    app([ ])
      where
        app(m) = if m eq [ ] then [2] else hd(m) :: app(tl(m)) fi;
      end
)

```
where
   app(m) = if m eq [] then [1] else hd(m) :: app(tl(m)) fi;
end
   where
      rev(x) = if x eq [] then [] else app(rev(tl(x))) fi
         where
            app(m) = if m eq [] then [%hd(x)%]
                  else hd(m) :: app(tl(m)) fi;
         end;
end
```

At this point we could expand the expression **app([ ])**, but, before we do, we will use the Elimination Rules again to simplify the whole expression. The expression as a whole is a **where** clause whose body has only one definition, that of **rev**. There are no longer any calls to the function **rev** other than those occurring in its own definition. This definition can therefore be discarded. Furthermore, since this definition is the only one in the clause in which it occurs, we can replace the whole clause by its subject, namely the expression

```
app(
   app([ ])
      where
         app(m) = if m eq [] then [2] else hd(m) :: app(tl(m)) fi;
      end
   )
   where
      app(m) = if m eq [] then [1] else hd(m) :: app(tl(m)) fi;
end
```

Now we can expand the expression **app([ ])**. Using the Calling Rule again, we get

```
app(
   if [] eq [] then [2] else hd([ ]) :: app(tl([ ])) fi
      where
         app(m) = if m eq [] then [2] else hd(m) :: app(tl(m)) fi;
      end
   )
   where
      app(m) = if m eq [] then [1] else hd(m) :: app(tl(m)) fi;
end
```

(Notice that the inner definition was the relevant one.) The Basis Rule allows us to reduce the substituted expression to **[2]** and the resulting 'working expression' becomes

> **app(**
> **[2]**
> **where**
> **app(m) = if m eq [] then [2] else hd(m) :: app(tl(m)) fi;**
> **end**
> **)**
> **where**
> **app(m) = if m eq [] then [1] else hd(m) :: app(tl(m)) fi;**
> **end**

and with the Elimination Rules it becomes

> **app([2])**
> **where**
> **app(m) = if m eq [] then [1] else hd(m) :: app(tl(m)) fi;**
> **end**

This can be transformed to

> **if [2] eq [] then [1] else hd([2]) :: app(tl([2])) fi**
> **where**
> **app(m) = if m eq [] then [1] else hd(m) :: app(tl(m)) fi;**
> **end**

using the Calling Rule; then it can be transformed to

> **2 :: app([ ])**
> **where**
> **app(m) = if m eq [] then [1] else hd(m) :: app(tl(m)) fi;**
> **end**

using the Basis Rule; and then to

> **2 :: if [] eq [] then [1] else hd([ ]) :: app(tl([ ])) fi;**
> **where**
> **app(m) = if m eq [] then [1] else hd(m) :: app(tl(m)) fi;**
> **end**

using the Calling Rule, to

> **[2 1]**
> **where**
> **app(m) = if m eq [] then [1] else hd(m) :: app(tl(m)) fi;**
> **end**

using the Basis Rule; and finally to

[2 1]

using Elimination Rules. We can easily extend our notion of symbolic evaluation to handle programs with input variables. Before beginning the evaluation, we replace all free occurrences of the input variables by constants denoting the corresponding inputs.

10. The Symbolic Evaluation of Iterative Programs

The transformation rules can also be used to 'evaluate' iterative programs using the special Lucid operators. Consider, for example, the following iterative program

> **f asa i eq 3**
> **where**
>   **i = 1 fby i + 1;**
>   **f = 1 fby f ∗ next i;**
> **end**

The first step is to use the Basis Rule and the appropriate instance of the equation

>   **x asa p = if first p then first x else next x asa next p fi**

to transform the program into

> **if first i eq 3 then first f else next f asa next i eq 3 fi**
>   **where**
>   **i = 1 fby i + 1;**
>   **f = 1 fby f ∗ next i;**
>   **end**

Next, we use the Substitution Rule to replace the first occurrence of i by **1 fby i + i**, giving

> **if first (1 fby i + 1) eq 3**
>   **then f**
>   **else next f asa next i eq 3 fi**
>   **where**
>   **i = 1 fby i + 1;**
>   **f = 1 fby f ∗ next i;**
>   **end**

We then use the Basis Rule, again with the equation

$$\text{first } (1 \text{ fby } i + 1) = 1$$

and our program becomes

> **if** 1 eq 3 **then first** 1 **else next** f **asa next** i eq 3 **fi**
> **where**
> i = 1 **fby** i + 1;
> f = 1 **fby** f * next i;
> **end**

Using the equation

$$1 \text{ eq } 3 = \text{false}$$

and those for **if–then–else**, it all reduces to

> **next** f **asa next** i eq 3
> **where**
> i = 1 **fby** i + 1;
> f = 1 **fby** f * next i;
> **end**

For the next step in our symbolic iteration, we again apply the **asa** equation and replace the first occurrence of **i** by its definition. This gives

> **if first next** i eq 3
> **then first next** f
> **else next next** f **asa next next** i eq 3 **fi**
> **where**
> i = 1 **fby** i + 1;
> f = 1 **fby** f * next i;
> **end**

The symbolic evaluation of the test involves the computation of **first next** i, i.e., of the second (time 1) value of **i**. First we substitute the expression **1 fby** i + 1 for **i**, and (as before) apply the Basis Rule with the equation

$$\text{next } (1 \text{ fby } i + 1) = i + 1$$

This gives us the expression **first** (i + 1). We now apply the Basis Rule with the equations

$$\text{first } (i + 1) = \text{first } i + \text{first } 1$$
$$\text{first } 1 = 1$$

and we obtain the expression **first** i + 1. This in turn can be transformed to **first (1 fby i + 1) + 1**, which becomes **first 1 + 1**, then **1 + 1** and finally **2** (using the Substitution and Basis Rules). The original expression is therefore now:

> **if 2 eq 3**
> **then first next f**
> **else next next f asa next next i eq 3 fi**
> **where**
> **i = 1 fby i + 1;**
> **f = 1 fby f * next i;**
> **end**

and this is quickly transformed to

> **next next f asa next next i eq 3**
> **where**
> **i = 1 fby i + 1;**
> **f = 1 fby f * next i;**
> **end**

On the next step in our symbolic iteration the subject of the clause becomes

> **if first next next i eq 3**
> **then first next next f**
> **else next next next f asa next next i eq 3 fi**

but this time the symbolic evaluation of **first next next i** yields **3**. The subject therefore reduces to the expression **first next next F**, and this in turn can be transformed to **6**. After discarding the **where** clause we obtain **6** as the final answer.

The above program, however, was not typical of Lucid programs in general—its value was constant in time (namely, constantly 6) and so the whole program could be reduced to one consisting of the numeral **6**. In general, though, the output of Lucid programs is not constant, and so the program cannot be rewritten in such a simple form. Most Lucid programs, such as

> **i**
> **where**
> **i = 1 fby i + 1;**
> **end**

produce an infinite number of different data values in the course of their lifetimes. A program like the above cannot possibly be equivalent to any expression involving only constants, and no variables. It is therefore not possible in general to symbolically evaluate a Lucid program in exactly the same way in which pIswim (for example) can be evaluated. The same is true of any member of the Iswim family (including HyperpIswim) based on an algebra of infinite data objects.

There is, however, still one sense in which it is possible to symbolically evaluate an arbitrary Lucid program. Suppose that T is a program and that t is a time. The expression

first next next ... next T

(with t **next**'s after the **first**) denotes the value of the program at tlme t. If this value is a 'healthy' object (i.e., is not $\perp$), we can use the transformation rules to reduce the above expression to one consisting of a constant denoting the value in question. Consider, for example, the program

> **f**
> > **where**
> > i = 1 **fby** i + 1;
> > f = 1 **fby** f * **next** i;
> > **end**

which produces the stream 1, 2, 6, 24, 120, ... of all factorials. The time 4 output of this function is 120, a fact which can be verified symbolically by transforming the expression

> **first next next next next (f**
> > **where**
> > i = 1 **fby** i + 1;
> > f = 1 **fby** f * **next** i;
> > **end**
> **)**

into **120** (we will not give the details).

Another way of formulating this idea is as follows: If the value of program T at time t is v (v not $\perp$), then T can be transformed into an expression of the form

$$E_0 \text{ \textbf{fby} } E_1 \cdots \text{ \textbf{fby} } E_{t-1} \text{ \textbf{fby} } c \text{ \textbf{fby} } E_{t+1}$$

where c is a constant denoting v. For example, we can transform the above program into

> **1 fby 2 fby 6 fby 24 fby 120 fby**
> > **next next next next next (f**
> > > **where**
> > > i = 1 **fby** i + 1;

$$f = 1 \textbf{ fby } f * \textbf{next } i;$$
$$\textbf{end}$$
$$)$$

The notion of evaluation given above applies to programs with input as well. Suppose that a program T with input variable V has output v at time t whenever the input values of V at times

$$r_0, r_1, r_2, \ldots, r_{k-1}$$

are

$$w_0, w_1, w_2, \ldots, w_{k-1}$$

respectively. Let H be an expression of the form

$$G_0 \textbf{ fby } G_1 \textbf{ fby } \cdots \textbf{ fby } G_{r_{k-1}-1} \textbf{ fby } G_{r_{k-1}}$$

in which each G_{r_i} is a constant denoting w_i, but the other G_j are distinct variables not occurring in T. Let T' be the result of substituting H for all free occurrences of V in T. Then the transformation rules can be used to transform T' to an expression of the form

$$E_0 \textbf{ fby } E_1 \cdots \textbf{ fby } E_{t-1} \textbf{ fby } c \textbf{ fby } E_{t+1}$$

In other words, we can use symbolic methods to verify that any particular finite amount of information about the input determines a corresponding particular finite amount of information about the output. Since the input/output function of a Lucid program is computable, the collection of all such finite relationships determines the input/output function as a whole.

Of course neither of these versions of the notion of 'evaluation' applies to a member of the Lucid family based on an algebra which already has infinite objects in it. We would have to reformulate it again, and use symbolic methods to derive finite amounts of information about particular output values.

11. Binding and Calling Conventions

The transformation rules can also be used to answer questions about 'calling conventions' for parameters of functions and about the binding of global variables. With imperative languages these issues are usually discussed in operational terms, and the conventions chosen seem somewhat arbitrary. In Lucid (and Iswim) the answers to these questions are already determined by the transformation rules, and so any other choice regarding calling or binding conventions would invalidate some of the rules.

Consider first the program

```
        r
            where
                a = 3;
                f(x) = x + a;
                r = s
                    where
                        a = 5;
                        s = f(1);
                    end;
            end
```

The question is, should the output of this (pIswim) program be 4 or 6? The function **f** is *defined* in a context in which the value of **a** is 3, but it is *used* (called) in a context in which the value is 5. Which value applies? If the defining context is the relevant one, the language is said to use *static* binding. If the calling context is the determining one, the language is said to use *dynamic* binding (LISP and POP-2 use dynamic binding, PASCAL uses static binding).

We can use our transformation rules to show almost immediately that binding in Iswim and Lucid must be static. One way to do this is to apply the substitution rule to the occurrence of **a** in the definition of **f**. The relevant definition is **a = 3**, so that the occurrence of **a** is replaced by **3**, and the program becomes

```
        r
            where
                a = 3;
                f(x) = x + 3;
                r = s
                    where
                        a = 5;
                        s = f(1);
                    end;
            end
```

The output of this program is clearly 4.

Another way to see this is to use the Local Variable Renaming Rule inside the inner **where** clause, and systematically replace **a** by **b**. The result is the program

```
        r
            where
```

```
a = 3
f(x) = x + a;
r = s
    where
        b = 5;
        s = f(1);
    end;
end
```

and again the output is clearly 4.

Finally, we could use the Definition Elimination Rule in the inner clause and discard the definition of a—there are no occurrences of **a** in this clause for which this definition is the relevant one. The result is again a program whose output is clearly 4.

We can conclude, then, that introducing dynamic binding into Iswim and Lucid would mean losing the Substitution, Renaming and Local Variable Elimination Rules (at least). Dynamic binding is inconsistent with the interpretation of Iswim definitions as equations.

Now consider the (slightly mysterious) program

```
f(3, 5)
    where
    f(x, y) = if x < 1 then 0 else f(x − 1, f(x, y + 1)) fi;
    end
```

The question is not which of two numbers will be output (0 is the only candidate). The question is whether or not there will be any output at all.

A PASCAL programmer would expect that this program would give rise to unending (nonterminating) computation. This is certainly what will happen when we run the analogous PASCAL program:

```
program test(input, output);
function f(x, y : integer) : integer;
begin
    if x = 0 then f := 0 else f := f(x − 1, f(x, y + 1))
end;
begin
    writeln(f(3, 5))
end
```

The call **f(3, 5)** will give rise to the call **f(3, 6)**, which will in turn give rise to the call **f(3, 7)** and so on indefinitely. The **write** statement will never be executed.

In Iswim and Lucid, however, the denotational semantics requires that the output be 0—and this is the value produced by a pIswim imple-mentation and (over and over) by the Lucid interpreter. It might not be obvious *how* this result is produced; but it is very easy, using our transfor-mation rules, to see *why* 0 must be the output. We can simply use the Calling and Basis Rules to evaluate the program. The first application of the Calling Rule gives

> **if 3 < 1 then 0 else f(3 − 1, f(3, 5 + 1)) fi**
> **where**
> **f(x, y) = if x < 1 then 0 else f(x − 1, f(x, y + 1)) fi;**
> **end**

and a little Basis Rule calculation simplifies this to

> **f(2, f(3, 6))**
> **where**
> **f(x, y) = if x < 1 then 0 else f(x − 1, f(x, y + 1)) fi;**
> **end**

At this point we *could* apply the Calling Rule to the call **f(3, 6)**; but we do not have to. Instead, we apply the Calling Rule to the *outer* call of **f**, the one whose actual parameters are **2** and **f(3, 6)**. (The Calling Rule does not require that the actual parameters be constants.) The resulting program is

> **if 2 < 1 then 0 else f(2 − 1, f(2, f(3, 6) + 1)) fi**
> **where**
> **f(x, y) = if x < 1 then 0 else f(x − 1, f(x, y + 1)) fi;**
> **end**

which after cleaning up becomes

> **f(1, f(2, f(3, 6) + 1))**
> **where**
> **f(x, y) = if x < 1 then 0 else f(x − 1, f(x, y + 1)) fi;**
> **end**

Continuing in this way we obtain

> **f(0, f(1, f(2, f(3, 6) + 1)) + 1)**
> **where**
> **f(x, y) = if x < 1 then 0 else f(x − 1, f(x, y + 1)) fi;**
> **end**

One more application of the Calling Rule (to the outer call, as always) gives

> **if 0 < 1 then 0 else f(0 − 1, f(0, f(1, f(2, f(3, 6) + 1)) + 1) + 1) fi;**

where
  f(x, y) = if x < 1 then 0 else f(x − 1, f(x, y + 1)) fi;
end

This time, however, the Basis Rule gives us

  0
    where
    f(x, y) = if x < 1 then 0 else f(x − 1, f(x, y + 1)) fi;
    end

which quickly reduces to **0**.

The reason that the PASCAL program never produces any output is that parameters of functions are called *by value*. This means that PASCAL attempts to evaluate all the actual parameters before 'entering' the body of the function, even if some of these values are not actually needed. PASCAL attempts to perform unnecessary computations, and if these unnecessary computations never terminate, no value will ever be produced.

The interpreters for PIFL and Lucid, however, do not attempt to evaluate any expression until it is certain that the result will be needed. When processing a function call, evaluation of the function body begins immediately and actual parameters are evaluated only when the evaluation of the body requires these values. This is call *by need* (sometimes called call *by name*). A call-by-value implementation of Iswim or Lucid would only be partially correct: any actual output which appears would be the right output, but the implementation might sometimes fail to deliver output specified by the denotational semantics and the transformation rules. Call-by-value is inconsistent with the Calling Rule; it corresponds to a more restricted version of this rule in which the actual parameters of the call are required to be constants.

12. Proving Assertions about Programs

The program transformation rules given in the last chapter allow only a very limited kind of formal reasoning *about* programs. We cannot use these rules to derive true assertions about programs (except assertions to the effect that a transformed program is equivalent to the original). In particular, we cannot prove that a given program is correct in that it corresponds to a specification written in some logical language.

The simplest way to permit reasoning about *Lucid(A)* programs is to take some formal logical system and allow Lucid expressions to appear as terms. One of the simplest choices is the second-order language *L* whose individual variables are the nullary Lucid variables and whose operation symbols are taken from the signature of A. (The language L is second order because it allows function variables.) We could generalise L to the language L^* by allowing any *Lucid(A)* term to appear in a formula anywhere an ordinary term is permitted. In this extended logic, assertions about programs are assertions about the values of programs, and are just formulas in which the program appears. For example, the fact that the pLucid program

> **fac(n)**
>> **where**
>> **fac(x) = if x eq 1 then 1 else x ∗ fac(x − 1) fi;**
> **end**

calculates the factorial of **n** might be formulated as

> **forall n (integer(n) and n >= 1 →**
> **n! = (fac(n)**
>> **where fac(x) = if x eq 1**
>>> **then 1**
>>> **else x ∗ fac(x − 1) fi; end))**

Notice that the assertion uses primitives (such as the symbol ! for factorial, the quantifier **forall** and the logical connective →), which are not available in pLucid. We have used a hypothetical linear representation of the logical symbols in the ordinary character set. Program equivalence statements can be expressed as equations between programs, with the input variables universally quantified.

This does allow reasoning about programs, but only about programs *as terms*. In other words, we can make statements only about the *output* of the program—and not about the internal values of variables. For example, given the program

> **f asa i eq N**
>> **where**
>> **N is current n;**
>> **i = 1 fby i + 1;**
>> **f = 1 fby f ∗ next i;**
> **end;**

it is only natural to observe that the value of **f** is always the factorial of the value of **i**. This statement, however, cannot be stated as a formula about the program itself. If we use the embedding approach, we can only talk about values of variables occurring *free* in a program, and their relation to the output. In particular, we could state that the output of the program is the factorial of the value of **n**, if that value is a positive integer. But we could not prove or even formulate any connection between the values of **f, i** and the program.

In reasoning about programs informally, and in documenting them, programmers often "annotate" them with comments (written, say, to the right of the text) which refer to the 'local' values of the variables. This concept is relatively easy to formalise, and can be used as the basis of a much more convenient method of program verification in Lucid (and Iswim).

The extended system works by treating all verification as a form of transformation. The transformations are applied to *annotated programs*—programs in which **where** clauses have added 'marginal' comments about the values of internal variables. There are rules for introducing annotations, for deriving new annotations from old, for moving annotations in and out of clauses and even for using annotations to modify the program itself.

The rules for annotated programs are, as was mentioned earlier, all transformation rules. The annotation rules and their restrictions are very similar to those presented in the previous sections for ordinary programs. We will therefore present only a brief summary of the annotation rules.

Among the most important is the Consequence Rule. It allows us to add to the commentary of a clause any formula which is a logical consequence of the formulas already in the commentary. Consequences derived using global reasoning are allowed. The Consequence Rule has a dual, the Discard Rule, which is much simpler. It allows us to delete *any* formula in a commentary.

The Basis Rule allows us to add to a commentary any formula true in $Lu(A)$ in all interpretations.

The Definition Rule allows us to add to the commentary the formula obtained by taking any definition in the clause and universally quantifying all the formal parameters.

The Export Rule allows us to add to the commentary of an outer clause any formula in the commentary of an inner clause. There are, however, strict controls in effect. It is necessary that no variable clashes result; none of the locals of the inner clause, or of a definition containing the inner (but not the outer) clause, may occur free. Fortunately, there is a small loophole in the restrictions. If the formula to be exported has free occurrences of **is current** declared variables, and if these variables appear in synchronic contexts, then an export is possible. However, it is necessary first to replace each declared variable by the right-hand side of the appropriate declaration. The Import Rule is the reverse of the Export Rule. The loophole is actually more useful for importing. For example, if a clause contains the declaration **N is current next n**, then the assertion **next n = i** can be imported as **N = i**, provided **i** is not a local of the clause.

The Subject Rule allows us to convert internal information about the subject of a clause into information about the clause itself. A simple formulation of this rule is as follows: suppose that a clause contains a definition of the form $V = W$, that W is a clause with subject S and that inside the commentary of W a formula containing S has been proved. Then the same formula may be added to the commentary of the outer clause, with S replaced by V, provided no locals of W appear in the formula after the replacement.

There is also a whole family of rules corresponding to the family of ordinary program transformation rules described in the last chapter. The annotated version of a rule is the same as the ordinary version except that the annotations are 'dragged along' with the code as it is moved about. The restrictions on the annotated versions are more complicated, because occurrences of variables in commentaries must be taken into account. For example, if we want to remove an equation from a clause body, it is not enough to make sure that there are no relevant occurrences in the clause of the variable defined by the equation. We must also check that there are no free occurrences of the variable in formulas in the commentary. However, apart from these complications, the rules are straightforward and we will not give details.

The rules just described so far all have the property that their use involves only a *one-way* flow of information *from* the actual program part (clause bodies) *to* the annotations. We therefore need an additional rule, the Modification Rule, which allows annotations to be used to modify the actual program text. This rule allows equations found as annotations to be used to rewrite definitions. Careful restrictions (which will not be given here) are required to prevent the least fixed point of the body of a clause being perturbed. The restrictions on the Modification Rule have the effect of ensuring that the definition being modified could not have been of any use in deriving the equation being employed. [We can sometimes avoid these restrictions by using the "cyclesum test" of Wadge (1981) to show that the transformed definition still has a *unique* fixed point.]

The annotation rules just described are almost independent of the particular logical formal system in which annotations are expressed. However, the approach works best when the logical system is one which is in harmony with the Lucid approach to iteration and time. For these purposes a conventional two-valued logic is definitely not the harmonious choice. A conventional, two-valued system forces the programmer to think in terms of static, infinite objects—exactly the opposite of the approach we have been urging throughout the previous chapters. Program verification will never enjoy much success as long as the language and concepts used to *reason* about programs differ radically from the language and concepts used to actually *write* them. What is needed is a form of logic which allows direct reasoning about values and properties which change with time—without the introduction of explicit time parameters and ugly explicit indexing.

In fact there already exists a branch of logic which allows reasoning about time directly. Systems of this type are called *tense logics* and their formal properties have been studied by logicians for many years. In tense logics formulas may be true at one instant and false at another, and primitives (such as **always** and **sometimes**) are available which take time into account. A great many tense logics are possible, depending on the notion of time involved and the primitives available. Tense logics were studied first by logicians interested mainly in the philosophical implications of nonstandard logical systems. Later, computer scientists put these systems to work as assertion languages for *describing* the behaviour of conventional imperative programs. Recently, these systems have been used to *specify* programs to be written, not just describe ones which already exist.

In Lucid this "prescriptive" approach to the use of tense logic has been carried to its logical conclusion. In Lucid the programs themselves are written in a language in which the values of expressions depend on a 'hidden' time parameter. Lucid programmers are encouraged to think about time in exactly the same 'dynamic' way which tense logic makes possible. It is only natural, then, that reasoning *about* Lucid should also take place in such a system.

The logic appropriate for reasoning about Lucid (or at least Luswim) programs is a particularly simple one in which the collection of time instants is (or is isomorphic to) the natural numbers together with the usual numeric ordering. The **always** and **sometimes** operators will not normally be needed, but we will use the Lucid primitives **first** and **next** as logical operators. For example, the formula **next** F is true at time t iff the formula F is true at time $t + 1$.

A number of minor technical difficulties arise (in particular, regarding the proper treatment of $\perp$), but the only real problem is distinguishing between 'local' and 'global' reasoning. In 'local' reasoning the verifier is drawing conclusions about the values of expressions at one particular time, while in global reasoning he, she (or it) is deriving assertions true at all times from hypotheses true at all times.

For example, one of the most important rules of inference (the Lucid Induction Rule) allows us to infer an annotation A from the annotations

first A and $A \rightarrow$ **next** A. The latter can be proved by assuming A and deriving **next** A, but only if the reasoning involved is local. We need to know that the fact that A is true at one particular instant implies that it is true at the next instant.

More information about the Lucid logical system can be found in Ashcroft and Wadge (1976). Naturally, the rules for manipulating annotations can be used for more than just assisting transformation. These rules can be used to *verify* a program, i.e., to show that it is correct with respect to some given specification. Annotations can even be used in program design: one could begin with the specification and gradually refine it into a working program. Unfortunately these topics are beyond the scope of this work, which is more concerned with Lucid as a practical tool rather than as an object of formal study.

13. Verification Aiding Transformation: An Example

We close this chapter by presenting (in outline) an example of how verification and transformation rules can be used together to massage a nontrivial (though still simple) program into an equivalent but very different form which performs the calculations using a very different algorithm.

The programs we will be working with all compute a 'running' standard deviation of their input: the output at time t will be the standard deviation

$$\sqrt{\sum_{i=0}^{t}\left\{a_i - \left[\sum_{i=0}^{t} a_i/(t + 1)\right]\right\}^2 \Big/ (t + 1)}$$

of the sequence $a_0, a_1, \ldots, a_t$ of values input so far.

Our first version is intended to be obviously correct, if inefficient.

```
sqrt(avg((a − MEAN) ∗ (a − MEAN)))
        where MEAN is current avg(a); end
    where
        avg(y) = s/n
                where
                    n = 1 fby n + 1;
                    s = y fby s + next y;
                end;
    end
```

It uses a naive algorithm and imitates as closely as possible the specification of the problem given above. With every number input it 'rewinds' its input stream all the way back to the beginning, runs through all the input it has seen so far to compute the new average and then rewinds and runs through these numbers again to compute the output. The algorithm is *quadratic*: the amount of work done (demands generated or arithmetic operations performed) in processing the first *n* input values is proportional to the *square* of *n*. It also needs more and more memory, because all the input values must be saved. Our goal is to transform it into a *linear* algorithm which uses *constant* space.

Our first step is to prove that **avg** is linear; we will add the formula

forall x: forall y: (rational(x) and rational(y)) ⇒
avg(x + y) = avg(x) + avg(y)

We do this by showing that the assumption **rational(x) and rational(y)** (used globally if we wish) allows us to transform **avg(x)** + **avg(y)** into **avg(x + y)**.

We begin this transformation by using the Calling Rule on **avg(x)** and **avg(y)** so that the sum becomes

> **s/n**
>   **where**
>   **n = 1 fby n + 1;**
>   **s = x fby s + next x;**
>   **end**
> **+**
> **s/n**
>   **where**
>   **n = 1 fby n + 1;**
>   **s = y fby s + next y;**
>   **end**

Next we apply the local renaming rule to both clauses and rename **n** and **s** as **n1** and **s1** and **n2** and **s2**, respectively. This clears the way for the amalgamation rule; it allows us to replace the sum of the two **where** clauses by the single clause

> **s1/n1 + s2/n2**
>   **where**
>   **n1 = 1 fby n1 + 1;**
>   **s1 = y fby s1 + next y;**
>   **n2 = 1 fby n2 + 1;**
>   **s2 = y fby s2 + next y;**
>   **end**

whose subject is the sum of the original subjects and whose body is the union of the two bodies.

We now introduce the two new definitions,

$$n = 1 \text{ fby } n + 1;$$
$$s = x + y \text{ fby } s + \text{next}(x + y);$$

into the clause, and derive the annotations

$$n = n1$$
$$n = n2$$
$$s = s1 + s2$$

using Lucid induction. Then we can substitute **n** for both **n1** and **n2**, giving us

$$s1/n + s2/n$$
where
$$n = 1 \text{ fby } n + 1;$$
$$s = x + y \text{ fby next}(x + y);$$
$$n1 = 1 \text{ fby } n1 + 1;$$
$$s1 = y \text{ fby } s1 + \text{next } y;$$
$$n2 = 1 \text{ fby } n2 + 1;$$
$$s2 = y \text{ fby } s2 + \text{next } y;$$
end

The definitions of **n1** and **n2** are now unused and can be eliminated. To get rid of **s1** and **s2**, we transform the subject to **(s1 + s2)/n** and then replace **s1 + s2** by **s** (we are using the Modification Rule here, but the cyclesum test ensures that it is safe). We are left with

$$s/n$$
where
$$n = 1 \text{ fby } n + 1;$$
$$s = x + y \text{ fby next}(x + y);$$
end

which we recognize as the result of using the Calling Rule to expand **avg(x + y)**.

Now that we have demonstrated the linearity of **avg**, we can return to the main clause. We use the binomial theorem to expand the square of **(a − MEAN)**, and the subject becomes

sqrt(avg(a ∗ a − 2 ∗ a ∗ MEAN + MEAN ∗ MEAN))
where MEAN is current avg(a); end

Since **avg** is linear, we can reduce this to

sqrt(avg(a ∗ a) − avg(2 ∗ a ∗ MEAN) + avg(MEAN ∗ MEAN))
where MEAN is current avg(a); end

We can also prove, without much difficulty, that **avg(MEAN * MEAN)** is **MEAN * MEAN** and that **avg(2 * a * MEAN)** is **2 * avg(a) * MEAN** (using the fact that **MEAN** in this context is a constant). The subject becomes

> **sqrt(avg(a * a) − 2 * avg(a) * MEAN + MEAN * MEAN)**
> **where MEAN is current avg(a); end**

and now **MEAN** occurs in a synchronic context only (in the subject of the inner clause). We can therefore replace **MEAN** by **avg(a)** and discard the inner clause. The whole program is now (after some cleaning up of the subject):

> **sqrt(avg(a * a) − avg(a) * avg(a))**
> **where**
> **avg(y) = s/n**
> **where**
> **n = 1 fby n + 1;**
> **s = y fby s + next y;**
> **end;**
> **end**

The program no longer rewinds its input to produce each output value, and does not need unbounded storage. It could still be improved, though. We can use the Calling Rule, expand all the calls to **avg** and then discard the definition. Next, we can use the amalgamation rule to combine all the clauses into one (as we have done before), and introduce some new variables for convenience. The manipulations are completely straightforward and eventually produce

> **sqrt(s2/n − (s1/n) * (s1/n))**
> **where**
> **s2 = a * a fby s2 + next (a * a);**
> **s1 = a fby s1 + next a;**
> **n = 1 fby n + 1;**
> **end**

This version is essentially the same as the previous one, but now it is clearer that it is using a more sensible algorithm. Instead of saving all its input and repeatedly rereading it, it keeps running sums of the input values and their squares. Its memory requirements are finite, and the amount of work performed is now linear in the amount of input.

Of course, the transformation need not stop here. The program is still numerically naive, because it is subtracting larger and larger quantities. If we introduce the new definition **d = s2 * n − s1 * s1**, we can clean up the subject:

$$\text{sqrt(d)/n}$$
$$\textbf{where}$$
$$\text{d = s2 } * \text{ n } - \text{ s1 } * \text{ s1;}$$
$$\text{s2 = a } * \text{ a fby s2 + next (a } * \text{ a);}$$
$$\text{s1 = a fby s1 + next a;}$$
$$\text{n = 1 fby n + 1;}$$
$$\textbf{end}$$

Now we change the program to compute **d** incrementally, rather than directly. Using the (easily derived) annotations

d = first d fby d + (next d − d)
first d = a ∗ a
next d − d = (n ∗ (next a) − 2 ∗ s1) ∗ (next a) + s2

we can modify the definition of **d** to be

d = 0 fby d + (n ∗ (next a) − 2 ∗ s1) ∗ (next a) + s2;

and even better improvements are possible.

The improvements in the performance of the new version are real enough, even on the pLucid interpreter. The interpreter is certainly slow, but the difference between a linear and a quadratic algorithm is still very noticeable. The interpreter always saves its input (because demand for input values is, in general, unpredictable). The new version running on its own will still require more and more buckets in the memory. However, if the program was converted to a filter (so that the values of **a** were not coming directly from the 'outside world'), the difference would be noticeable. A filter based on the original algorithm would endlessly redemand early values of its input and prevent the interpreter's garbage collector from collecting the buckets. The new version would not 'revisit' its input, and eventually these buckets would be retired and collected if they were not being used elsewhere.

The objection could be made that the programs are not really equivalent, because rounding errors will cause different values to be produced. This is certainly the case, and indeed the last transformation was made with the *intention* of getting different, better output. This does not mean, however, that formal equivalence between programs computing with approximations to real numbers is an unrealistic concept. In general it will be true that transformed programs will give different results in spite of being formally equivalent. Nevertheless, if we have used the transformation rules correctly, we can be confident that any differences between the programs are due *solely to rounding errors*. If the original was correct 'in theory', then so is the second, and any problems can be blamed on errors in calculation. This knowledge can be extremely useful. Otherwise, if a numerical program does not work, there is no simple way to decide whether a logical error is at fault (and debugging is required) or whether the numerical techniques are inadequate. The presence of numerical inaccuracy makes *formal* transformation and verification more, not less, important. Program bugs are much harder to find through testing because the random numerical errors provide excellent camouflage.

VII BEYOND LUCID

The language pLucid, described in the preceding chapters, is remarkably simple (at least when compared to ADA or PL/I) and yet remarkably versatile. We have shown that a wide variety of applications can be programmed in pLucid, including many (like the screen editor given in the pLucid manual) that might be thought beyond the reach of a functional language. Recall that pLucid is only one member of a family, and that applications which are difficult to program in pLucid might be easier in another member of the family with more appropriate data types and operations.

Nevertheless, the examples in the preceding chapters have revealed a number of limitations in pLucid and in the whole Lucid family. In this chapter we will examine some of these limitations, and propose tentative solutions. We will consider adding type checking and abstraction, adding multioutput filters, adding arrays, adding a greater variety of computation/subcomputation interfaces and adding higher-order functions. In each case we will give a few sample programs written in the extended language. We must warn the reader that as of this writing none of the added features have been implemented and as a result none of the programs have been tested. We should also emphasise that the proposals are tentative, and that they should not be considered as 'official' extensions to Lucid.

Although the five proposals presented are somewhat speculative, we feel that they are useful and practical and conform to the design methodology described in Ashcroft and Wadge (1982). Operational ideas are used to *inspire* the new feature; denotational concepts are used to *specify* it; and then operational ideas (possibly new ones) are used to *implement* it. (The reference just cited is slightly ambiguous about the 'inspirational' role of operational concepts.) We are confident that the proposed extensions can still be understood and implemented within the broad context of dataflow. Moreover, it seems that the demand-driven, tagged dataflow model can easily be extended to handle arrays, hyperfilters and higher-order functions—although there are some subtle problems with the last of these. At any rate, even with the proposed extensions Lucid would still be a "dataflow programming language".

1. Types and Type Checking

A reader who took a quick glance at this book might be rather shocked that we are proposing a typeless language. In recent years undisputed progress has been made in enriching programming languages (even imperative ones) with a range of data types far more varied than the machine word of assembly language or the array of FORTRAN. Indeed PASCAL's data constructs are its only novel feature and almost the only basis for any claim that the language is superior to its predecessor, ALGOL 60.

In fact Lucid is not really a typeless language. Given any notion of data type (any algebra), there is a member of the Lucid family which allows dataflow programming with 'datons', representing elements of the universe of the algebra. Of course, there is no uniform way of *implementing* the entire Lucid family; but at least the user is not limited in principle to a particular collection of data objects and operations.

The parameter of any *particular* member of the Lucid family is a *single* sorted algebra. It could be argued, then, that each particular member of the family (such as pLucid) is a typeless language. In a sense this is true; in pLucid, the member of the family used in most of this book, there are no type declarations; any operation can be applied to any collection of operands. Nevertheless, the universe of pLucid's algebra in fact contains a wide variety of data objects (strings, lists, words and numbers). The language pLucid allows four different 'types' of data. pLucid is typeless only in the sense that there are no *a priori* syntactic constraints on what may be combined with what. In other words, there is no syntactical *type checking* of any kind. In practice, though, unusual combinations (like the sum of two strings) produce only the error object, so that programmers, if they want to write a sensible program, must follow some implicit type discipline. pLucid is not typeless in the the way that a systems programming language like C is. The pLucid user cannot get across to the machine representation of (say) words, and do arithmetic on them. (Clever programmers can do this even in PASCAL.)

Of course, it would be quite easy to add PASCAL-style strong typing to Iswim or Lucid. When a variable is defined, its type could be declared immediately; for example,

$$i : \text{integer} = 1 \text{ fby } i + 1;$$

For user-defined functions, the types of the formal parameters could be declared as well, as in PASCAL, in the form

sublist(i : integer, j : integer, S : list) : list = ⋯⋯

Checking the consistency of such typed programs is completely straight-forward. The underlying algebra determining a member or instance of strongly typed Lucid would be many sorted, of course.

Is it a good idea to have a language which is completely typeless in the sense that Lucid is now? A typeless language is certainly much simpler— we have avoided types up to now for exactly that reason. The basic principles of dataflow programming in Lucid can be demonstrated and employed without any formal (built-in) type discipline. On the other hand, strong typing forces the programmer to think more carefully about what is being done. Strong typing is also extremely useful in detecting errors; most programming errors cause type anomalies which the type checker automatically detects. A careful type analysis of a program can also help the implementation. For example, if the programmer is syntactically re-strained from ever using a string in a context in which a list is expected and vice versa, the representation can be simplified: there is no need to be able to distinguish them at run time. Type checking eliminates the danger of 'puns'.

On the other hand, a strong type-checking system can be very con-straining. It often prevents a programmer from writing in a form that is concise and correct but too subtle for the limited capabilities of the type checker.

PASCAL programmers well know the feeling of trying to program in a straightjacket. For example, PASCAL programmers using lists cannot have a single type **list** and (as in pLucid) a single **hd** and a single **cons** function. They must write different versions for every type of data that might be stored in a list. An even worse example of this kind of constraint is given by PASCAL arrays. In PASCAL you need a different sorting procedure for every possible length of array (if the array to be sorted is a parameter). Furthermore, the endless type declarations required in a strongly typed language can be extremely tedious. Programmers would justifiably resent having to declare **i** as an integer in

$$i : \text{integer} = 1 \text{ fby } i + 1$$

when the fact that **i** is always an integer is perfectly obvious from the definition.

It is our opinion that a simple-minded pigeonholing type system like PASCAL's, based on a many-sorted algebra, is more trouble than it is worth. The contortions and irregularities introduced by the programmer to get around the system (e.g., multiple copies of procedure definitions) entail an enormous waste of human effort and can introduce as many bugs as the checker eliminates. Finally, it should be apparent that the merits of a PASCAL-like type system can be appreciated quite independently of the merits of Lucid's approach to dataflow and iteration. It was felt that incorporating a type checking discipline into the language (especially one of dubious worth) would distract the reader from the basic ideas of Lucid.

Our feeling is that type checking can be very useful provided it is sophisticated enough to

(i)   allow polymorphism, so that for example the function **hd** can be applied to any list and produce an object of the appropriate type;

(ii)   allow one type to be a subtype of another, so that for example integers could also be real numbers (it should not be necessary to distinguish 3 and 3.0);

(iii)   allow parameterised types, so that (e.g.) for each type **t** there is a type **listof(t)** of lists with components of type **t**; and

(iv)   have a type checker capable of interpolating most types, so that the user can omit almost all declarations.

There already exists a functional language with a type system and checker with properties (i), (iii) and (iv): the language ML described in Gordon *et al.* (1977). One can define in ML a function **rev** which reverses lists, omitting any type declarations. The ML type checker nevertheless concludes that **rev** has type

$$\textbf{listof(alpha)} \rightarrow \textbf{listof(alpha)}$$

(**alpha** is a *generic* type variable—it represents an arbitrary type). It would not be particularly difficult to adapt the ML system for Lucid. This could provide the ideal combination of discipline and flexibility. The ML system does not, however, support requirement (ii). Shamir and Wadge (1976) might prove a theoretical basis for a an ML-like system which allows subtypes as well.

The ML approach to types is very different to that of PASCAL, and not just because it is more flexible. Type declarations in PASCAL cannot be omitted because they contribute semantic information. One cannot always determine the meaning of a PASCAL expression without knowing the types of variables involved. In ML, by contrast, an expression has some meaning (which might be an error object) no matter what types the values of the variables in the expression may have. In other words, type assertions are properties of the values of expressions. Some values are integers, others are not, some are lists, others are not. The meaning of the program can be defined independently of any knowledge of the classification of values into types. The type declarations are *assertions about the meanings of the variables*. Type checking is therefore a special kind of program verification.

The success of the ML approach makes it possible to avoid making any *a priori* choice of type system. We can first define the semantics of the language as we have done, in terms of a single sorted algebra. We can then select some classification of the single universe into types, together with a corresponding type discipline.

There is, however, one respect in which the present Lucid approach to data structures is inherently inadequate: it is not completely *abstract*. An abstract approach to data types means allowing the user to use the data types and operations in a completely representation-independent way. Any particular member of the Lucid family is completely abstract in its treatment of the data types supplied by the underlying algebra. In pLucid, for example, the programmer is presented with lists, and not with any particular representation of them (such as one using pointers). However, if a programmer wishes to use a data type not already available in the particular family member being used, he or she must either (i) simulate the data type with the types available or (ii) use another member of the family. There is no way in which the Lucid programmer can expand the collection of data types presented abstractly (the same criticism applies to PASCAL).

Suppose, for example, that you wanted to do some work with polynomials in Lucid. It is easy to represent polynomials as lists (lists of coefficients) and write functions which implement addition, multiplication, division, and so on. If you were clever you would write all your polynomial programs using only these primitives to handle polynomials. For example, you would never take the head of a polynomial. The advantages of this discipline are (i) that it makes programs simpler to read and write, since neither reader nor writer has to keep implementation details in mind and (ii) that it makes modification much simpler; if you devise a new representation (which is more efficient, or correct where the first was not) you need only change the definitions in your polynomial 'package'. You do not have to go searching through all your polynomial programs changing the way polynomials are dealt with.

This is a very effective methodology. The problem is that with Lucid (or Iswim, or even PASCAL) it is only that: there is no way of having it enforced. Programs which violate the discipline are still legal. It is up to the users to check that they really have used the new types in an abstract way. What is required is some way for the user to stipulate new types, and new operations to be used on these types, in such a way that the type checker rejects any attempt to work with other than the provided operations. We need a 'module' facility, which will allow us to encapsulate information about the representation of the type so that it is not available outside.

This is not particularly difficult if the underlying type system is a pigeonholing one of the PASCAL variety. Here is a hypothetical fragment of a extended Iswim program which defines the new type **poly** (the syntax is *ad hoc*):

```
(poly : type,
 degree(poly) : integer,
 psum(poly, poly) : poly,
 pprod(poly, poly) : poly,
 scalprod(poly, rational) : poly,
) =
    (poly, degree, psum, pprod)
      where
        poly = listof(rational);
        degree(x) = lengthof(x);
        psum(p, q) = if null(p) then q elseif null(q) then p else
            hd(p) + hd(q) :: psum(tl(p), tl(q)) fi;
        pprod(p, q) = if null(p) then [ ]
                    else psum(scalprod(hd(p), q), 0 :: pprod(tl(p), q)) fi;
        scalprod(s, p) = if null(p) then [ ]
                    else s * hd(p) :: scalprod(s, tl(p)) fi;
      end
```

If we want our language to be usable, however, the module facility must be based on a looser, ML-like type system. This is undoubtedly possible (ML has such a feature), but subtle technical difficulties arise. In any case, these difficulties are not particular to Lucid or dataflow, and so will not be discussed further.

2. Tupling, or Filters with Multiple Outputs

The reader may have noticed one strange restriction which we seem to have placed on dataflow nets: nodes may have only one output. For example, consider the merge sorting algorithm given in a previous chapter. The network given could be considerably simplified if we had a two-output **deal** node which divided its input stream into two, sending alternate datons to alternate paths (rather like a dealer distributing cards to two players). Double output nodes are easily incorporated into our net-drawing methodology: a node is considered as having one main output which is sent straight on the main pipeline, plus 'auxiliary' outputs sent at right angles. Here is a net for the merge sort which uses a **deal** node:

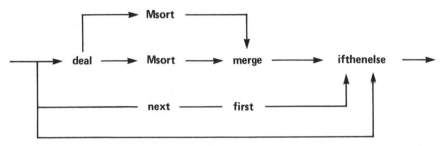

The nets which we have presented have, up to now, all been just graphical representations of textual/algebraic (Iswim-like) programs. This is the reason that nodes have had only one output: nodes in graphs correspond to functions, and in Iswim functions return only one value. Therefore, if we want graphs with multiple-output nodes, and if we still want every graph to correspond to some textual program, then we must extend Lucid (i.e., textual Lucid) to allow functions with more than one output.

Fortunately, it is possible to extend Lucid (and Iswim) to allow multiple output functions without really tampering with the fundamental notion of "function" on which these languages are based. Instead, we simply extend any given underlying algebra by adding to its universe all finite sequences (we call them *tuples*) of data objects. (We do this even when the algebra has sequences in some other form, say as lists.) A 'multiple-result function' can then be represented as a single-result function whose single result is a tuple. In programs, we can use a comma/parentheses notation for tuples; for example, **(a, b, c)** will represent a tuple with the three components **a, b** and **c**. We avoid introducing component selector operations by allowing tuples of variables to appear on the left-hand side of definitions (this corresponds most closely to the graphical form).

We should emphasise that a tuple is *not* the same as a list. We want to distinguish between a filter with one output line which carries a stream of lists, and a filter with several output lines.

Here, for example, is the textual form of the merge sort, using **deal**.

```
Msort(a)  = if iseod first a
              then a
              else merge(Msort(b0), Msort (b1)) fi
            where
              (b0, b1) = deal(a);
            end;
```

We could define **deal** with the following equation:

$$\textbf{deal(x) = (x whenever p, x whenever not p)}$$
$$\textbf{where p = true fby not p; end;}$$

There are many natural operations that yield more than one value. One example is the 'inverse' of **fby**, which we call **ybf**. This function can be defined by the equation

$$\textbf{ybf(x) = (first x, next x);}$$

The following definition of **whenever** uses **ybf**:

$$\textbf{whenever(x, p) = if P0 then X0 fby v else v fi;}$$
$$\textbf{where}$$
$$\textbf{(X0, y) = ybf(x);}$$
$$\textbf{(P0, q) = ybf(p);}$$
$$\textbf{v = whenever(y, q);}$$
$$\textbf{end}$$

and the graph of this program is

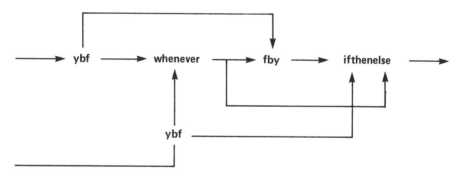

Even simple iteration often benefits from the tuple notation. Here is a program to compute the greatest common divisor of inputs **a** and **b**.

$$\textbf{x asa x eq y}$$
$$\textbf{where}$$
$$\textbf{A is current a;}$$
$$\textbf{B is current b;}$$
$$\textbf{(x, y) = (A, B) fby if x < y then (x, y − x)}$$
$$\textbf{else (x − y, y) fi;}$$
$$\textbf{end}$$

In this form it is especially clear that x and y are varying together, 'in step'.

Tupling is an example of a 'feature' that seems simple enough, but is semantically surprisingly difficult, or at least subtle, if we want to avoid the explicit detupling operations and allow tuples on the left-hand sides of definitions (as we have done in our examples). We would like to allow 'structured' left-hand sides, but at the same time we want to preserve the vital principle that the statements in a program really are equations.

The ability to have expressions on the left-hand side, however, introduces the possibility that that the definition, considered as an equation, may have *no* solution. Consider, for example, the equation

$$(x, y) = 8;$$

(in some conventional algebra). The number 8 is not a tuple; there are no values of **x** and **y** that make the equation true. As a result, our definition of the semantics of a Lucid program does not necessarily extend to programs that use tupling in an arbitrary way.

There is, of course, an easy way to assign meanings to such programs—if that is all we want to do. We introduce symbols for the component extraction (or 'projection') operations: in general let $\mathbf{P}i\text{–}j$ select the jth component from a tuple of length i. Given a program with tupling on the left-hand side, we 'massage' it into a normal program by replacing a definition like

$$(x, y, z) = w;$$

by the three definitions:

$$x = \mathbf{P3\_0(w)};$$
$$y = \mathbf{P3\_1(w)};$$
$$z = \mathbf{P3\_2(w)};$$

(We can stipulate that a selection function returns $\perp$ when given something which is not a tuple, or not one of the appropriate length.) We can then decree that the meaning of the original program is the meaning of the new, massaged one.

Unfortunately, this procedure is not quite honest. There is no guarantee that the solutions to transformed equations are solutions to the originals. For example, the equation

$$(x, y) = 8;$$

is transformed to the pair;

$$x = \mathbf{P2\_0(8)};$$
$$y = \mathbf{P2\_1(8)};$$

of equations; and their solution sets requires both **x** and **y** to be $\perp$. But

$(\perp, \perp)$ is certainly not 8. If we proceeded to think and reason about such a program on the basis of our principle that statements really are equations, we could get in trouble. We must restrict programs with tupling in such a way that solutions of the transformed equations are solutions of the originals, and vice versa (then the *least* solution will be the same in both cases). We must check that when an equation like

$$(x, y, z) = w;$$

appears, that **w** really is a tuple of length three.

This checking is simple enough when the right-hand side expression directly involves tupling as well, as in

$$(A, b, C) = (3,5 * i, K - L);$$

We can be a little more generous and allow tuple expressions on both arms of an **if–then–else**; as in

$$(A, b) = \text{if } x > y \text{ then } (x - y, x) \text{ else } (x, y - x) \text{ fi};$$

However, tupling is not very useful if we restrict the Lucid user to these forms alone. It amounts to adding a kind of nonprocedural multiple assignment facility. Sooner or later the programmer will want to give a name to a tuple and use the name in an expression; for example, by writing

$$a = \text{if } x > y \text{ then } a0 \text{ else } a1 \text{ fi};$$
$$a0 = (x - y, y);$$
$$a1 = (x, y - x);$$

More generally, the programmer will want to define tuple-valued functions (as we did earlier in our examples). Since we definitely want this (recall that in terms of dataflow networks a tuple-valued function is a filter with more than one output line), we cannot make the restriction that all tuples be 'anonymous'.

Unfortunately, if we allow variables to denote tuples, the checking becomes much more involved. Suppose, for example, that we have a definition such as

$$(m, N) = \text{if } V < 0 \text{ then } (-1, 1) \text{ else } z \text{ fi};$$

in our program. In order to be able to give this equation a clean bill of health, we must look up the relevant definition of **z** and verify that its value is in fact a tuple of length 2. If this definition is of the form

$$(z, w, h) = \text{bleen}(k, l);$$

then we must check that the function **bleen** always yields a tuple of length

3, whose first component is in turn one of length 2. This involves checking the body of the definition of **bleen**, and it may turn out that **bleen** makes assumptions about the tuplicity of its arguments; for example, it may be that **bleen** assumes that its second argument is a quadruple. It may even be the case that some parts of the tuple structure of the value of **bleen** depend on that of its arguments; for example,

$$\textbf{bleen(g, h)} = \textbf{(g, c, d) where (c, d, e)} = \textbf{h; end;}$$

and if this is the case, tuple checking must be performed on the actual parameters of any 'call' of **bleen**. It is easy to see that tuple checking may propagate through whole program.

The consistency checking also needs to be done to verify that expressions of the form *A* **fby** *B* give the results expected. We must ensure that *A* and *B* have the same tuplicity. If we allow the tuplicity of a variable to change with time, we are forced to give up any hope of syntactically determining the tuplicity of expressions.

Special difficulties arise when the output tuplicity of a recursively defined function depends directly or indirectly on itself. For example, consider the definition

$$\textbf{divs(a, d)} = \textbf{if a} < \textbf{d then (0, d) else (q1 + 1, r1) fi}$$
$$\textbf{where}$$
$$\textbf{(q1, d1)} = \textbf{divs(a} - \textbf{d, d);}$$
$$\textbf{end;}$$

(**divs(a, d)** returns the quotient and remainder which result when **a** is divided by **d**). The question is, do we consider an expression of the form **divs(x, y)** to be a tuple or not?

The checking algorithm described informally goes into a loop; it tells us that **divs** returns 2-ple iff **divs** returns 2-ple! All is well as long as the computation of a particular 'call' of **divs** converges, but what about those that do not (such for **divs(2, −2)**)? In this case the result is ⊥—apparently not a tuple! This conundrum appears in Lucid in a sharper form: Is

$$\textbf{(x, y) asa p}$$

a tuple whether or not **p** is eventually true? The tuple checking is a form of type checking, and should therefore avoid performing any 'real' computation. It should not be necessary to check if loops terminate (which is impossible anyway). On the other hand, it is hard to find fault with the equation

$$\textbf{(a, b)} = \textbf{(x, y) asa p;}$$

Still, we want our statements-as-equations principle to hold. Perhaps all that is necessary is to require that

$$(\perp, \perp, ..., \perp) = \perp;$$

so that $\perp$ has all tuplicities. We do not know if this approach works, although we conjecture that it does.

3. Arrays, or Frozen Streams

We have already seen that one can easily do nontrivial problems in Lucid without using anything like an array, even though the corresponding PASCAL programs make heavy use of arrays. The explanation is that PASCAL programs often use arrays where a corresponding Lucid program uses streams. Arrays in PASCAL are usually scanned in order (accessed sequentially rather than randomly). The essential difference between *arrays* and *streams* is that the first represents an ordered series of items *at rest*, whereas the second represents an ordered series of items *in motion*. The imperative languages are based on the idea of processing data at rest, so it is only to be expected that arrays play a crucial role. When dataflow algorithms are programmed in imperative languages, streams are often simulated by arrays.

Lucid, however, is based on data in motion and streams play a crucial role. When dataflow algorithms are programmed in Lucid, streams appear as streams and there is no need to represent them statically. The arrays disappear.

Sometimes, however, Lucid programs involving streams have a somewhat awkward or unnatural flavour even if they are technically simple. In many cases a little reflection shows that the programmer is being forced to do the exact opposite of what happens in PASCAL; the programmer is forced to represent, as a stream, data which is better thought of as being *at rest*.

Consider, for example, the recursive definition of **merge** (of two increasing streams of integers):

> **merge(x, y) = if first x < first y**
> **then first x fby merge(next x, y)**
> **else first y fby merge(x, next y)**
> **fi;**

Thinking of **x** and **y** as *streams* (data in motion) is somehow not quite right; the program is far easier to understand if we imagine all the infinite number of values of **x** and **y** laid out all at once. We compare the initial elements of **x** and **y**, choose the smaller, and then merge one of **x** and **y** with what remains of the other.

This point is easier to appreciate if we use **rest** instead of **next**, but with the same meaning. This word is fully appropriate in

$$\begin{aligned}&\textbf{merge(x,y) = if first x < first y}\\&\quad\quad\quad\quad\textbf{then first x fby merge(rest x, y)}\\&\quad\quad\quad\quad\textbf{else first y fby merge(x, rest y)}\\&\textbf{fi;}\end{aligned}$$

On the other hand, the use of **rest** in

$$\textbf{s = first x fby s + rest x;}$$

is completely inappropriate. The difference, of course, is that in the **merge** definition it is natural to think of all the components of the sequence as being present simultaneously, whereas in the second it is natural to think of the values of **s** being generated in succession, as the values of **x** become available. In the second it is quite natural to imagine that at any given time only one or two components of **s** or **x** are present.

It is our experience that lack of understanding of the dynamic point of view is often the greatest obstacle for people who want to read and write Lucid; they see that the formal semantics is given in terms of infinite sequences and assume that this is the way the programmer is supposed to think. Definitions like that of **merge** offer no problems, but simple equations like the definition of **s** are absolutely baffling. People who misunderstand Lucid in this way often ask why we use **next** instead of **rest** or **tail**. (And such people find **is current** and mixed freezing absolutely beyond the reach of human comprehension.)

In Lucid the dynamic view is the intended one, hence the words **next**, **whenever**, **current** and so on. Thinking and writing in terms of static histories is a gross misuse of the language. Sometimes, however, the static approach is appropriate; and in these circumstances the dynamic point of view represents a serious misunderstanding. In Lucid as it stands, however, the dynamic point of view is essentially forced on the programmer, and the fault lies with the language instead.

One solution to this difficulty would be to provide **rest** as a synonym for **next** (and **initial** as a synonym for **first**) and advise the programmer to use whichever is appropriate. This idea breaks down, though, when the user tries to write a program involving both the dynamic and the static points of view. For example, we might want to write an iterative program in which each value of a loop variable is an entire 'static stream'.

The deficiency in Lucid is therefore deeper than syntax and is not just a matter of attitude. Lucid genuinely lacks a static analog of streams. Of course, we could always treat static streams as just another data type, and use a member of the Lucid family based on algebras with static streams.

However, this would be far from satisfactory. The notion of a static stream is obviously intimately linked with the analogous dynamic concept (might want to convert between the two). This notion is not inherently connected with any particular data types, i.e., with any particular algebras.

If streams are objects that vary in *time*, the corresponding static objects ought to vary in *space*. This suggests modifying the semantics of Lucid [in particular, the definition of $Lu(A)$] to allow space as well as time parameters. This is the solution we describe here. The space-varying objects are called *ferds*. (*The Oxford English Dictionary* lists "ferd" as an obsolete word meaning "a warlike array".)

Time and space are not, however, quite symmetric. For one thing, time-varying objects are intended to be thought of in parts (in terms of individual values), whereas space-varying objects are thought of as a whole. Furthermore, although there is only one time parameter, there is no reason to have only one space parameter as well. In fact, multidimensional ferds are almost unavoidable. We want to allow streams of ferds (as above); and we want to be able to 'package up' any stream as a ferd. But when we package a stream of ferds, the result will be a ferd of more than one dimension.

This is the road we choose to follow. To avoid bothersome type distinctions, our ferds will all be notionally infinite dimensional.

The language Flucid (ferd Lucid), which we now introduce and describe informally, is based on an algebra-producing operation *Flu* in exactly the same way as Lucid is based on *Lu*. The elements of $Flu(A)$ are streams of 'hyper-arrays' with individual values determined by one time parameter and infinitely many space parameters. In other words, they are functions from

$$N \times N^N$$

to the universe of A (N being the set $\{0, 1, 2, ...\}$ of natural numbers). The value of one of these objects F, given time parameter t and space parameters $\langle s_0, s_1, s_2, ... \rangle$, we will write as $F_t^{s_0 s_1 s_2 \cdots}$. Ordinary data operations are, of course, extended pointwise in space as well as time.

The most basic ferd operations are the space analogs of **first**, **next** and **fby**. These are called **initial**, **rest** and **cby** (continued by). In general,

$$initial(F)_t^{s_0 s_1 s_2 \cdots} = F_t^{0 s_0 s_1 s_2 \cdots}$$
$$rest(F)_t^{s_0 s_1 s_2 \cdots} = F_t^{s_0 + 1 s_1 s_2 s_3 \cdots}$$
$$cby(F, G)_t^{s_0 s_1 s_2 \cdots} = F_t^{s_1 s_2 s_3 \cdots} \quad (s_0 = 0)$$
$$= G_t^{s_0 - 1 s_1 s_2 \cdots} \quad (s_0 > 0)$$

(here *initial*, *rest* and *cby* are **initial**$_{Flu(A)}$, **rest**$_{Flu(A)}$ and **cby**$_{Flu(A)}$, respectively). The following equations must therefore always hold:

$$\textbf{F} = \textbf{initial F cby rest F}$$
$$\textbf{initial (F cby G)} = \textbf{F}$$
$$\textbf{rest(F cby G)} = \textbf{G}$$

Obviously, the definitions of **initial**, **rest** and **cby** are similar to those of **first**, **next** and **fby**, but thought of differently. Given a ferd **F**, **initial F** is the first component of **F**; **rest F** is the result of dropping that component; and **x cby F** is the result of sticking **x** on to **F** as the initial component.

Notice one important difference between the space operations and the corresponding time operations: **initial F** is not the first component of **F** stretched out in space in the same way as **first x** is the first time component of **x** stretched out in time. It is only the first component of **F**, and is not necessarily equal to **initial initial F**. The latter is the initial component of the initial component of **F**. In that sense, the three space operations correspond more closely to the list operations **hd**, **tl** and **cons**.

Our ferds do not have any explicit rank, but an implicit rank can often be assigned. For example, the value of an individual component of **F** may depend on s_0, s_1 and s_2 only. In such a case, **F** can be thought of as 'really' just a three-dimensional object. The 'rank' of **rest F** is therefore usually that of **F**, but the 'rank' of **initial F** is at least one less than that of **F**. If **x** is rank $n - 1$ and **F** is rank n, then **x cby F** is rank n. Notice that we can define ferds of infinite rank; for example, with the equation

$$\textbf{F} = \textbf{F cby 2;}$$

The object defined here has a 'singularity' at the space point $\langle 0, 0, 0, ... \rangle$ (the value at this position is $\perp$).

The next most important ferd operations are those for converting streams into ferds and vice versa. The operation **all** takes a stream as its operand and returns as its result the entire history as a ferd; it converts time to space, so that if **i** is the stream of natural numbers defined by

$$\textbf{i} = \textbf{0 fby i + 1;}$$

then **all i** is the array of all natural numbers. The function **all** is defined by the equation

$$all(X)_t^{s_0, s_1, s_2, \cdots} = X_{s_0}^{s_1, s_2, \cdots}$$

Notice that the value of **all x** is independent of time; it is a constant. The companion of **all** is **elt** (element), and it converts space back into time. If **F** is a ferd which is constant in time, **elt F** is the stream of components of **F**, i.e., the value of **elt F** at time t is the tth component of **F**. If **F** itself varies with time, **elt** performs a 'gather' in that the value of **F** at time t is the tth component of the (ferd) value of **F** at time t. The operation *elt* is defined by the equation

$$elt(F)_t^{s_0 s_1 s_2 \cdots} = F_t^{t s_0 s_1 s_2 \cdots}$$

The two functions are 'not quite' inverses, in the following sense: we have

elt all x = x

for all values of **x** but

all elt F = F

only if **F** is constant. The operations **all** and **elt** are useful when we want to define a stream function in a manner more appropriate to arrays or when an array is to be defined by generating its components in order.

For example, we can define the merge operation on streams (after all, the operation itself is quite naturally understood as a binary filter) as follows:

```
merge(x, y) = m
  where
    a = all x fby if p then rest a else a fi;
    b = all y fby if p then b else rest b fi;
    p = initial a < initial b;
    m = if p then initial a else initial b fi;
  end;
```

This is an example of a program which has loops with ferd-valued loop variables. At any given point in time the value of **a** is an *entire* ferd; and on each iteration this entire value can change. Naturally, since ferds are infinite, there is no simple corresponding PASCAL loop.

The relationship between space and time can be clarified by reconsidering the 'sieve' algorithm to produce primes. In its original Lucid form:

```
sieve(n)
  where
    n = 2 fby n + 1;
    sieve(x) = first x fby sieve(x whenever x mod first x ne 0);
  end
```

it could be thought of as specifying a dynamic pipeline with a new filter added for every prime found (this was the way McIlroy thought of it).

However, a static view is also possible:

```
sieve(n)
  where
    n = all i where i = 2 fby i + 1 end;
    sieve(X) = initial X cby sieve(X wherever X mod initial X ne 0);
  end
```

with **wherever** being the obvious spatial analog of **whenever**. The above, however, is clearly a recursive version. Here is an iterative one:

```
sieve(N)
  where
    N = all i where i = 2 fby i + 1 end;
    sieve(a) = all p
      where
        A is current a;
        m = A fby m whenever m mod p ne 0;
        p = initial m;
      end;
  end
```

but now **sieve**, being no longer recursively defined, can be eliminated from the program. After a little tidying it becomes

```
all p
  where
    i = 2 fby i + 1;
    m = all i fby m wherever m mod p ne 0;
    p = initial m;
  end
```

In this form it is much more evident that the program is correct. It is quite easy to see that at each step in the iteration **m** is the array of all numbers not divisible by any prime less than the value of **p** at that step.

From a conceptual point of view, ferds are easily incorporated in the informal iterative/dataflow operational model, which we have been recommending as a programming guide. After all, one should have no difficulty in *imagining* infinite data objects flowing through a network. As for the actual implementations, those which are based on demand-driven dataflow could easily be adapted. Adding ferds means only that the tag of a daton has a third extra 'field', for the code for the space parameters, in addition to the existing ones for the codes for the time and place parameter. Ferds are much more in the spirit of Lucid and dataflow than (say) the infinite lists used by LISP-oriented functional languages.

4. lLucid, Lucid with Multidimensional Time

We have already seen that the simple primitives of 'ordinary' Lucid allow for an amazing variety of different kinds of computation. However, ordinary Lucid still provides only two forms of interaction between a computation and a subcomputation. Programmers often find Lucid somewhat restrictive in this sense. People used to conventional imperative languages perceive it as an inability to "do I/O in a subcomputation." Suppose, for example, that we wanted to perform a lexical analysis of a stream of input characters. We want to bundle up groups of characters into lexical units ("lexons") and output the stream of lexons. A PASCAL programmer would write a main loop which produces a lexon 'each time round', with a subloop that on each invocation runs through as many characters as are needed for the next lexon. The PASCAL program cannot be transcribed directly into Lucid because the interface between the main loop and the subloop is not one of the two supplied by Lucid. The subloop is not running in parallel with the main loop, nor is it being invoked once for each input item. In fact the program is not particularly hard to write using **whenever** and **upon** (instead of using a subcomputation); but after writing a number of such programs, one quickly gets the impression that these two operators are being used to 'simulate' something which should be made more directly available.

Of couse, there would be no real difficulty in adding other forms of computation/subcomputation to the language. Suppose, for example, that we want an inner variable V to have on the tth invocation of the subcomputation the sequence of values

$$e_t, e_{t+1}, e_{t+2}, \ldots$$

where e is the value of some expression E. (This would allow the subcomputation to 'look ahead' in the main computation.) We could always extend the syntax to allow declarations of the form

$$V \textbf{ is remaining } E;$$

and make the appropriate changes to the definition of the semantics of **where** clauses; but this seems is a little *ad hoc,* and contrary to the algebraic approach of Lucid.

It is possible to extend Lucid's algebraic approach to handle the interface problem, but we must first extend the notion of a history. The total activity of a variable defined in a deeply nested iteration cannot be described by a single infinite sequence. To specify a particular value of such a variable, we need to know which step the innermost iteration has reached; and which step the next enclosing iteration has reached; and which step the next enclosing iteration has reached; and so on. We need *multidimensional* histories.

The simplest way to proceed is to define a *generalised history* to be a function of the entire infinite sequence $t_0, t_1, t_2, \ldots$ of time parameters. In other words, a generalised history (or *hyperstream*) is a function whose domain is the set N^N of all infinite sequences of natural numbers. These objects are in a sense streams whose dimensions are formally infinite. In actual programs, though, the values of any particular variable will depend on only finitely many of the time parameters. It is extremely important to understand that time is parametrised from the inside out; t_0 is the time in the current local computation, t_1 that in the enclosing computation, t_2 that in the next enclosing computaton and so on.

It is not hard to see how to define the data operations and normal Lucid operations on hyperstreams; they are simply extended pointwise to the $t_1, t_2, t_3, \ldots$ parameters. The value of **next(a)** is the stream *next(a)* where

$$next(a)_{t_0t_1t_2\ldots} = a_{(t_0+1)t_1t_2\ldots}$$

because **next(a)** is the value **a** has on the next step of the *local* computation. From the global point of view, this is the value which **a** has on the *immediately* succeeding step of the computation. It is the value obtained when only the innermost computation is advanced one step, i.e., when all the enclosing computations remain suspended. In the same way, the hyperstream operations **first** and **fby** are defined by

$$
\begin{aligned}
first(a)_{t_0t_1t_2\ldots} &= a_{0t_1t_2\ldots} \\
fby(a, b)_{t_0t_1t_2\ldots} &= a_{0t_1t_2\ldots} \qquad (t_0 = 0) \\
&= b_{(t_0-1)t_1t_2\ldots} \qquad (t_0 > 1)
\end{aligned}
$$

Finally, we need special hyperstream operators which give the various nesting effects. We could define these operators directly, one for each interface, but it is possible instead to give a set of primitive operations from which the others can be defined.

Among the hyperstream primitives there are only two which actually change the 'dimension' of a hyperstream. The remaining operations take t_1 into account but do not alter dimension.

The dimension 'shifting' operations are called **active** and **contemp**, and are defined as follows:

$$
\begin{aligned}
active(x)_{t_0t_1t_2\ldots} &= x_{t_0t_2t_3\ldots} \\
contemp(n)_{t_0t_1t_2\ldots} &= n_{t_0t_0t_1t_2\ldots}
\end{aligned}
$$

The meaning of **active** can best be grasped if we assume that the value of **x** is independent of t_1, t_2, t_3 and so on; in other words, that x is 'really' just a sequence of the form

$$\langle x_0, x_1, x_2, ... \rangle.$$

In this case the value of **active(x)** depends only on t_0 and t_1, and is 'really' the double sequence

$$\langle \langle x_0, x_1, x_2, ... \rangle, \langle x_0, x_1, x_2, ... \rangle, \langle x_0, x_1, x_2, ... \rangle, ... \rangle.$$

(with t_0 the index of the inner sequences and t_1 the index of the outer sequences). This can be interpreted as follows: the value of x inside each subcomputation is the same *stream* as outside; on each invocation it is restarted and runs through its complete set of values. The variable is *active* inside the subcomputation.

The operation **contemp** can also be understood in terms of double sequences. Informally speaking, it collapses a double sequence into a single sequence by sampling. It turns

$$\langle \langle a_0, a_1, a_2, ... \rangle, \langle b_0, b_1, b_2, ... \rangle, \langle c_0, c_1, c_2, ... \rangle, ... \rangle$$

into

$$\langle a_0, b_1, c_2, ... \rangle.$$

The value of **contemp(x)** is the value which x has inside a loop when the inner time (t_0) 'catches up' with the outer time (t_1); it is the *contemporary* value of x. It is therefore easy to see that **contemp(active(x))** is the same as x.

The function **active** in a sense gives nesting without freezing. If we want freezing as well, we need another function to do it (but this function does not have to change dimensions). The obvious name for the new function is **current**; it is defined as follows.

$$current(y)_{t_0 t_1 t_2 ...} = y_{t_1 t_1 t_2 t_3 ...}$$

In terms of double sequences, **current** transforms

$$\langle \langle a_0, a_1, a_2, ... \rangle, \langle b_0, b_1, b_2, ... \rangle, \langle c_0, c_1, c_2, ... \rangle, ... \rangle$$

into

$$\langle \langle a_0, a_0, a_0, ... \rangle, \langle b_1, b_1, b_1, ... \rangle, \langle c_2, c_2, c_2, ... \rangle, ... \rangle.$$

In the same way the 'from now on' effect can be obtained with the function **remaining**, where

$$remaining(x)_{t_0 t_1 t_2 ...} = x_{(t_1 + t_0) t_1 t_2 ...}$$

The function **remaining** transforms the sequence

$$\langle\langle a_0, a_1, a_2, ...\rangle, \langle b_0, b_1, b_2, ...\rangle, \langle c_0, c_1, c_2, ...\rangle, ...\rangle$$

into

$$\langle\langle a_0, a_1, a_2, ...\rangle, \langle b_1, b_2, b_3, ...\rangle, \langle c_2, c_3, c_4, ...\rangle, ...\rangle$$

The functions **current** and **remaining** can be defined in terms of still simpler operations, operations which are the t_1 analogs of **first**, **next** and **fby**. We will not give details.

We can use these definitions to specify an operator Llu on algebras, which takes a data algebra A and returns an algebra $Llu(A)$ of hyperstreams. Given any A, we can form the language $Iswim(Llu(A))$ and write Luswim-like programs with nested iterations. Here are two simple $Iswim(Llu(P))$ programs which use this explicit algebraic approach to specifying subcomputations.

```
contemp(y asa y > n)
   where
      n = current active n;
      y = remaining active x;
   end
```

```
contemp(maxsofar eq current active p)
   where
      maxsofar = active(p) fby if maxsofar > active p
         then maxsofar
         else active p fi;
   end
```

The first finds the first-encountered present or future value of x which is greater than the present (current) value of **n**. The second tests if the current value of **p** is the greatest so far.

These various strange operations on hyperstreams (we could call them *hyperfilters*) may seem rather farfetched. We can still think of programs using hyperfilters in terms of pipeline dataflow, but a realistic implementation along those lines could be very complicated. Fortunately, however, hyperstreams and hyperfilters are quite simple from the tagged-dataflow point of view. The pLucid interpreter already handles multidimensional 'time tags'; with very little work it could be made accept programs with hyperfilters. There is therefore much to be gained by extending Lucid with hyperstreams. We could greatly increase the power and simplicity of the language, without at the same time greatly increasing the complexity of the implementation.

One serious problem with this approach is that **active** has to be explicitly applied to all the 'global' variables of a subcomputation. The programmer has to explicitly write all these applications, and this could be very tedious. For example, in the second of the programs given above, **p** is a global of the subcomputation. As a result, all four occurrences of **p** inside the **where** clause have to be as an argument of **active**. If we did not apply **active** to these occurrences, strange results would be produced.

What is still required is a linguistic way of enforcing the discipline and saving the poor programmer the worry of balancing **active-contemps**'s. The easiest way to do this is to generalise the way in which Lucid links the Iswim **where** clause (which really only hides definitions) and the idea of subcomputation. We do this by redefining the meaning of **where** so that **active** is automatically (and 'secretly') applied to the globals of a **where**, and **contemp** is automatically and secretly applied to the result. The resulting language (which we might call "Llucid") is much more convenient. Here are the preceding two examples written in Llucid

$$
\begin{aligned}
&\textbf{y asa y > n}\\
&\quad \textbf{where}\\
&\qquad \textbf{n = current n;}\\
&\qquad \textbf{y = remaining x;}\\
&\quad \textbf{end}
\end{aligned}
$$

$$
\begin{aligned}
&\textbf{maxsofar eq current p}\\
&\quad \textbf{where}\\
&\qquad \textbf{maxsofar = p fby if maxsofar > p then maxsofar else p fi;}\\
&\quad \textbf{end}
\end{aligned}
$$

We can even reconcile Llucid with ordinary Lucid by defining "is" to be "nonrecursive" definitional equality (the form that was the default in Landin's original Iswim).

This approach, however, still has drawbacks. Llucid is not a member of the Iswim family, and this causes serious difficulties when we try to define hyperfilters with **where** clauses. It seems very unsatisfactory to introduce hyperstreams and hyperfilters and still have to modify the semantics of the **where** clause. Ideally, we would like to be able to write programs with subcomputations in a language which really is a member of the Iswim family. Llucid is much more general than Lucid but is still not, in this sense, strictly kosher. $Iswim(Llu(A))$ is tantalizingly close, but the goal remains outside our grasp.

5. Lambda Lucid, Lucid with Higher-Order Functions

The reader will have undoubtedly noticed another serious restriction on Lucid: the lack of functional parameters. One Lucid function cannot appear as the argument of another function. Functions cannot even appear as the arguments of operations (presupplied functions). In other words, functions cannot be handled as data objects in their own right—they can never appear in public without being accompanied by an argument. The Lucid programmer can talk about $f(3)$ or $f(H - G)$ or $f(x)$ (the values of f for given arguments) but never about f itself. In this respect Lucid is more restrictive than PASCAL or even FORTRAN (but, ironically, not ADA).

There are many excellent reasons for wanting to process a function as a data object. One reason is to avoid cluttering up a program with 'dummy' variables and to make clearer the way in which filters and functions are built-up from simpler ones. Suppose, for example, that we have written a compiler for some language in Lucid, and that the program has the form

$$\textbf{comp(P)} = \textbf{optimise(codefor(parsetreeof(lex(P))))}$$
$$\textbf{where}$$
$$\textbf{lex(X)} = \cdots$$
$$\textbf{parsetree(L)} = \cdots$$
$$\textbf{codefor(T)} = \cdots$$
$$\textbf{optimise(C)} = \cdots$$
$$\textbf{end.}$$

The part of the program above the **where** simply says that the filter **comp** is formed by putting the filters **lex**, **parsetree**, **codefor** and **optimise** in series. The variable **P** is just a dummy; a temporary name for the input to **comp**, which appears (with this meaning) only in one other place, namely, directly on the other side of the equals sign (but not in the body of the program). Nothing called **P** really has anything to do with the way **lex**, **parsetree**, and so on, are combined to form **comp**. The dummy could have been **Q**, or **W**, or almost any other variable. But in any case, the Lucid programmer is forced to choose *some* variable.

The relationship between **comp**, **lex**, **parsetree**, and so on, is made much clearer by the dataflow diagram

$\longrightarrow$ lex $\longrightarrow$ parsetree $\longrightarrow$ codefor $\longrightarrow$ optimise $\longrightarrow$

In UNIX notation, we can make it equally clear by defining **comp** to be the filter

$$\textbf{lex | parsetree | codefor | optimise;}$$

but in Lucid we are not allowed to refer to any of the filters in the absence of an argument. We therefore have to invent a dummy argument to accompany them.

The dummy variable **P** could easily be avoided if Lucid had a reverse *function composition* operation. It would be convenient to add such an operator to Lucid (we could use the symbol |) so that the program given above could be rewritten as

> **computation = lex | parsetree | codefor | optimise**
> **where**
> > **lex(X) = ⋯**
> > **parsetree(L) = ⋯**
> > **codefor(T) = ⋯**
> > **optimise(C) = ⋯**
> **end**

The reason we cannot add this operation to Lucid as it exists now is that it is *higher order*; neither its arguments nor its results are streams of simple data objects.

Of course 'piping' is a relatively simple operation, and we could easily devise a preprocessor which would remove this and similar 'inessential' uses of higher-order functions. There are, however, other, more essential uses of higher-order objects which cannot be handled so simply.

Suppose, for example, that in the course of writing a program we need to find (an approximation to) a root of a function **f** which is negative at 0 and positive at 1. A simple binary search algorithm can easily be written in Lucid, as follows:

> **l asa abs(u − l) < 0.0001**
> > **where**
> > **u = 1 fby if mval > 0 then m else u fi;**
> > **l = 0 fby if mval <= 0 then m else l fi;**
> > **m = (l + u)/2;**
> > **mval = f(m);**
> > **end**

Suppose, however, that we later need to find the roots of functions **g** and **h** in the same way. (Algorithms with 'parameters' which are functions are very common in numerical analysis.)

The obvious solution is a single **Root** function, defined as follows:

> **Root(f) = l asa abs(u − 1) < 0.0001**
> > **where**
> > **u = 1 fby if f(m) > 0 then m else u fi;**

$$l = 0 \text{ fby if } f(m) <= 0 \text{ then } m \text{ else } l \text{ fi;}$$
$$m = (L + u)/2;$$
end

Again, this is not legal Lucid as it stands. A Lucid implementation's syntax checker would completely miss the point, and complain that **f** is being used inconsistently (with different arities).

Clearly, there is a case to made for higher-order objects being made available; even for solid, mainstream, 'meat-and-potatoes' computing (such as numerical analysis). It is therefore worth investigating how the Lucid approach to dataflow can be combined with a higher-order functional language. Unfortunately, certain problems arise with higher-order functions, which are not encountered when we extend Lucid with more ordinary data objects.

Suppose, for example, that we want to have arrays in Lucid—that we want to write dataflow programs which manipulate (finite) multidimensional arrays. We simply define an operator *Arr* which takes an algebra *A* of arbitrary data types and operations and returns an algebra *Arr(A)* which extends *A* by adding multidimensional arrays with components from the universe of *A*. [The extra operations over *Arr(A)* could be those of APL.] Once we have the operation *Arr*, the rest is easy. The language *Lucid(Arr(A))* extends *Lucid(A)* by adding arrays and array operations as desired.

In a sense, the Lucid concept of stream here takes precedence over the APL idea of arrays. We have streams of arrays, but not arrays of streams. [The latter can be found in *Iswim(Arr(Lu(A)))*, a very strange language.]

In trying to combine Lucid and functions, the issue is not so clear cut. We could define an operation *Fun* which extends an algebra *A* by adding all functions of all levels over *A*. [*Fun(A)* could have an explicit function application operation.] Then we could extend *Lucid(A)* to *Lucid-(Fun(A))*.

This language has higher-order functions—but only higher-order *data* functions. We could write definitions like the following:

$$f = \backslash x: x \text{ fby } \backslash x: x * f(x);$$

which define streams whose individual values are functions. We cannot, however, define piping, because it is an operation on filters.

The language *Lucid(Fun(A))* allows filters but not operations on filters. We could define a reverse composition operation but it would still be a filter. It would accept two streams of data functions and compose them pointwise. The trouble is that in *Lucid*(*Fun*(*A*)) the concept of stream takes precedence over that of function. We have streams of higher-order functions, but not higher-order stream functions.

Another possible approach is to make the notion of function primary, and use a language like *Iswim*(*Fun*(*Lu*(*A*))). This approach genuinely extends Luswim as it is now (but including nesting is a problem). All the Lucid functions like **next** and **fby** can be found in the domain. And it does allow higher-order functions. We can have filter piping, since | (reverse filter composition) can also be found.

This solution is better but still not completely satisfactory. We might well want to write programs which process streams of functions. If function streams are not allowed, if a variable cannot take on a function value, then functions are second class data objects in comparison with integers or lists. This is totally against the spirit of the Lambda Calculus languages. At the same time, it would mean that some algorithms (which operate on functions) could be expressed recursively but not iteratively. This is against the spirit of Lucid.

The problem, it seems, is that sometimes we want the notion of "stream" to be primary, sometime "function"; we must have both available in the same domain.

The difficulties encountered in just *specifying* a higher-order dataflow language may well be symptomatic of a certain conflict or antagonism between the notions of iteration and recursion. In ordinary Lucid these the two features are available and cooperate in harmony, but only because one of them (recursion) is severely restricted.

There are a number of possible solutions to the problem, but the simplest appears to be the most obvious: to have 'function filters'. By this we mean allowing streams of data functions, and also allowing filters which operate on these streams—in other words, *Iswim*(*Fun*(*Lu*-(*Fun*(*A*)))).

When we come to specify the operations, however, we must be careful. It seems, at first sight, that we need two different function application operations. The first is ordinary application, used for applying an element of $L \rightarrow L$ to an element of L (L being *Lu*(*Fun*(*A*))). The second is what we might call "data function application", which we will (temporarily) denote with the symbol :. This second operation is used to apply a stream of data functions (elements of $A \rightarrow A$), and the value of **x** is a stream of data objects (elements of A), then the value of **f** : **x** would be the stream of results resulting by applying values of **f** to corresponding values of **x**.

In fact, this duplication is unnecessary. Every function stream f already determines a corresponding filter f^* which transforms streams by applying the values of f pointwise; in other words

$$f^*(x) = \langle f_0(x_0), f_1(x_1), f_2(x_2), \ldots \rangle$$

Not every filter g is of the form f^* for some f, because any f^* has the crucial property that the value of $f^*(x)$ at time t depends only on the value of x at time t; in other words, f^* is always *synchronic* (recall that g is synchronic iff

$$g(x)_t = g(\langle x_t, x_t, x_t, \ldots \rangle)_t$$

for all x and t). It can be proved that a function g is synchronic iff it is of the form f^* for some stream function f; indeed f is the stream whose tth value is the data function k, where

$$k(d) = g(\langle d, d, d, \ldots \rangle)_t$$

for any data object d.

The synchronic filters can therefore be considered as function streams as well. This means there is no need to have a separate application operation. When evaluating **f(x)**, if the meaning of **f** is a stream f (of functions), we apply f^* to the meaning of x.

By the same token, there is no need to restrict the stream operations like **first** and **next** to operate only on streams. If g is synchronic, then it is 'really' a stream $\langle f_0, f_1, f_2, \ldots \rangle$ of functions (with $g = f^*$), and $next(g)$ should obviously be the synchronic function corresponding to $\langle f_1, f_2, f_3, \ldots \rangle$; in other words $(next(f))^*$. Of course, not every g is synchronic; but given any g we can still form an f using the equation given, and we can still return $next(f)^*$. If g is not synchronic, the result will be rather strange, but we should not expect otherwise; nonsynchronic filters are not really streams anyway. We see, then, that every element of L can be coerced into a stream if it is not one already, or coerced into a filter if it is not one already.

This approach (we will omit the details) seems to give the desired hybrid of functional programming and dataflow programming. A definition

$$\mathbf{f(x)} = E$$

makes the value of f the least element of $L \to L$ which satisfies the equation. The expression $\backslash x : E$ is the function defined by the equation **f(x)** = E (provided **f** does not occur in E). There is only one kind of application and only one lambda.

The program

> **pow(odd)**
> **where**
>   **pow = \x : x fby \x : x * pow(x);**
>   **odd = 1 fby odd + 2;**
> **end**

outputs the stream 1, 9, 125, ... ($=1^1$, 3^2, 5^3, ...), and the program

> **(next pow)(odd)**
> **where**
>   **pow = \x : x fby \x : x * pow(x);**
>   **odd = 1 fby odd + 2;**
> **end**

outputs 1, 27, 625, ... ($=1^2$, 3^3, 5^4, ...). At the same time the definition

$$\textbf{pipe(P, Q) = \textbackslash x : Q(P(x));}$$

defines piping, so that our original sample program given in the introduction could have been written with **pipe(sqroot, pipe(avg, square))** as the subject.

REFERENCES

Ackerman, W. B. (1979). Data flow languages, *Proc. Nat. Comput. Conf.*, pp. 1087–1095; and AFIPS Press, Arlington, Virginia.

Arsac, J. (1977). "La construction de programmes structurés." Dunod, Paris.

Arvind, and Kathail, V. (1981). A multiple processor dataflow machine that supports generalized procedures, *Ann. Symp. Comput. Arch.,* 8th, pp. 291–302.

Ashcroft, E. A., and Wadge, W. W. (1976). Lucid—A formal system for writing and proving programs, *SIAM J. Comp.* **5,** 519–526.

Ashcroft, E. A., and Wadge, W. W. (1977). Lucid, a nonprocedural language with iteration, *Comm. ACM* **20,** 519–526.

Ashcroft, E. A., and Wadge, W. W. (1979). "Structured Lucid." Tech. Rep. CS-79-21, Comp. Sci. Dept., Univ. of Waterloo, Ontario, Canada.

Backus, J. (1978). Can programming be liberated from the von Neumann style? *Comm. ACM* **21,** 613–641.

Backus, J. (1981). Is computer science based on the wrong fundamental concept of program? An extended concept, *in* "Algorithmic languages" (J. W. de Bakker and J. C. van Vliet, eds.), pp. 133–165. Elsevier North-Holland, Amsterdam.

Burstall, R. M., Collins, J. S., and Popplestone, R. J. (1971). "Programming in POP-2." Edinburgh Univ. Press, Edinburgh.

Church, A. (1941). "The calculi of lambda-conversion." Annals Mathematical Studies 6, Princeton Univ. Press, Princeton, New Jersey.

Conway, M. E. (1963). Design of a separable transition-diagram compiler, *Comm. ACM* **6,** 396–408.

Darlington, J., and Burstall, R. (1973). A system which automatically improves programs, *Proc. IJCAI, 3rd, Stanford, California,* pp. 479–485.

Davis, A. L. (1978). The architecture and system method of DDM1: A recursively structured data driven machine. *Ann. Symp. Comput. Arch. 5th,* pp. 210–215.

Dennis, J. B., Misunas, D. P., and Leung, C. K. C. (1977). "A highly parallel processor using a data flow machine language." Computation Structures Group Memo 134, Lab. for Comp. Sci., MIT, Cambridge, Massachusetts.

Dijkstra, E. W. (1965). Computer programming as a human activity, *Proc. IFIPS Congress 65,* pp. 213–217, Elsevier North-Holland, Amsterdam.

Dijkstra, E. W. (1968). Go to statement considered harmful, *Comm. ACM* **11,** 147–148.

Dijkstra, E. W. (1976). "A discipline of programming." Prentice-Hall, Englewood Cliffs, New Jersey.

Farah, M. (1977). Correct compilation of a useful subset of Lucid, Ph.D. dissertation, Univ. of Waterloo, Ontario, Canada.

Faustini, A. (1982). The equivalence of a denotational and an operational semantics for pure data flow, Ph.D. dissertation, University of Warwick, Comp. Sci. Dept., Coventry, United Kingdom.

Friedman, D., and Wise, D. (1976). CONS should not evaluate its arguments, *in* "Automata, Languages and Programming" (S. Michaelson and R. Milner, eds.), pp. 257–284. Edinburgh Univ. Press, Edinburgh.

Gordon, M., Milner, R., Morris, L., Newey, M., and Wadsworth, C. (1977). "A metalanguage for interactive proof in LCF." Tech Rep. CSR-16-77, Dept. Comput. Sci., Univ. of Edinburgh.

Henderson, P. (1980). "Functional programming: Application and implementation." Prentice-Hall International, London.

Henderson, P., and Morris, J. M. (1976). A lazy evaluator, *Proc. Symp. Principles Prog. Lang., 3rd.,* pp. 95–103. ACM, New York.

Hoare, C. A. R. (1969). An axiomatic basis for computer programming, *Comm. ACM* **12,** 576–580.

Hoare, C. A. R. (1978). Communicating sequential processes, *Comm. ACM* **21,** 666–677.

INMOS (1982). "OCCAM, INMOS Ltd" (company publication). Whitefriars, Lewins Mead, Bristol.

Kahn, G. (1974). The semantics of a simple language for parallel processing, *Proc. IFIP Congress 74,* pp. 471–475. Elsevier North-Holland, Amsterdam.

Kahn, G., and MacQueen, D. B. (1977). Coroutines and networks of parallel processes, *Proc. IFIP Congress 77,* pp. 993–998. Elsevier North-Holland, Amsterdam.

Keller, R. M., Lindstrom, G., and Patil, S. S. (1979). A loosely-coupled applicative multi-processing system, *AFIPS Conf Proc.* **46,** pp. 613–622.

Landin, P. J. (1966). The next 700 programming languages, *Comm. ACM* **9,** 157–166.

McCarthy, J. (1960). Recursive functions of symbolic expressions and their computation by machine, *Comm. ACM* **3,** 184–95.

McCarthy, J. (1965). Problems in the theory of computation, *Proc. IFIPS Congress 65,* pp. 219–222. Elsevier North-Holland, Amsterdam.

McCarthy, J., Abrahams, P. W., Edwards, D. J., Hart, T. P., and Levin, M. I. (1962). "LISP 1.5 programmer's manual." MIT Press, Cambridge, Massachusetts.

McIlroy, M. D. (1968). "Coroutines." Internal report, Bell Telephone Laboratories, Murray Hill, New Jersey.

Ostrum, C. B. (1981). "The Luthid 1.0 manual." Dept. Comput. Sci. Univ. of Waterloo, Waterloo, Ontario, Canada.

Pilgram, P. (1983). Translating Lucid dataflow into message passing actors, Ph.D. dissertation, Univ. of Warwick.

Reynolds, J. (1970). GEDANKEN—A simple typeless language based on the principles of completeness and the reference concept, *Comm. ACM* **13,** 308–319.

Shamir, A., and Wadge, W. W. (1976). Data types as objects, *Proc. ICALP 4th,* pp. 465–479. (Springer LNCS 52).

Sargeant, J. (1982). Implementation of structured lucid on a dataflow computer, M.Sc. dissertation, Univ. of Manchester.

Smith, D. E. (1929). "A source book in mathematics." McGraw-Hill, New York.

Strachey, C. (1971). Systems analysis and programming, *Sci. Am.* **215** (3), 112–124.

Turner, D. A. (1979). A new implementation technique for applicative languages, *Software Pract. Exper.* **8,** 31–49.

Uchida, S. (1982). Towards a new generation computer architecture—Research and development plan for computer architecture in the fifth generation computer project. TR/A-001, Tech. Rep. Res. Lab. of the Inst. New Generation Comput. Tech.), Tokyo, Japan.

Wadge, W. (1981). An extensional treatment of dataflow deadlock, *Theoret. Comp. Sci.* **13**, 3–15.

Wadge, W. (1984). "Viscid, a vi-like screen editor written in pLucid." Univ. of Victoria, Comp. Sci. Dept., Tech. Rep. DCS-40-IR, Victoria, British Columbia, Canada.

Watson, I., and Gurd, J. (1982). A practical data flow computer, *Computer* **15** (2), 51–57.

Yourdon E., and Constantine, L. L. (1979). "Structured design." Prentice-Hall, Englewood Cliffs, New Jersey.

APPENDIX

THE pLUCID PROGRAMMER'S MANUAL

A. A. Faustini
A. A. G. Yaghi*
S. G. Matthews†

Department of Computer Science
Arizona State University
Tempe, Arizona

* Present address: Department of Computer Science, University of Warwick, Coventry, England.
† Present address: Department of Computer Science, University of Victoria, Victoria, British Columbia, Canada.

1 INTRODUCTION

The language *pLucid* can best be described as a functional dataflow programming language. We use the term *dataflow* because a *pLucid* program defines a dataflow net and we use the term *functional* because for each node in the net, the entire output history is a function of the entire input history.

A brief look at *pLucid's* pedigree shows that its block structuring mechanism is the **where** clause from P. J. Landin's ISWIM, and that its data types are those of POP-2, i.e. integers, reals, booleans, words, character strings and finite lists. The language pLucid is *typeless* and so there are neither type declarations nor compile-time type checking. Those programmers who are familiar with programming the UNIX shell will feel at home programming in pLucid. The reason for this is that basic to both pLucid and UNIX are the concepts of *filter* and *data stream*.

A pLucid program is *an expression*, and a program execution is an *expression evaluation*. For example, consider the simple expression

x + y

which constitutes a complete pLucid program. When evaluated this program repeatedly demands values for **x** and **y** and outputs their sum. Note that the free variables in a pLucid expression are assumed to be inputs. The above program induces an endless interaction between the user and the evaluator that might proceed as follows:

x(0): 2	*The first demand for a value of* x.
y(0): 3	*The first demand for a value of* y.
output(0): 5	*The first value of the sum.*
x(1): 1	*The second* ......
y(1): ~8	
output(1): ~7	
x(2): 2.73	*The third* .....
y(2): 1	
output(2): 3.73	
x(3):	*A fourth demand for* x, *for which the user has not yet supplied a value.*

In section 5 we explain how these apparently endless computations can be made to terminate in a graceful manner.

Another example program is the following:

hd(tl(L))

When this program is evaluated it repeatedly demands values for L (which are assumed to be finite lists) and outputs the head of their tail (i.e. the second element of the input list). This is another example of a continuously operating program evaluation. For this program a listing of the interaction between the user and the evaluator of might look as follows:

```
      L( 0): [42 7 5]
output( 0): 7
      L( 1): [3 [2.4 8] 9]
output( 1): [2.4 8]
      L( 2): [2]
output( 2): ?          (the pLucid error object)
      L( 3): [5 1 2]
output( 3): 1
           .   .
           .   .
           .   .
```

Note that, given an input which is not a finite list of length at least one, the resulting output is the error value ?.

One important property shared by the above examples is that they can all be thought of as filters. The first example can be thought of as an addition filter, i.e. it takes two streams of inputs and produces the stream of their sums. The following sequence of snapshots of the dataflow computation:

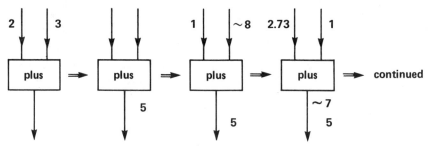

note: in pLucid negative numbers are prefixed by the symbol ~ as in ~8 (minus 8).

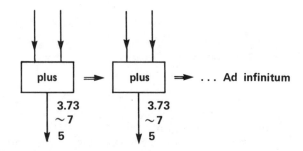

Similarly the second example is a combination of two filters. The first, called the tail filter, takes one input stream and produces the stream of tails. The output of this filter is *piped* to the input of the second filter, namely, the head filter. This second filter produces as its output the heads of the sequence of finite lists input. The following is a sequence of snapshots of the computation:

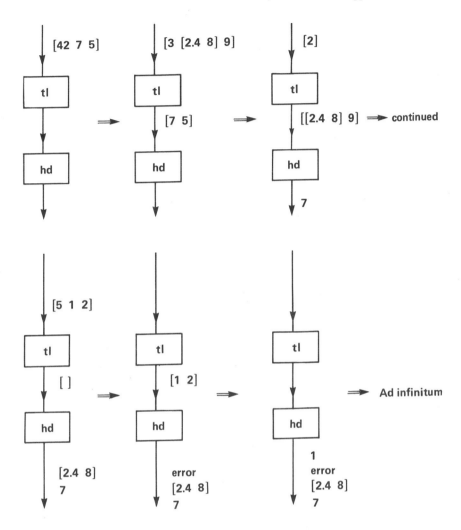

Simple filters like the above are usually memoryless, but there is no reason why this should be the case for more complex filters. It is possible for a filter to produce as output values that depend upon values already processed. An example of a filter with memory is one that takes as input a sequence of numbers, one at a time, and produces as output the smallest and the largest of the numbers read so far. Initially the program reads the first number and gives this number as both the smallest and the largest read so far. Then it asks for the next input and if this input is smaller than the smallest, it replaces the old smallest and in addition is output as the current smallest. If this input is larger than the largest, it becomes the largest and is output as the current largest. In the case of it being the same value as the current smallest or the current largest, the input is ignored. Note that if the input is anything but a number,

...en the output will be the special error value. This program can be written in pLucid as follows :

```
[% "smallest", s , "largest", h %]
    where
        s = x fby if next x <  s then next x else s fi;
        h = x fby if next x >  h then next x else h fi;
    end
```

A sequence of snapshots of a computation is illustrated in the following diagram:

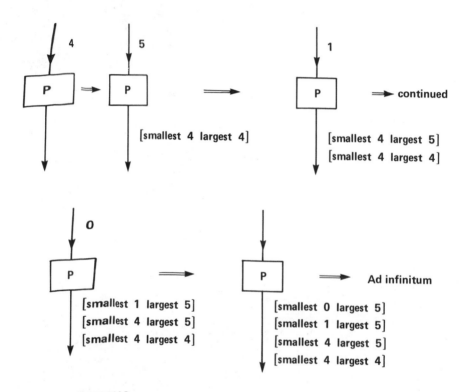

2 LUCID EXPRESSIONS

2.1 THE where CLAUSE

The **where** clause is pLucid's means of structuring programs, just as the *block* is the means in Algol and Pascal. As mentioned earlier, a pLucid program is an expression, and is thus a composition of subexpressions. To avoid horrendously long and complicated expressions we use the **where** clause to replace subexpressions by variables. For example, the following three programs are all equivalent.

i. (x ** y) / (x**y div z)

ii. temp / (temp div z) where temp = x ** y; end

iii. temp1 / temp2
            where
                 temp1 = x ** y;
                 temp2 = temp1 div z;
            end

Moreover, **where** clauses may be nested to arbitrary depths. For example, the following two programs are equivalent:

i. (x-2)*(x+3)+y+z

ii. a+b
     where
       a = w1*w2
            where
                w1 = x-2;
                w2 = x+3;
            end;
       b = y+z;
     end

In this last program, the expression **a+b** is called the *subject part* of the (outermost) **where** clause. The *body* of this **where** clause consists of two *definitions*, the first defining **a**, and the second defining **b**. The subject part of the innermost **where** clause is **w1*w2**, and its body consists of two definitions, namely those of **w1** and **w2**.

2.2 THE OPERATORS next, fby and first

Variables in pLucid are similar to variables in most conventional programming languages. They are dynamic objects in the sense that their values change as the program execution proceeds. Often, in the execution of a particular **where** clause, it is possible to think of an execution as a sequence of steps in which the values of the local variables of the **where** are updated simultaneously. For example, suppose we wish to write a program to read in a stream of numbers and output the partial sums, i.e., after each number is read the sum of the numbers read so far is output. For this we can use two variables, one called i, which at any step holds the last number read in, and another called s, which at any step holds the sum of the numbers read so far. At each step in the program execution the variables i and s are updated. At any step the next value of i is the next value to be read, while the next value of s is the present value of s plus the next value of i. In pLucid s is defined as follows:

s = i fby s + next i ;

This definition is read: The first value of **s** is the first value of i, while at any step in the program execution, the next value of **s** is the present value of **s** plus the next value of **i**. The complete pLucid program to generate the stream **s** of partial sums is:

s where
    s = i fby s+next i;
end

This program uses the two pLucid operators **next** and **fby** (pronounced "followed by"), which we will now introduce. **next** is a prefix operator which, when applied to a variable at any step in the execution, returns the value which that variable has after the next step of the execution. Of course, in a conventional language we do not know what the next value of a variable will be; however, in pLucid this value can be computed from the definition. For example, suppose that a variable **x** is defined in terms of a variable **y** by the pLucid definition

x = next y;

then at any step in the program execution the value of **x** will be the next value of **y**, i.e., the value of **y** after the next execution step. Hence if, as we go through the execution steps, **y** takes on successive values from the stream 2,4,6,8,10,..., then **x** takes on the successive values from the stream 4,6,8,10,... . Thus, **x** is 4 when **y** is 2, **x** is 6 when **y** is 4, and so on.

As well as being able to talk about the next value of a variable we can also talk about the next value of an expression. For example, suppose **x** and **y** are as above, then at any step the next value of **x+y** will be the sum of the next values of **x** and **y**. So, if **z** is a variable such that at any step **z** is the next value of **x+y**, then in pLucid **z** is defined by:

z = next(x+y);

Let us now turn our attention to the infix operator **fby**. As described earlier, in pLucid we regard variables as dynamic objects, dynamic in the sense that their values change as the program execution proceeds. In the programs we have introduced so far, the values of all the variables are simultaneously updated at each computation step. In fact, for each variable we can talk about the "stream of values" it assumes during the course of a program execution. For example, we can interpret statements such as, "the variable **x** takes the values 2 followed by 4, followed by 6 etc.", to mean that after the first execution step **x** is 2, after the second step **x** is 4, after the third step **x** is 6, and so on.

In general, definitions using the infix operator **fby** usually have the following form:

x = <*expression1*> fby <*expression2*> ;

This can be read as follows : The stream of values of **x** is the initial value of the <*expression1*> followed by each of the successive values of the <*expression2*>. An alternative reading is: The initial value of **x** is the initial value of the <*expression1*>, and at any step in the program execution, the next value of **x** is the present value of <*expression2*>.

The final operator to be introduced in this section is the prefix operator called **first**. For any expression <*expr*>, if the variable **x** is defined by

x = first <*expr*> ;

then at any step in the program execution, the value of **x** is the first (i.e., initial) value of <*expr*>. For example, suppose **nat** is a variable having the values 0 followed by 1, followed by 2, followed by 3, etc. Then the expression, **first nat**, takes the values, 0 followed 0, followed by 0 ,etc. in other words, **first nat** is equivalent to the constant **0**.

Now that **next**, **fby** and **first** have been introduced we consider examples of their use. The first example is a filter that produces as output the stream 0,1,2,... ,etc., of natural numbers

```
nat where
    nat = 0 fby 1+nat;
end
```

The program execution begins by producing the initial value of **nat**, i.e., 0. From then on, the execution repeatedly adds 1 to **nat** and outputs the result. The filter just described is so useful that the pLucid system supports a constant called **index** that produces the same values as the above filter. Thus the following program:

```
index
```

is equivalent to the one above.

The next example is a filter that produces as output the stream of squares 0,1,4,9,16,... ,etc.

```
sq where
    nat = 0 fby 1+nat;
    sq  = 0 fby sq+2*nat+1;
end
```

As in the previous program the variable **nat** takes on the successive values 0,1,2,3,... . The first value of **sq** (i.e., the square of 0) is 0, while at any step the next value of **sq** is the present value of **sq** plus two times the present value of **nat** plus 1. Note that we have used the fact that for any n,

$$(n+1)(n+1)=n^2+2n+1$$

The next example is a filter that uses Newton's algorithm to output a stream of approximations to the square root of the input. Roughly speaking the algorithm goes as follows: to calculate the square root of a number n, take the first approximation to be 1, and thereafter take each successive approximation to be $\dfrac{(a+\frac{n}{a})}{2}$, a being the previous approximation. In pLucid we might code this up as follows:

```
approx
    where
    approx = 1 fby (approx+first n/approx)/2;
end
```

(For improvements on this example see sections 2.4 & 2.5.)

2.3 USER DEFINED FUNCTIONS (UDF'S)

Pointwise functions (or operators) in pLucid are similar to pure functions (i.e., functions without side effects) in other programming languages. For example, the following program repeatedly reads in integers and outputs the corresponding factorial.

```
fac(n)
where
  fac(n) = if n eq 0 then 1 else n*fac(n-1) fi;
end
```

The function **fac** defined in the body of the **where** clause can be thought of as a machine or *black box* which continuously consumes values of **n** and produces values of **fac(n)**. In other words it is a filter in the UNIX sense, the only difference being that this *black box* filters integers rather than characters. The following is a sequence of snapshots for a particular sequence of inputs:

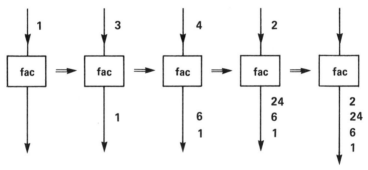

The filter produces each of the factorials **fac(n)** 1,6,24,2 as **n** takes each of the values 1,3,4,2. However, pLucid programmers are not restricted to only pointwise filters. A pLucid filter may have internal memory and/or it may produce outputs at a different rate than that at which it consumes inputs.

The following non-recursive udf has internal memory. It computes the average of the last three numbers input.

```
avg3(input)
  where
  avg3(n) = avg
            where
            avg = (one+two+three)/3;
            one = n;
            two = next n;
            three = next next n;
            // This is a comment
            // A simpler way of writing this whole
            // where clause would be as the following
            // expression
```

```
        // (n + next n + next next n)/3
        end;
end
```

Another example of a program using a udf is one which reads in a stream of finite lists and outputs a stream of the atoms in those lists; e.g., if the list [*1*, [*3.7*], *true*] is input, then the atoms 1, 3.7, and *true* will be output.

```
flatseq(x)
  where
    flat(x) = if x eq nil then nil
                elseif isatom( x ) then x fby nil
                   else join(flat(hd x),flat(tl x))
                fi;
    join(x,y) = if first x eq nil then y
                   else x fby join(next x,y)
                fi;
    flatseq(x) = join(flat(first x),flatseq(next x));
  end
```

The function **flatseq** consumes a stream of finite lists and produces a stream of all the atoms in those lists, while the function **flat** consumes just one list and produces its atoms. The function join consumes two streams of atoms, for example, 1,2,[],[],[],.... and 3,4.75,[],[],[],.... and produces the stream 1,2,3,4,75,[],[],[],.... . The filters **flat**, **join** and **flatseq** could in principle be implemented as three concurrently running processes. Note that **flatseq** produces values faster than it consumes them, as for each list going into **flatseq** many atoms may be produced as output.

Another example of a simple program with functions is the following. The program generates the prime numbers using the *sieve of Eratosthenes*.

```
sieve(n)
  where
  n     = 2 fby n+1;
  sieve(i) = i fby sieve(i whenever i mod first i ne 0);
  end
```

2.4 THE OPERATORS asa,whenever,upon

asa

If **asa** were not a predefined infix operator it could be defined as follows:

```
asa(x,y) =if first y then first x
          else  asa(next x,next y) fi;
```

Although this is a concise and precise way of defining **asa** it may be better at this stage to give a more operational description, such as the following. We can imagine that the **asa** operator computes by repeatedly reading in pairs of values of **x** and **y** until (if ever) **y** has the value *true*. Assuming a *true* is eventually read then the value taken by the **asa** operator will be the value of **x** corresponding to the *true* value of **y**. Moreover the **asa** takes on this value everywhere. In this respect the **asa** operator can be thought of as a constant. For example, if **x** takes the values 0,1,2 and **y** the values *false, false, true* then **x asa y** takes the values 2,2,2,.... . Another example is if **x** takes the values *abc*, *3*, [*d,e*] and **y** the values *false, true, false*, then **x asa y** produces as output the stream of values 3,3,3,... .

(Actually, the pLucid evaluator implements **asa** in a more clever fashion than just described: it does not try to compute the values of **x** which it does not need. But there is usually no harm in imagining that it works in the manner described.)

The following program illustrates a use of the **asa** operator. The program is a slightly different version of the Newton's algorithm program of section 2.2.

```
(approx asa count eq 10) fby eod
  where
    approx = 1 fby (approx+first n/approx)/2;
    count  = 1 fby count+1;
  end
```

Given a number 42, say, as input (i.e., the variable **n** is a free variable in this program and is therefore assumed to be an input variable), the program outputs the 10th approximation to its square root, i.e., 6.48.

whenever

The predefined infix operator **whenever** (sometimes written **wvr**) could be defined recursively as follows:

```
whenever(x,y) = if first y then x fby z else z fi
                where
                  z = whenever(next x,next y);
                end
```

Again, at this stage, a more operational description will be of more benefit to the reader. The operator **whenever** is best thought of as a process that filters out some elements (possibly none) from the stream **x** according to a control stream (i.e., booleans) **y**. In terms of machines (see the factorial example in section 2.3), **whenever** repeatedly takes pairs of values for **x** and **y**; if **y** is true then **x** is output and if **y** is *false* then **x** is discarded. For example, suppose at each step in the computation **y** takes on successive values from the stream *true, false, true, false,...*, i.e.,

```
y = true fby false fby y;
```

In addition, suppose at each step in the computation **x** takes on successive values from the stream 0,1,2,... i.e.

```
x = 0 fby x+1;
```

If **x** and **y** take on successive values as described above, then **x whenever y** will produce as output successive values from the stream 0,2,4,6,... of even numbers. The following is a pictorial description of the computation:

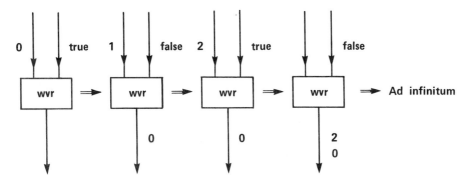

(For another example of **whenever** see the prime number program of section 2.3).

upon

The **whenever** operator is best thought of as a filter that selectively passes on values that it receives as its input. The Lucid operator **upon** is a dual to **whenever** in the sense that it selectively 'stretches out' its input stream by repeating some of the values that it receives. Again we can give a concise definition of **upon** in terms of a recursive user defined function as follows:

```
upon(x,y) = x fby
        if first y
        then upon(next x,next y)
        else upon(x,next y)
        fi;
```

If we think of **upon** as a black box then we can describe its behaviour as follows. The first output of the box is whatever shows up as the first value of **x**. If the corresponding value for **y** is *true* then the box will advance looking for the next value of **x**. However, if the corresponding value of **y** is *false* the next value output will again be the current value of **x**. Thus our 'black box' output is controlled by the boolean values sent along **y**. The following is an example of a program to stretch out the stream 0,1,2,3,... of natural numbers.

```
stretch where
    x = 0 fby x+1;
    y = true fby false fby y;
    stretch = x upon y;
end;
```

The following is a pictorial description of the computation:

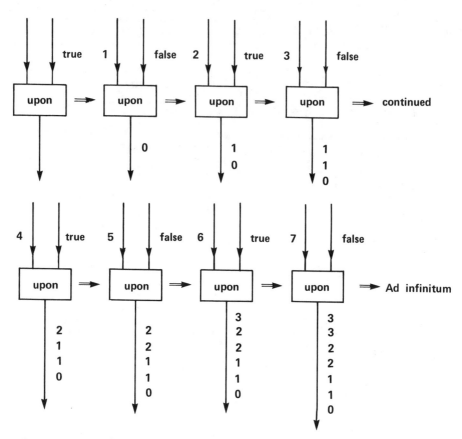

Another example of a program that uses **upon** is the following merge program. The streams to be merged (i.e., **xx** and **yy**) are assumed to be streams of numbers in increasing order. Let us define the stream associated with **xx** to be 2,4,8,16,32,64,..., and the stream associated with **yy** to be 3,9,27,81,.... Then the ordered merge of these two streams will be the stream 2,3,4,8,9,16,27,32,64,81,.... The following is the pLucid program that computes this ordered merge:

```
merge
  where
    merge = if a<b then a else b fi;
    a = xx upon a eq merge;
    b = yy upon b eq merge;
    xx = 2**i;
    yy = 3**i;
    i = 1 fby i+1;
  end;
```

attime

The last operator (filter) to be described is **attime.** If this was not a predefined infix operator we could define it with the following udf:

attime(x,y) = (x asa index eq first y) fby attime(x, next y);

Note: **index** has been defined in section 2.2. In fact, using **attime** it is possible to give the following non-recursive definition for **upon** and **whenever.**

```
wvr(x,p) = x attime t2
      where
        t1 = if p then index else next t1 fi;
        t2 = t1 fby t1 attime t2+1;
      end;

upon(x,p) = x attime t1
      where
        t1 = 0 fby if p then t1+1 else t1 fi;
      end;
```

2.5 THE is current DECLARATION

In this section we introduce a pLucid construct that allows the programmer to write programs which involve nested iteration. This construct is the **is current** declaration.

Suppose we wish to write a program which repeatedly takes pairs of non-negative integers and raises the first to the power of the second, e.g., 2 to the power of 3 is 8. A typical approach to designing such a program would be first to write a smaller program to produce the power of just one pair of inputs and second to embed this program in another that executes the first program indefinitely. In pLucid the first program could be written as follows:

```
p asa index eq first n
    where
      p = 1 fby p * first x;
    end
```

It is a simple loop program where, each time round the loop, **p** is multiplied by the first value of **x**. The loop continues until **index** (which is a simple counter) equals the first value of **n**, at which point the value of **p** is the first value of **x** raised to the power of the first value of **n**. We now attempt to place this program within a nonterminating loop program. The resulting program has two loops, one nested within the other; however, whenever the inner loop (i.e., the above program) is executed, the expressions **first n** and **first x** would always have the same value. Consequently the power of only the first pair of inputs would be repeatedly computed. Obviously this is not what we require. We can try to resolve the situation by replacing **first n** and **first x** by **n** and **x**, respectively. Unfortunately this does not help either since we require **n** and **x** to remain constant during each execution of the inner loop. Thus we require that **n** and **x** be outer loop variables which only change between executions of the inner loop. This is clearly impossible when we think of **x**, **n**, **index** and **p** as variables which are all updated simultaneously. To overcome this problem we use the **is current** declaration with **n** and **x** in the above program. The effect of this is to set up an outer loop in which **x** and **n** only get updated between executions of the inner loop. The resulting program is the following:

```
p asa index eq first N
    where
    X is current x;
    N is current n;
    p = 1 fby p * first X;
    end
```

Note the informal convention used, i.e., that the variables that are introduced by an **is current** declaration use upper case. Although any variable name could have been used, the use of upper case letters makes programs involving nested iterations easier to understand. The inner loop variable **X** only ever has one value which is the current value of **x**, hence as **index** and **p** get updated, **X** stays constant. Similarly **N**, the current value of **n**, stays constant during the execution of the inner loop. Remember, **x** and **n** are outer loop variables, while **X** and **N** are inner loop variables which restart life anew at the beginning of each inner loop execution. In general, the effect of the **is current** declaration is to set up a nested iteration.

An improvement in the above program is to replace **first X** by **X** and **first N** by **N**. This does not change the meaning of the program as **X** and **N** remain constant during each execution of the inner loop. This results in the following program:

```
p asa index eq N
    where
    X is current x;
    N is current n;
    p = 1 fby p * X;
    end
```

Now, suppose we had wanted to write a program which took a power (the first value of **n**) and then raised each of a sequence of inputs to that power; e.g., it might compute the squares of all its inputs. The program would then use **is current** with **x** but not with **n**.

```
p asa index eq first n
    where
    X is current x;
    p = index fby p*X;
    end
```

Note that the expression **first n** cannot be replaced by **n** as **n** is a variable that is active in the inner loop, and we require **n** to be the same for each execution of the inner loop. In a similar way we can write a program which takes an integer (the first value of **x**) and raises it to each of a sequence of powers; e.g., it might compute powers of 2. The program uses **is current** with **n** and not **x**.

```
p asa index  eq N
  where
    N is current n;
    p = 1 fby p * first x;
  end
```

As with **n** in the previous program, we cannot replace **first x** by **x**.

Another example of a program using **is current** is one to calculate the exponential e^x using the series

$$e^x = 1 + x + \frac{x^2}{2!} + \frac{x^3}{3!} + \cdots$$

The program is

```
expsum asa next i eq 10
      where
        X    is current x;
        i    = next index;
        term  = 1 fby (term/i)*X;
        expsum = 0 fby expsum+term;
      end
```

The body of the outer loop asks for the present value of **x** to be input, and then outputs an approximation to e^x. The inner loop takes the current value of **x**, i.e., **X**, and computes an approximation to e^x by adding the first ten terms of the above series. The body of the inner loop computes the next term of the series and adds it to **expsum.** Hence each time the inner loop is called it executes its body ten times. If the stream of values 1, 2, 0.5, ~1, ... are the inputs for **x** then the stream 2.718, 7.389, 1.649, 0.369, ... will be output.

The next example is an improvement of Newton's algorithm for computing a square root given in section 2.1. Given a stream of numbers we compute approximations to their roots by applying Newton's algorithm to each of them 10 times.

```
approx asa count eq 10
  where
    X is current x;
    approx = 1 fby (approx+ X/approx)/2;
    count = 1 fby count+1;
  end;
```

Inputting the numbers 2, 2.213, 26.7, ... produces 1.414, 1.487, 5.167, ... as output.

The general form of the **is current** declaration is:

<*variable*> **is current** <*expression*> ;

Our next example uses **is current** in its more general form, namely with an expression on the right-hand side. It computes the roots of the polynomial

$$a\,x^2 + b\,x + c = 0$$

in the obvious way, calculating the square root as in the previous example. The roots are output as a two element list.

```
[%r1,r2%]
   where
   r1    = (-b+sqroot)/(2*a);
   r2    = (-b-sqroot)/(2*a);
   sqroot = approx  asa  count eq 10
         where
           X is current b*b-4*a*c;
           approx = 1 fby (approx+X/approx)/2;
           count  = 1 fby count+1;
           end ;
   end
```

3 THE pLucid DATA TYPES

So far we have described the Lucid operators which are available in pLucid. Such operators are common to all members of the Lucid family of languages. Each particular member of the family is distinguished by the choice of data types on which the Lucid operators are applied. However, the members of the Lucid family are typeless, in the sense that there are no type declarations and no type checking at compile-time.

The data types of pLucid are integers, reals, words, strings, finite lists - the basic types of POP-2. In addition, there are two special objects, *error* and *eod*. In this section we give a brief informal introduction to pLucid expressions using these types (for more formal details see section 6).

3.1 Numeric Expressions

Numeric expressions in pLucid are basically the same as in most other programming languages supporting mixed integer and real arithmetic. Numbers, i.e., reals and integers, are represented by numeric constants. As with APL, pLucid distinguishes between the sign of a number and the operator applied on that number. The binary subtraction operator on numeric expressions is represented by the symbol -; but the negative sign of a numeric constant is represented by the symbol ~. The symbol + is the binary addition operator on numerics, but the positive sign for numeric constants should not be written, as it is assumed by default. For example the following are numeric constants

$$1 \quad 42 \quad \sim 6 \quad 1.0 \quad \sim 5.324 \quad 42.127$$

the following are not numeric constants

$$+2 \quad -4 \quad -1.0 \quad .12$$

At present there is no provision in pLucid for the exponent representation of reals.

Apart from the additional operator **isnumber**, pLucid's numeric operators are essentially the same as those in most other programming languages.

isnumber is an operator which tests its argument to see if it is numeric. It returns the word *true* if its argument is either an integer or a real, and returns the word **false** otherwise. For example, the following program checks whether its input is a number. If it is, it outputs the square of that number, then asks for the next input, and so on. If the input is not a number, the program outputs an error message:

```
if isnumber(x)
then x*x
else 'The input was not numeric\n' fi
```

To finish this section on numeric expressions we will, by way of examples, describe the pLucid division and modulus operators. The remaining numeric operators need no explaination beyond that given in section 6.

pLucid has two division operators; **div** for integer division, and **/** for real division. For any numbers n and m, n **div** m is the largest integer such that (n **div** m)*m is not greater than n. The following are example pLucid expressions together with their equivalent integer constants.

12 div 5	is equivalent to	**2**
60 div ~5	is equivalent to	**~12**

The second division operator is for real division. **/** accepts numeric operands and yields a numeric result, e.g.,

123 / 5	is equivalent to	**24.6**
0.123 / 0.123	is equivalent to	**1**
~1.0 / 3	is equivalent to	**~0.33333**

Remember that the accuracy of **/** is dependent upon the accuracy of the pLucid implementation.

The modulus operator **mod** is the mathematical modulus function. For any numbers n and m,

n **mod** m equals $n - m*(n$ **div** $m)$&

For example,

9 mod 5	is equivalent to	**4**
~9 mod 5	is equivalent to	**~4**
4.5 mod 1.2	is equivalent to	**0.9**

3.2 Non-Numeric Data Processing

Besides numeric computation, pLucid allows non-numeric data processing. This is done using the types word, string and finite list. These types, which are similar to those in POP-2, are discussed in this section.

3.2.1 Word Processing

A word is determined by a sequence of characters of one of the following forms,

- an arbitrarily long sequence of alphanumerics
  starting with a letter
  (e.g., this t23r Warwick)
- an arbitrarily long sequence of signs, where
  a sign is one of
  + - * / & = < > : # ^
- a bracket, where a bracket is one of
  ( )   (% %)   [% %]
- a separator, where a separator
  is either ; or ,
- a period
- a double quote

The following are examples of words

   yes   *true*   "   %]   ++   , *false*

A word constant is simply a sequence of characters determining the word, enclosed in double quotes. For example, the pLucid word constants representing the above words are

   "yes"   "true"   "."   """"   "%]"   "++"   ","   "false"

The distinction between words and word constants is important and should must be clearly understood. The following example is instructive:

   "fred"

is a word constant representing the word **fred**. On the other hand

   fred

is an identifier (i.e., a variable).

   Word constants, like other constants, are pLucid expressions, and can be used to define values for variables in programs. For example, the definition

   x = "dog";

defines the value of the variable **x** to be the word **dog**.

   The boolean values in pLucid are the words *true* and **false,** i.e., they obey the rules for the type word, i.e., **isword(true)=true** and **isword(false)=true**. Note that the programmer may assume that the variables **true** and **false** have been predefined to be the words **"true"** and **"false"**. Thus it is as if every pLucid program has the following definitions included automatically:

   true = "true";
   false = "false";

However, for the sake of clarity, we shall talk about these two special words separately in section 3.2.2.

   Beside those operators described in section 3.2.2, which apply to the words **"true"** and **"false"**, there are four other operators applicable to words in general. These operators are **isword**, **mkword** and the polymorphic operators **eq** and **ne** which can be used to compare words.

The operator **isword** recognizes words, it yields "**true**" if its argument is a word, and "**false**" otherwise. For example :

    isword ("pLucid") is the word "**true**",
    isword (123)   is the word "**false**", as the argument is a
        number.

The operator **mkword**, read *make word*, takes a string as an argument. If the characters in this string make up a legal word it returns that word. Otherwise, it returns the error object. For the definition of what a string is see section 3.2.3. The following are some examples of the use of the operator **mkword**:

    mkword ('this') has the same value as the word constant "**this**",
    mkword ('this ') returns the error object,
    mkword ('123') returns the error object,

The binary operators **eq** and **ne** are for comparing two words. **eq** returns the word *true* if its arguments are equal, and returns **false** otherwise. **ne** returns *true* if the arguments are different, and **false** otherwise. It is worth mentioning here that these operators can be applied to any pLucid data object. For example :

    (z eq "dog") or not (isword (z))

can be viewed as a filter with input **z**.

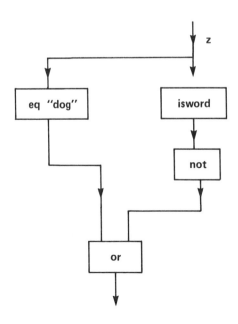

The above machine continuously asks for inputs. If the input is either not a word, or is the word **dog,** then the output is the word *true*, otherwise the output is *false*.

3.2.2 Boolean Expressions and Predefined Variables

The pLucid programmer is provided with six predefined variables (actually, they are constants, because they cannot be redefined). These variables are **index** (discussed earlier), **true, false, nil, error** and **eod**. The variables **true** and **false** have as values the words "true" and "false" respectively. The value of the variable **nil** is the empty list. It is as if the pLucid programmer has the following definitions included in his program.

```
true  = "true"
false = "false"
nil   = []
```

The variable **error** has as its value the error object and the variable **eod** has as its value the eod (end of data) object. (For more about these last two objects, see section 3.3.)

PLucid has the usual boolean operators, namely **or, not** and **and.** These operators yield their usual boolean results when applied to the words *true* and *false*. However when one of their arguments is neither *true* nor **false** the operators may yield the error object. (For further details see section 3.3.)

Apart from many of the usual logical operators found in other languages, pLucid includes the operators **isnumber, isword, isstring, isnull, islist, iserror**, and **iseod**. These will be defined in the appropriate sections.

3.2.3 String Processing

A string, in pLucid, is determined by a sequence of zero or more ASCII characters. Strings must not be confused with words, they form a completely different data type. Any attempt to apply a string operator on a word, or vice versa will yield the error object.

Every string in pLucid can be represented by a string constant. A string constant representing a given string can be obtained first by replacing each character by its pLucid representation and secondly enclosing the resulting sequence between ' and ' For example, the following are string constants:

```
':: yes, ~ #'
'this is a string ? '
'pLucid is non procedural '
```

For string processing in pLucid, we have the following operators: **isstring** takes one argument and returns the word **true** whenever this argument is of type string; otherwise it returns the word **false**.

˄ (string concatenation)

The operator ˄ is the string concatenation operator. It takes two strings and forms a new one by concatenating the second to the end of the first.

However, if one of its arguments is not a string, it yields the error object.

substr

The operator **substr**, read as *substring*, takes three arguments. The first of these is a string, and the other two are positive integers. These two integers determine a range for extracting a substring from the first argument of **substr** (the first argument must be a string). Hence, the first integer should be less than or equal to the second, which should be less than or equal to the length of the string. Mathematically, the operator **substr** can be defined as follows:

> If the value of the string S is the sequence of
> characters $S_1 S_2 \cdots S_n$
> where k and m are integers such that $k <= m <= n$,
> then **substr**$(S,k,m) = S_k \cdots S_m$
> Otherwise, the result will be the error object.

mkstring

The operator **mkstring,** read as *make string*, takes its argument, which should be a word, and makes a string out of it. If the argument is not a word, the result will be the error object. Consider the following example pLucid expressions and their equivalent string constants:

> **mkstring(**"hello"**)** gives **'hello'**
> **mkstring(**"t1239"**)** gives **'t1239'**
> **mkstring(123)**   yields the error object

length

The operator **length** returns the length of a string, that is the number of characters contained in the string. Note that internally characters are stored unescaped. That is to say that \b, backspace is not stored as two characters, backslash and b, it is stored as the character backspace.

Note: **length** can be applied to words and lists as well as to strings.

Examples

The following is an example program that takes one input **x** and checks whether or not it is a string.

> **if isstring x**
>   **then**   x ^ **' is a string, well done'**
>   **else**   **'Sorry, it is not a string, try again'**
> **fi**

If **x** is a string the program outputs **x** concatenated to the string

> **' is a string, well done'**

Otherwise the program outputs

> **'Sorry, it is not a string, try again'**

3.2.4 List Processing

The third non-numeric type in pLucid are the finite lists. A list in pLucid is essentially a sequence of zero or more items, each of which is either a number, a word, a string, or a list. The lists in pLucid are almost identical to those of POP-2 and (therefore) also very similar to those of LISP.

List Constants

A list constant is a sequence of items enclosed in square brackets. Each of these items is either a numeric constant, a word constant less the quotes, a string constant, or a list constant. Quotes, single and double, around string and word constants act as delimiters. However, it is obligatory in pLucid to write the string quotes, it is necessary to drop the quotes of the word constants when written as items in a list constant. Whenever ambiguity occurs, a space can be used to seperate two successive words. So the following two list constants have the same value

   i. **[" dog "]**
   ii. **["dog"]**

but the following do not

   i. **["dog"]**
   ii. **[dog]**

Moreover, the following two list constants are different

   i. **[this is pLucid]**
   ii. **['this' is pLucid]**

because the sequence of letters, this, occurs in the first list as a word constant, while in the second it is a string constant.

A list expression is either an expression built up using the :: (cons) operator or a sequence of zero or more pLucid expressions enclosed in %-square brackets (**[%** and **%]**) and separated by commas. To make this clearer, consider the following examples:

1. The followings are expressions in pLucid, as they are all constants,

    "dog" 'c a t' [this is pLucid]

The list expression, built from these expressions, can be written as

    "dog" :: 'c a t' :: ("this" :: "is" :: "pLucid" :: nil) :: nil
    [% "dog", 'c a t' , [this is pLucid] %]

The value of either list expression is equal to the value of the list constant

    [dog 'c a t' [this is pLucid]]

2. The value of the list expression

    [% i+3 , tl (y) , 'S T R' , [% "programming" %] %]

depends on the values of **i** and **y**. Assuming that **i** equals 2 and **y** is the list **[hello world]**, then the list expression above will be equivalent to the constant

[5 [world] 'S T R' [programming]]

3. The sequence of characters **[% "dog" %]** in the list constant

[the [% "dog" %] sat on the mat]

is not a list expression, it is a sequence of five word constants, each of which is considered as an item in the main list. Note that every item in a list constant should be a constant.

pLucid facilitates list processing by means of the following four operators.

hd.

The prefix operator **hd**, read as *head*, yields as its result the first element of the argument list. This may be a word, a number, a string, or a list. When the argument to **hd** is a list of one element, the result will be that element. If the argument to **hd** is either the empty list or a non-list then **hd** yields the error object.

tl

The prefix operator **tl**, read as *tail*, yields as its result the argument list, but with its head (i.e., the first object in the list) removed. Unlike **hd**, the tail operator yields the empty list when its argument is a one object list. If the argument is either the empty list or a non-list, **tl** yields the error object.

<> (append)

The infix operator **<>**, read as *append*, takes two lists and yields a new list constructed by appending the second list to the end of the first. If one of the arguments is a non list, it yields the error object.

:: (cons)

The infix operator **::**, read *construct*, yields (constructs) a new list from its two arguments, the right-hand argument must be a list. The new list has as its head the left-hand argument and as its tail the right-hand argument. If the right argument is not a list, the result will be the error object.

eq and ne

The operators **eq** and **ne** are for comparing data items in pLucid and have been explained before.

isnull

The operator **isnull** takes a list and returns the word **true** if the list is the empty list and **false** if it is not. It returns the error object if the argument is not a list.

islist

The operator **islist** returns **true** if its argument is a list, and *false* if it is not.

Examples

The following examples illustrate the use of **hd**

hd([hello world])
    has the same value as the word constant "**hello**"

hd([% [this 'is'] pLucid %])
    has the same value as the list constant **[this 'is']**

hd([[[a b] c] d [e]])
    has the same value as the list constant **[[a b] c]**

The following expressions return the error object

hd([])   **hd** is applied to the empty list,
hd("this")   the argument is not a list,
hd(nil)   the argument is the empty list.

The following examples illustrate the use of **tl**

tl([hello world])
    has the same value as the list constant **[world]**

tl([hello [world]])
    has the same value as the constant **[[world]]**

tl([programming])   returns the empty list

tl([% 1+3, 'S T R', [% "programming" %] %])
    has the same value as the list constant
              ['S T R' [programming]]

The following expressions return the error object

tl("what")   the argument is not a list
tl(nil)   the argument is the empty list

The following examples illustrate the use of the operator <>

[[pLucid] is a] <> [[non] procedural language]
    has the same value as the list constant
            [[pLucid] is a [non] procedural language]

[Lucid] <> 'with POP2'
    returns the error object because one of the arguments
    is not a list

The following examples illustrate the use of the construction operator ::

[programming] :: [languages]
    has the same value as **[[programming] languages]**

'pLucid is'::[Lucid]
    has the same value as **['pLucid is' Lucid]**

[the language] :: [% "Iswim" ,700 , 'iteration' %]
  has the same value as
    [[the language] Iswim 700 'iteration']

'##87' :: nil   has the same value as **['##87']**

[pascal] :: 'triangle'   returns the error object, because
    the second argument is not a list.

Example

Any expression above, whether it is a constant or an operator with some operands, can be written as a program by itself. For example, the expression

  hd(x)

is a program which repeatedly asks for values for the variable **x**, expecting each to be a list and producing as output the head of each. It yields the error object if the input is not a list. The program could be thought of as a filter for which a typical computation sequence might be as follows:

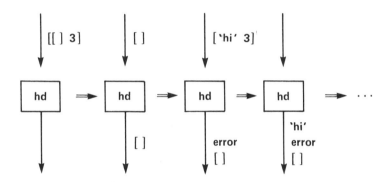

Example

When the program

  rotate where

      t = x fby tl t <> z ;
      z = hd(t) :: nil ;
      rotate =if t eq first x and counter ne 0 then eod
                      else t fi;
      counter = 0 fby counter + 1 ;
    end

is run on the machine, it will ask for a value for the variable **x**, expecting it to be a list. Then it produces all the possible rotations for this list. Instead of asking for the next value of **x**, it gives the object *eod*, which terminates the whole program. So supplying the list constant **[a b c d]** as an input, the program will give the result

[a b c d]
[b c d a]
[c d a b]
[d a b c]

and then terminate.

3.3 The objects eod and error

Among the data objects of pLucid there are two special ones which are completely distinct. These are the *error* and *eod* (each could be considered as constituting a separate data type on its own).

The object error

We have mentioned, while defining the data types of pLucid, the cases where an operator yields the object *error*. Informally speaking, the error object results from applying an operator of certain type to operands which are of types different than the ones which such an operator expects. For example, trying to add two words, find the head of a string, or divide a number by a list.

In a program we represent the object *error* by the predefined identifier **error**. Hence, the value of the expression

error

is the stream of error objects. It is worth noting here that the above expression differs from the expression

"error"

The first represents the error object, while the second is the word constant representing the word *error* (the error object is not a word).

While the error object is represented, in a program, by the predefined identifier **error**, its representation as an input, or as an output, is dependent on the implementation of the language. In the Arizona State University implementation it is represented by the symbol **?**. (For further details see section 5.)

the object eod

In a program, this object will be represented by the predefined identifier **eod**. Unlike the object *error*, trying to output the object *eod* will cause the machine to terminate the execution of the program. For example, the program

1 fby 2 fby eod

will output the numbers 1, 2 and then terminates. The representation of the eod object as an input is again dependent on the implementation. In the Arizona State University implementation it is represented by the character control-D or the *at* character (see section 5 for more details). Again, the distinction between the eod object represented by the reserved identifier **eod**, and the word *eod* represented by the word constant **"eod"**, should be clear.

Furthermore, the special identifiers **error** and **eod** are not considered as proper constants. Hence, they cannot be written as items in list constants, as such items must be constants. So the items in the list constants

[error]   [eod]

are, respectively, the words *error* and *eod*. Of course, they can appear in **[% - %]** expressions, but the value of any such expressions will be *error* or *eod*.

Examples

The value of the expression

[% error %]

is the error object. This is because the above list expression is really an abbreviation of the expression

error :: nil

which evaluates to the object *error*. However, the value of the list expression

[% "error" %]

is a list of one item. This item is the word *error*.

Similarly, the value of the expression

[% eod %]

is the object *eod*.

[% "eod" %]

is a list of one item. This item is the word *eod*.

If the argument to an operator is the object *eod* (or the object *error*) then, except for certain operators, the object yielded by that operator will be the object *eod* (or the object *error*). The only prefix operators that yield values other than *eod* or *error* when one of their arguments is *eod* or *error* are **iserror** and **iseod**. These operators are for recognizing the objects *error* and *eod*. When the argument of the operator **iserror** is the object *error*, it yields the word *true*. If the argument is the object *eod* it yields the object *eod*. Otherwise it yields the word *false*. On the other hand, when the operator **iseod** is applied to the object *eod* it yields the word *true*. Otherwise it yields the word *false*.

The boolean operators **and** and **or** can also return values other than *eod* and *error* when given these two objects as arguments. The result of applying these operators to the objects *error* and *eod* are given in the following table.

It is worth mentioning here that these operators are commutative when applied to 'proper' data objects, i.e., the following two rules hold for any 'defined' **P** and **Q**

P or Q = Q or P
P and Q = Q and P

Unfortunately, this rule may fail if the one of the computations required to produce **P** or **Q** fail to terminate. This is because the pLucid evaluator is sequential and evaluates the first operand before the second. If this first computation fails to terminate, no value is produced, even if the value of the second operand is available and determines the overall result

P	Q	P and Q	P or Q
true	error	error	true
false	error	false	error
true	eod	eod	true
false	eod	false	eod
error	eod	eod	eod
error	error	error	error
eod	eod	eod	eod

3.4 pLucid Conditional Expressions

The simplest conditional expression in pLucid is the expression **if then else**. The expression

if <*expr1*> **then** <*expr2*> **else** <*expr3*> **fi**

expects the values of <*expr1*> to be of type boolean, while the values of <*expr2*> and <*expr3*> could be of any type. The pLucid conditional expression works as the logical function **if then else**. It evaluates the expression <*expr1*>, if it is the word *true* the result will be the value of the expression <*expr2*>, and if it is *false* the result is the value of <*expr3*>. If the expression <*expr1*> is not a boolean, i.e., its value is not a truth value, the **if then else** expression will output the error object. The word **fi** appearing at the end in the above expression is a terminator for the **if then else** expression.

Example

The pLucid program

if X <= Y then Y else X fi

asks for the values of **X** and **Y** as inputs. It evaluates the expression **X <= Y**, if it is *true* it returns the value of **Y**, if *false* it returns the value of **X**. If one of the inputs is not numeric it outputs the error object. Then it asks for new values for **X** and **Y**, and so on. This expression could be used to define a function which takes two arguments and yields their maximum by writing

max (X,Y) = if X <= Y then Y else X fi ;

pLucid conditional expressions could be nested to many levels by using the reserved word **elseif** instead of **else**. The word **elseif** acts as **else** for the outer **if** expression and as **if** for the new one, i.e., there is no need to write the word **if** after **elseif**, and no need for the corresponding **fi**'s. Hence the expression

> **if** x **then** y **elseif**
> z **then** m **elseif**
> n **then** q **else** r **fi**

is equivalent to the expression

> **if** x **then** y
> **else if** z **then** m
> **else if** n **then** q
> **else** r
> **fi**
> **fi**
> **fi**

Example

The following is a legitimate expression in pLucid, it expresses a simple salaries system,

> **if** (status eq "single") **then** basicsalary
> **elseif** (status eq "married") **then** basicsalary * 1.30 +
> children * 40
> **else** specialsalary **fi**

When this program is run the evaluator asks for a value for the variable **status**. If the value of **status** is the word *single*, it asks for the value of **basicsalary** and outputs it. If the value of **status** is the word *married*, it asks for the values of **basicsalary** and **children**, then outputs the value of the expression **basicsalary * 1.30 + children * 40**. Otherwise, it asks for the value **specialsalary** and outputs it. Then it asks for the next value of **status**, and so on.

pLucid case Expression

Another way of writing conditional expressions in pLucid is by using the pLucid **case** expression. The **case** expression provides a clearer way for writing long, nested **if** expressions. The example above could be written using the **case** expression as follows:

> **case** status **of**
> "single" : basicsalary ;
> "married" : basicsalary * 1.30 + children * 40 ;
> default   : specialsalary ;
> **end**

The **case** expression consists of two parts, the *selector part* and the **case** body. The selector part is the expression which comes between the words **case** and **of**, see the above example. The **case** body is a list of switches, terminated by the word **end.** Each switch is of the form

> *expression : expression*

and must be terminated by a semicolon. One of these switches must be the default switch, which is a switch whose left-hand-side is the word **default** (it must appear last). Evaluation of the **case** expression proceeds as follows: the selector part, which is an expression, is evaluated, then its value is compared with the value of the left-hand-side expression of each switch in the **case** body. If there is an expression which is equal to the selector, then the value of the right-hand-side expression of that switch is the value of the **case** expression. Otherwise, the value of the **case** expression is the value of the expression to the right of the word **default.** In the event of two expressions in the **case** body with the same selector value, the first one to appear in the list is chosen.

The **case** expression, like the **if** expression, can be nested to arbitrarily many levels. This is done by writing another **case** expression as the right-hand-side of a switch in the outer **case** expression. For example, suppose we want to split the case of being married in the above example, so we write

```
case status of
  "single" : basicsalary ;
  "married" : case  arechildren of
                   "none"  : basicsalary * 1.20 ;
                   "many"  : basicsalary * 1.30 +
                             numchildren * 40 ;
                   default : error;
              end;
  default   : specialsalary ;
end
```

pLucid cond Expression

Another way of writing conditional expressions in pLucid is by using the pLucid **cond** expression. The **cond** expression provides a clean mechanism for the writing of long nested if-expressions. The example above could be written in terms of the **cond** expression:

```
cond
  status eq "single" : basicsalary ;
  status eq "married" : basicsalary * 1.30 + children * 40 ;
  default            : specialsalary ;
end
```

The **cond** expression consists of a body which is a list of switches, terminated by the word **end.** Each switch is of the form

> **expression : expression**

and must be terminated by a semicolon. One of these switches should be the

default switch, which is a switch whose left-hand-side is the word **default**.
Evaluation of the **cond** expression proceeds as follows: the expressions to the left
of the **:** are evaluated from top to bottom and if one is found to be true then the
value of the **cond** is the expression on the right-hand-side of the **:** and if no
expression to the left of a **:** is true then the value of the **cond** is the default value.
In the case of there being two expressions in the **cond** body that are true, the
first encountered is chosen.

The **cond** expression, like the **if** and **case** expressions, can be nested to
many levels.

4 SCOPE RULES

The scope of an occurrence of a variable, in a pLucid **where** clause, is either
local or *global*. It is local if the relevant declaration or definition is in the same
clause. The only declaration we have in pLucid is the **is current** declaration. The
variable occurring to the left of the declaration is local to that clause, while any
variable occurring in the expression to the right occurs globally. Moreover, if a
variable is neither declared nor defined in the clause then any occurrence is
global.

If an occurrence is global to a clause its value is expected to come from an
outer clause, the first outer clause in which that variable is local. This also
applies on the outermost clause. If a variable is left global in that clause, its
value is supposed to come from an outer clause, which is the user environment.
Consequently, the machine asks for that value as an input. For example:

```
X + y + z where
     X is current x + y ;
     y = 12 + z ;
     end
```

The occurrences of **X** and **y** in **X + y + z** are local to the **where** clause as is the
first occurrence of **X** in **X is current x + y**   Also y in **y = 12 + z** is local. The
occurrence of **y** and the occurrence of **x** in **X is current x + y** are both global to
the clause, as is that of **z** in **y = 12 + z**.

5 RUNNING PLUCID UNDER UNIX

5.1 The Basics

This section of the manual explains how a pLucid program runs in the UNIX
environment.

The pLucid evaluator is itself a UNIX process and as such has associated
with it an input stream (the standard input), an output stream (the standard
output) and an output stream for reporting of errors (the standard error). On
most implementations of UNIX the standard input is associated with the user's
keyboard and the standard output and standard error with the user's screen. It
is possible in UNIX to redirect input and output to places other than the screen

and keyboard and for this the reader is referred to the UNIX manual. The following diagram shows how the pLucid evaluator interfaces with the user:

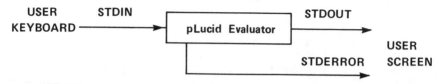

Many useful pLucid programs never need use more than these three basic streams. The **filter** operator decribed in the next section explains how more input and output streams may be associated with a pLucid program.

Let us begin with the most trivial of pLucid programs, namely, the expression:

x

In this simple program there is no definition for **x**, in other words, **x** is a free variable of the expression. In pLucid each free variable occurring in an expression is associated with its own pLucid input stream and all pLucid input streams take their input from the standard input (see above). Thus if we run the above program the following prompt will a appear on the screen

x(0):

(Prompts for input and output are sent along the standard error, thus they can be discarded if they are of no help.) If we input a constant such as **4.3**, **[2 3 [4]]**, **'a string'** or the word **fred**; then our program will echo the input, e.g.,

```
        x(0): 4.3
   output(0): 4.3
        x(1): [ 2 3 [ 4 ]]
   output(1): [ 2 3 [ 4 ]]
        x(2): 'a string'
   output(2): 'a string'
        ...        ...
        ...        ...
```

Note that when words are input, such as the input for x(2), they must be input unquoted. Thus if we input **nil** then we are inputting the word **nil** and not the empty list. To input the empty list we use square bracket notation, i.e., **[]**.

Similarly, if we want to input the special object *error* we shall use the symbol **?**, e.g.,

```
        x(3): ?
   output(3): ?
```

The special object *eod* is input as control-D (or whatever the local UNIX convention is for end of file), e.g.,

```
        x(4): ^D
   %
```

where % is the UNIX shell prompt. Thus the special object *eod* can be used to gracefully terminate the evaluation of a continuously operating program. What is happening in effect is that the pLucid input stream associated with **x** is closed after an *eod* has been read. All future inputs on that particular pLucid stream are deemed to be *eod*.

Pop Input versus Character Input

In UNIX processes communicate to each other by sending streams of characters. For example, the date command sends a stream of characters on its standard output to the user's screen. This stream of characters is that which makes up the current date and time. In pLucid there are no objects of type character, so how does pLucid manage to run in the UNIX environment ?

When a pLucid program is run, it normally expects all of its inputs and outputs to be either numbers, words, strings or finite lists, successive inputs and outputs being separated by white space. However, there are options available that allow input or output or both to take a different form.

Character Input

In this mode the values read from the standard input are assumed to be raw characters. As far as the pLucid program is concerned, a character is a string of length one. Note that these characters could be control characters and non-printable characters. These characters are represented in pLucid strings by the following escape sequences.

'\b'	for backspace
'\n'	for newline
'\t'	for tab
'\f'	for formfeed
'\r'	for carriage return
'\\'	for \
'\''	for '

In addition an arbitrary byte-sized bit pattern can be generated by writing

\DDD

where **DDD** is one, two or three octal digits. For example:

'\014'	is formfeed
'\33'	is the character escape

The option for running the evaluator in character input mode is given in the UNIX manual entry (the -c option). Note that Pop and character input cannot be mixed. Programs that use only the basic input stream must be evaluated either in Pop input mode or character input mode.

Character Output

This mode is similar to the normal output mode except that there is no white space to separate successive outputs, string constants are stripped of their quotes and escaped characters such as \n and **\33** are output as the characters they denote. The option for running the evaluator in character output mode is given in the UNIX manual entry (the -s option). Again programs must be evaluated either in Pop output mode or in character output mode.

A Simple Program

The following is an example of a pLucid program (or filter) to compress the blanks in a file:

input whenever not (input eq ' ' and next input eq ' ')

It reads from the standard input, character by character, converting each character to the corresponding string of length one. If we want output in character form, then the -s option must be used. If we type the above program into a file called **compressblanks,** we can then compile this program to get the pLucid intermediate code in the file **compressblanks.i**. If we run the evaluator as follows:

luval -c -s compressblanks.i < text

the result is that the file text will be printed on the screen with all blanks compressed.

Programs with More Than One Free Variable

In the following program

x or y

there are two free variables, **x** and **y,** and thus the evaluator associates with each variable it's own pLucid input stream. To evaluate the program, successive values for **x** and **y** must be obtained from the user. The first value required is the first value for **x,** this is because the **or** operator evaluates its argument left to right, e.g.,

```
      x(0):  true
      y(0):  false
 output(0):  true
      x(1):  ...
```

If the object *eod* is input as a value for one of these variables, say **x,** the effect will be to close the input stream for that variable. Nevertheless, this does not terminate the program, as, according to the algebra associated with pLucid,

eod or true = true

Thus if the evaluator receives *eod* as input for **x** it will close the stream associated with **x** (i.e., all future input on **x** are *eod*). However, since the input stream for **y** is still open and since, given eod as its first argument, the **or** operator need not terminate, the evaluator will demand the next input for **y**. If the input is **true,** the evaluator outputs **true** and continues evaluation. Note that values of **x** will no longer be required since the input stream for **x** is closed. Thus only values of **y** are demanded, and so long as these values are **true** the computation continues, any other value for **y** will cause the program to terminate.

A simpler example of a program with two free variables is

x + y

When this program is run, it will ask for values for the variables **x** and **y**. If one of the input values for **x** or **y** is **eod** then the program terminates. This is because in the algebra associated with pLucid, *eod* + *z* = *eod* for any value *z*.

pLucid Programs as Standard UNIX Processes

As pLucid programs run as standard UNIX processes we can do all the usual things:

> **luval lex.i < filename**

if the file **lex** contains the program

> **x**

then this will read in constants (i.e., **[1 [2 3] 4]**, **'a string'**, **3.33**, **~9**) from file **filename** and output them to the terminal. Similarly

> **luval lex.i > fllename**

will read constants one by one from the terminal and output them to the file **filename**. We can also combine these to read constants from one file and output them to another. Our program is then in effect a filter.

> **luval lex.i < file1 > file2**

5.2 The filter and arg Operators

The **filter** function enables pLucid programs to interact in a simple manner with many useful UNIX utilities. The **filter** function is used as follows:

> **filter(*expression1*,*expression2*,*expression3*)**

The evaluation of a filter expression entails the following. First, evaluate *expression1*, which should evaluate to a string. This string is taken to be the name of a UNIX process. The pLucid evaluator then spawns a UNIX process named by this first argument. The second argument to the function **filter** is the stream of values that are to be sent to the standard input of the newly created process. Values produced by the newly created process are passed along its standard output back into the pLucid program and appear as the result of the function **filter.** The third argument of filter should again be of type string. This string is used to specify how the pLucid program is to interact with the process spawned by **filter**. The options for this are as follows:

's' Write to the stream associated with output to the filter in Character output mode.

'c' Read the stream associated with input from the filter as a stream of raw charaters. That is use Character input to read the stream produced by the the process spawned by filter.

'I' The filter requires no inputs.

'p' For every input sent to the filter it will guarantee to return one value. i.e., the filter is pointwise.

The third argument can be the empty string **''** which means that input and output to this filter should be in Pop mode. Note that the above options can be combined in the same string, e.g., **'csi'**. The last two options have been included for reasons of efficiency, but it is beyond the scope of this manual to explain why they are needed. The following diagram illustrates what happens when a filter is spawned by a pLucid program:

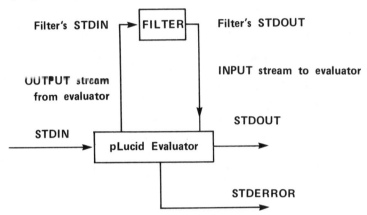

Note that due to the UNIX limitations on the number of processes and pipes that can be active at any one time, it is not advisable to include a **filter** function in a recursive function definition where it can be called upon to spawn large numbers of processes.

Note: The **filter** function may also be used to interface programs written in other languages with a pLucid program. The only requirement is that the the process written in the other language acts as a filter with respect to its input/output behaviour. This means that programs written in assembly language, Pascal, Fortran, PL/1 ..., can be used in conjunction with a pLucid program.

An Application of the Filter Function

In pLucid it is possible to supply a program with input from a file via the standard input. For many applications this method (i.e., **luval prog.i < filename**) is not satisfactory because it forces the standard input to be the named file. One way around this problem is to use the **filter** function which does not interfere with the evaluator's standard input. The following function definition could be included in a pLucid program. The function **file** expects its argument to evaluate to a string, which it takes to be the name of a file. The function then returns the stream of characters contained in the named file terminated by the eod object.

> **file(name) = filter('cat <' ⌢ filename, " , 'ci')**
> **where filename = first name; end;**

This facility means that we can choose dynamically the name of the files from which we require input.

5.3 Runtime Errors

If a pLucid program compiles, then the only errors that can occur at runtime will be type clash errors or errors that occur from giving a program strange inputs. A runtime type error will produce an error message which will give the exact location in the original source (i.e., file name, line number and cursor position of the error). If we run the following program:

```
moment where
    avg(x) = s / n
        where
        s = x fby hd s + next x;
        // We have included a deliberate mistake
        // The above definition should be
        // s = x fby s + next x;
        n = 1 fby n + 1;
        end;

    a = 7 fby 2 fby 4;

    moment = avg((a-m)*(a-m))
        where
         m is current m;
        end;

    m = avg(a);
end
```

the evaluator will give the following runtime error messages:

```
Evaluation begins ........
output(  0) : 0
```

```
Evaluation time error on line 4, of file bug
                    s = x fby hd s + next x;
.............................^
arg of hd must be a list, not  7

Evaluation time error on line 4, of file bug
                    s = x fby hd s + next x;
.................................^
left arg of numeric binary operator
or condition of wvr or upon is ?

Evaluation time error on line 2, of file bug
            avg(x) = s / n
.................^
```

        ... and so on

Error messages like the above will appear on the screen if a program containing type clashes is evaluated. Notice the propagation of errors. It is possible to turn off error reporting (see the UNIX manual entry).

Note: If the source program is changed, the program must be recompiled; otherwise the runtime error messages given by the evaluator will be with reference to the source program used to produce the current .i file.

If a program has a bug in it which is not a type error, that is, some form of logical error, then the **filter** function can be used to probe variables in much the same way as a technician uses a scope and probe to debug a piece of faulty hardware. A function **probe** could be defined as follows:

probe(name,expr) = filter('tee '⁀filename,expr,'')
where filename = first name; end;

Note that in the above example the values of the suspect variable have been tapped and stored in a file. On a system that allows a screen to be divided into multiple windows the values of the suspect variable could be displayed in one of the windows.

The arg Function

When invoking the evaluator it is often desirable to supply the evaluator with the names of one or more files as arguments. For example, if we wanted to write the UNIX **cat** filter in pLucid, we would need to supply the name of the file that we wanted to **cat**. To achieve this, pLucid has the prefix operator **arg**. The **arg** operator expects its argument to evaluate to a positive integer, which is used to select a string from the argument list associated with the invocation of the evaluator. To invoke the evaluator it is necessary to type the luval command, which has the following syntax:

luval <option list> <filename>.i <argument list>

(See UNIX manual entry for more details.) All that we need to say here is that the **arg** function will select a string from the <argument list> of an evaluator invocation. If the argument of **arg** is not a positive integer or there is no argument with that index, then **arg** yields the error object; otherwise it yields the appropriate string in the argument list.

5.4 A Facility for File Inclusion

A simple file inclusion facility is provided. To include a file (containing perhaps some function definitions) in another, just say

include *"filename"*;

Note: That any other statement on the same line as the **include** is ignored.

Included files may also have **include** statements, up to a level of ten.

There is also a standard inclusion directory where many useful functions are kept. In order to include files from this directory in your program, use angle brackets instead of quotes, that is, say

include *<filename>*;

where *filename* is a library file found in **/ud/cscfac/faustini/lu/lib** (this directory name will be different on your machine)

5.5 UNIX Manual Entry for plucid

lucomp, luval ∧ pLucid compiler and evaluator

Synopsis:

> **lucid** *filename*
> **lucomp** *filename*
> **luval** [*option*] ... *filename*

Description

   pLucid is a Arizona State University implementation of the language pLucid which runs on the Berkeley 4.1 UNIX. To run a pLucid program it must first be compiled using *lucomp*, which compiles pLucid programs into intermediate expression code. If the input argument is the file name "file" then the intermediate expression code will be output to a file named "file.i", which is then used as an argument to *luval*.

   luval evaluates the intermediate code in a file whose name must end with ".i". The following options are understood by *luval*:

-d   Produces a dump of the intermediate expression file onto the standard error (usually the terminal).

-c   Forces the evaluator into character input mode. In this mode all objects that travel along the input streams associated with the standard input are assumed to be of type character. Thus each character input (including newline) is treated by the evaluator as a string of length one (i.e. character is not a type in pLucid). Note if the -c option is not used then the inputs are assumed to be a stream of Pop2 data types separated by white space (i.e., newline, tab, etc.)

-s   Forces the evaluator into string output mode. In this mode all objects that travel along the output stream associated with the standard output are output as normal except for the following. When strings are output they are stripped of their quotes and escaped characters (i.e., \n for newline, \33 for the character escape,...) are output as the characters themselves. In addition no white space separates succesive outputs as it would when the -s option is not used.

-p   Used to inhibit prompting of input and outputs, i.e., the evaluator does not print output(10): before producing the 11th output. Similarly, it does not input x(7): when asking for the 8th input for x.

-t0   Prints a message every time a request is made for a variable during execution of the program.

-t1   Prints a brief message about garbage collection each time that it occurs during execution of the program.

-t2   Prints more information about garbage collection each time it occurs.

-t5   Prints information about action on the display as it occurs.

-t6   Print information each time a variable is defined by the evaluator.

-t9   In its usual mode the interpreter reports all non-fatal runtime error on the standard error. When trace 9 is set these run time errors are discarded.

-t30   Prints a demand trace for variables. This is usually run to the exclusion of all other trace options. A record can be made of the trace by piping the standard error to a file.

-t*   New traces (and options) may be added to the system. To find out what they are, interrupt the evaluator by using control-C and type h for help.

The evaluator can also be interrupted during execution to set or reset any of the traces and to inquire as to how much memory is used up so far, and in what fashion. Regular UNIX commands can also be run and then the program resumed. To interrupt the program, hit the interrupt key. Then the following commands are available to you:

q   Quit the evaluator.

c   Continue interpreting.

sN   Set trace option number N.

rN   Reset trace option number N.

m   Request information about memory usage.

!xxx Execute xxx as a UNIX command.

a   Print out the retirement age of variables. (The garbage collector uses a retirement scheme to collect 'old' variables.)

d   Dump the intermediate code.

t   Print out a list of all the strings used in the program (including those entered dynamically).

h   Print out the current height and limits of the evaluator's run time stacks.

For more information see the pLucid programmers manual. *lucid* is a macro file that compiles and runs pLucid programs.

Bugs

When too many UNIX filters are spawned by the filter function, there may be problems because of the limit on processes and pipes imposed by the UNIX operating system.

It is possible that when using a filter there may be problems with the number of inputs needed by the child process to respond to the parent. The evaluator is demand driven, UNIX is data driven, therefore a UNIX process may require additional inputs (i.e., it is data driven) to produce the required output.

Please report all bugs (however insignificant) to A. Faustini (i.e. mail faustini)

TABLES AND RULES

3.1 Tables of Operators

Numeric operators

operation	syntax	type of operands	type of result
addition	+	numeric	numeric
subtraction	-	numeric	numeric
multiplication	*	numeric	numeric
integer division	div	integer	integer
real division	/	numeric	numeric
exponentiation	**	numeric	numeric
modulus	mod	integer	integer
numeric	isnumber	anything	boolean
less than	<	numeric	boolean
greater than	>	numeric	boolean
equal	eq	numeric	boolean
less than or equal	<=	numeric	boolean
greater than or equal	>=	numeric	boolean
not equal	ne	numeric	boolean
sine	sin	numeric	numeric
cosine	cos	numeric	numeric
logarithm	log	numeric	numeric
tangent	tan	numeric	numeric
square root	sqrt	numeric	numeric

absolute value	**abs**	*numeric*	*numeric*
log10	**log10**	*numeric*	*numeric*

Word operators

operation	*syntax*	*operand type*	*type of result*
make a word out of a string	**mkword**	*string*	*word*
recognize a word	**isword**	*anything*	*boolean*

Boolean operators

operation	*syntax*	*type of operands*
conjunction	**and**	*boolean*
disjunction	**or**	*boolean*
negation	**not**	*boolean*

String operators

operation	*syntax*	*type of operands*	*type of result*
make a string out of a word	**mkstring**	*word*	*string*
string recognition	**isstring**	*anything*	*boolean*
string concatenation	**^**	*string*	*string*
form a substring	**substr**	*(string, integer, integer)*	*string*
length	**length**	*anything*	*number*

List operators

operation	*syntax*	*operand1*	*operand2*	*result*
the head of a list	**hd**	*list*	*--*	*anything*
the tail of a list	**tl**	*list*	*--*	*list*

appending two lists	<>	*list*	*list*	*list*
construction operator	::	*anything*	*list*	*list*
is the list empty?	**isnull**	*list*	--	*boolean*
is it an atom (not a list)	**isatom**	*anything*	--	*boolean*
is it a list	**islist**	*anything*	--	*boolean*

onditional expressions

f expression

    if
boolean expression
then
expression
else
expression
fi

ested if expression

    if
boolean expression
then
expression
        elseif
boolean expression
then
expression
else ... fi

case expression

case
expression
of
    expression   : *expression*   ;
    expression   : *expression*   ;
    . . . .
    expression   : *expression*   ;
    default : *expression* ;
    end

cond expression

> **cond**
>> *boolean expression : expression ;*
>> *boolean expression : expression ;*
>>
>> . . . .
>>
>> *boolean expression : expression ;*
>> **default** : *expression* ;
>> **end**

Lucid operators

operator	*syntax*	*operand* **1**	*operand* **2**	*result*
first	**first**	*anything*	---	*anything*
next	**next**	*anything*	---	*anything*
followed by	**fby**	"	*anything*	"
whenever	**whenever**	"	*boolean*	"
whenever	**wvr**	"	*boolean*	"
at time	**at time**	"	*integer*	"
as soon as	**asa**	"	*boolean*	"
upon	**upon**	"	*boolean*	"

current declaration

> *identifier* **is current** *expression*

6.2 Associativity and Precedence Rules

Associativity of Operators

An infix operator is said to be 'right associative', e.g. **fby**, if for any expressions E1, E2, and E3, the expression

> **X fby Y fby Z**

is always interpreted as

> **X fby (Y fby Z) .**

Similarly, an infix operator is said to be 'left associative', e.g **asa**, if for the expressions E1, E2, and E3, the expression

> *E1* **asa** *E2* **asa** *E3*

is always interpreted as

$$(\; E1 \; \textbf{asa} \; E2 \;) \; \textbf{asa} \; E3$$

The following table gives the associativity of infix operators in pLucid:

Associativity	*Operators*
left	+ , - , * , / , div , mod , or , and , ** , asa , attime, whenever , wvr, upon , if then else, case
right	:: , <> , fby , ^

Precedence Rules

These are rules to avoid clogging up programs with unnecessary brackets. For example, if we say that '* has higher precedence than +' then an expression like **2 + 4 * 5** is always interpreted as **2 + (4 * 5)**.

We list here the hierarchy of precedences amongst pLucid operators. Operators with lowest precedences are at the top of the list, and ones with highest precedences are at the bottom.

1	asa, upon, whenever, wvr, attime
2	fby
3	if then else fi, case, cond
4	:: , <>
5	or
6	and
7	not
8	eq, ne, < , <= , > , >=
9	+ , -
10	* , div , / , mod
11	**
12	^
13	first, next, sin, cos, tan, log, log10, hd, tl, isnull, isnumbe, isatom, isword, isstring, mkword, mkstring, lserror, iseod, sqrt, abs, arg, islist

The where-clause

The where-clause has the lowest precedence amongst other constructs in pLucid, so if E1, E2, and E3 are expressions, then for any operators in pLucid, say fby and next, the expression

E1 **fby** *E2* **fby next** *E3* **where**

. . .

. . .

. . .

end

is always interpreted as

$$(E1 \text{ fby } E2 \text{ fby next } E3) \text{ where}$$
$$...$$
$$...$$
$$...$$
$$\text{end}$$

6.3 Reserved Words

These identifiers are reserved as keywords

if	hd	true
then	tl	false
else	isatom	sin
elseif	isnumber	cos
fi	isnull	log
case	nil	is
of	div	current
default	mod	eod
where	and	error
end	not	isword
first	or	isstring
next	eq	iserror
fby	ne	iseod
asa	log10	substr
whenever	tan	mkstring
wvr	abs	mkword
upon	sqrt	length
cond	filter	attime
arg	include	islist

7 MISCELLANEOUS

7.1 plucid Grammar

We define here the pLucid syntax using the BNF formalism, where

::= is read as <meta variable> is defined as <meta variable>,

| is read as <meta variable> or <meta variable> ,

{ } denotes possible repetition zero or more times
of the enclosed construct .

<program> ::= <expression>

```
<expression> ::= <constant>
          | <identifier>
          | error
          | eod
          | <prefix operator> <expression>
          | <expression> <infix operator> <expression>
          | filter(<expression>,<expression>,<expression>)
          | substr(<expression>,<expression>,<expression>)
          | length <expression>
          | arg <expression>
          | <list expression>
          | <if expression>
          | <case expression>
          | <cond expression>
          | <function call>
          | <where clause>

<constant> ::=   <numeric constant>
          | <word constant>
          | <string constant>
          | <list constant>

<numeric constant> ::=   <integer constant>
              | <real constant>

<integer constant> ::=   <digit> { <digit> }
              | <n-sign> <integer constant>

<real constant>   ::=  <integer constant> . { <digit> }

<n-sign> ::= ~

<word constant>::= <quote> <word constant less the quotes> <quote>

<word constant less the quotes> ::=   <letter> { <alphanumeric> }
                    | <sign> {<sign>}
                    | <bracket>
                    | <period>
                    | <separator>
                    | <quote>
```

`<sign> ::= + | - | * | | & | = | < | > | : | # | ^` `<quote>` `::= " <bracket> ::= ( | ) | [%`
`[%] | (% | %) <period> ::= . <separator> ::= , | ;`

`<string constant> ::= '{<character>}'`

`<character> ::= <Any ASCII character except the closing single quote ' >`

```
<list constant> ::=  nil | [ ]
              | [ {<list constant element>} ]

<list constant element> ::=  <numeric constant>
                   | <word constant less the quotes>
                   | <string constant>
                   | <list constant>

<alphanumeric> ::=  <digit> | <letter>

<digit> ::=  0 | 1 | 2 | 3 | 4 | 5 | 6 | 7 | 8 | 9

<letter> ::= A | B | C | D | E | F | G | H | I | J | K | L | M
       | N | O | P | Q | R | S | T | U | V | W | X | Y | Z
       | a | b | c | d | e | f | g | h | i | j | k | l | m
       | n | o | p | q | r | s | t | u | v | w | x | y | z

<identifier> ::= <letter> { <alpahnumeric> }

<prefix operator> ::=  <p-numeric operator>
             | <p-word operator>
             | <p-string operator>
             | <p-list operator>
             | <p-lucid operator>
             | <p-special operator>

<p-numeric operator> ::= sin | cos | tan | sqrt | abs | log10| log | isnumber

<p-word operator>  ::= isword | not | mkstring

<p-string operator> ::= isstring | mkword

<p-list operator> ::= hd | tl | isatom | isnull | islist

<p-lucid operator> ::= first | next

<p-special operator> ::= iseod | iserror

<infix operator> ::=   <i-numeric operator>
             | <i-word operator>
             | <i-string operator>
             | <i-list operator>
             | <i-lucid operator>

<i-numeric operator> ::= + | - | ** | * | div | mod | /
             | eq | ne | <= | < | > | >=

<i-word operator>  ::= and | or | eq | ne

<i-string operator> ::= ^ | eq | ne
```

<i-list operator> ::=   <> | :: | eq | ne

<i-lucid operator> ::= fby | whenever | wvr | upon | asa | attime

<list expression> ::= [%%]
              | [% {<expressions list>} %]

<expressions list> ::= <expression item>
              | <expression item> , {<expressions list>}

<expression item> ::=   <expression>
              | <list expression>

<if expression> ::= if <expression> then <expression> <endif>

<endif> ::=   else <expression> fi
         | elseif <expression> then <expression> <endif>

<case expression> ::= case <expression> of <cbody> end

<cond expression> ::= cond <cbody> end

<cbody> ::= {<expression> : <expression> ;} <defaultcase>

<defaultcase> ::= default : <expression>;

<function call> ::= <identifier> (<actuals list>)

<actuals list> ::=   <expression>
              | <expression> , <actuals list>

<where clause> ::= <expression> where <body> end

<body> ::= <declarations list> <definitions list>

<declarations list> ::= { <current declaration> ; }

<current declaration> ::= <identifier> is current <expression>

<definitions list> ::= { <definition> ; }

<definition> ::=   <simple definition>
            | <function definition>

<simple definition> ::= <identifier> = <expression>

<function definition>::=
     <identifier> (<formals list>) = <expression>

<formals list> ::=   <identifier>
              | <identifier> , <formals list>

7.2 Syntax Diagrams

In this section we introduce the syntax diagrams for pLucid. The reserved *words* of the language appear underlined. However, signs, numbers, and brackets are not, as this might lead to ambiguity

program :

→—— expression ————→

expression :

→—┬—→ constant ——————————————————→—————————————→
   ├—→ identifier ——————————————→
   ├—→ **error** ——————————————→
   ├—→ **eod** ——————————————→
   ├—→ prefix operator ——→ expression ————→
   ├—→ expression ——→ infix operator ——→ expresssion ——→
   ├—→ list expression ——————————→
   ├—→ if expression ——————————→
   ├—→ case expression ——————————→
   ├—→ cond expression ——————————→
   ├—→ function call ——————————→
   ├—→ where clause ——————————→
   ├—→ **substr** ——→ (—→ 3expression ——→) ——————→
   ├—→ **filter** ——→ (—→ 3expression ——→) ——————→
   ├—→ **length** ——————→ expression ——————→
   └—→ **arg** ——————————→ expression ——————→

constant :

→—┬—→ numeric constant ——→——→
   ├—→ word constant ——→
   ├—→ string constant ——→
   └—→ list constant ——→

numeric constant :

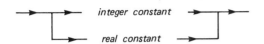

integer constant :

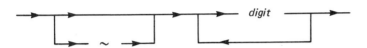

real constant :

word constant :

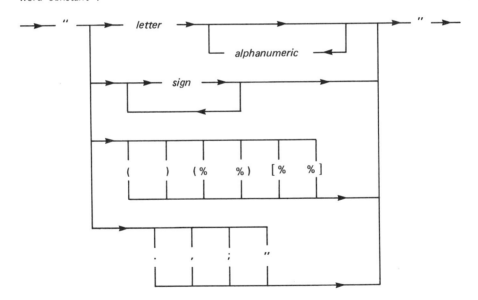

sign :

string constant :

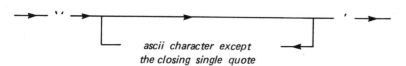

list constant :

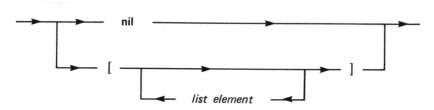

list element :

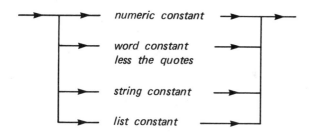

alphanumeric :   *letter* :

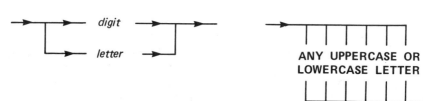

digit :

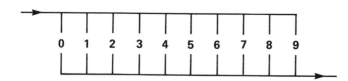

identifier :

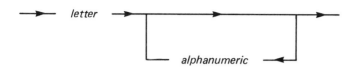

prefix operator :

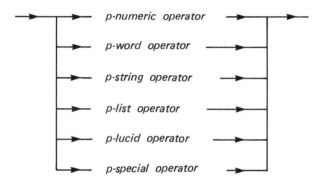

p-numeric operator :

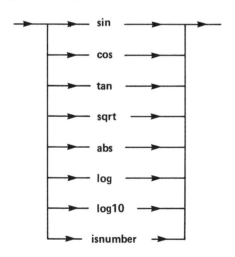

p-word operator :

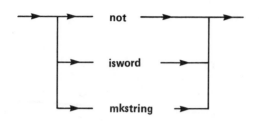

p-string operator :

p-list operator :

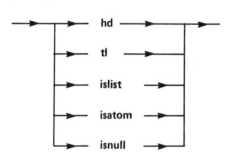

p-lucid operator :

p-special operator :

infix operator :

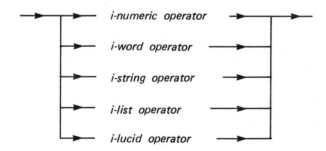

i-numeric operator :

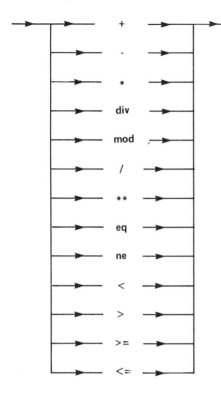

i-word operator :

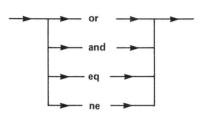

i-string operator :

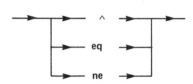

i-list operator :

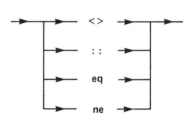

i-lucid operator :

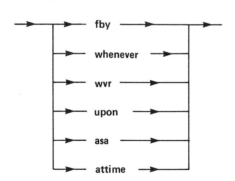

3expression

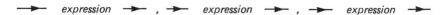

list expression :

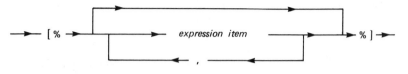

expression   item :

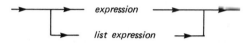

if expression :

→ **if** → *expression* → **then** → *expression* → *endif* →

endif :

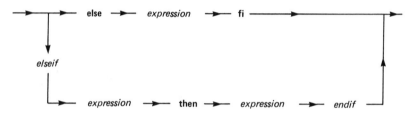

case expression :

→ **case** → *expression* → **of** → *case body* → **end** →

case body :

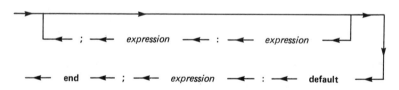

cond expression :

→ **cond** ──────────────── *cond body* → **end** →

cond body :

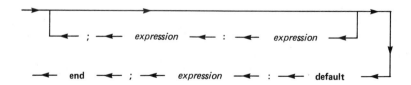

function call :

→— identifier —→— (—→— actual list —→—) —→

actuals list :

→— expression
            └— expression —←— , —←

where clause :

→— expression —→— **where** —→— body —→— **end** —→

body :

→
  └—←— declaration —←—   └—←— definition —←—

declaration :

→— identifier —→— **is current** —→— expression —→— ; —→

definition :

→
  ├—→ simple definition —→
  └—→ function definition —→

simple definition :

→— identifier —→— = —→— expression —→— ; —→

function definition :

→— identifier —→— (—→— identifier —→—) —→
                      └—←— , —←
  └—←— ; —←— expression —←— = —←

7.3 Programming Example

The following is an example of how a large program would be organised in pLucid. The example is of a screen editor and it illustrates many of the features of the pLucid system. Wadge (1984) discusses in detail the design and operation of a more elaborate (and more robust) version.

The macro used to run the screen editor

```
trap 'reset' 2
stty -echo cbreak;
luval -t10 -c -s screen.i 1 2>prompts;
stty echo -cbreak
```

```
// viscid - a vi-like-screen-editor-in-Lucid

chargen(cdecode(C))

where

cdecode(C) =    //turn raw stream of chars into stream of commands
cmd
 where
  include "cdecoder";
 end;

chargen(cmd) =    //generate the control chars from the commands
chars
 where
  include "chargen";
  include "workingtext"; //variables representing the current state
                    of the working text
  include "escseqs";    // control sequences for the vt100
  include "strings";    // useful string operations
  include "gather";    // functions for turning lists into streams
                // and vice versa
 end;

end
```

The file **cdecoder**.

```
namedcmd =                   //the command named by C
          case C of
          'i':"beginsert"; //begin inserting text
          'h':"left";     //move cursor left
          ' ':"right";    //move cursor right
          'k':"up";       //move cursor up one line
          'j':"down";     //move cursor down one line
          'o':"open";     //open a line below the cursor
          'x':"chdel";    //delete character
```

```
              'w':"write";     //write to file
              'X':"linedel";   //delete current line
              'D': "ldel";     //delete line to right of cursor
              'Z':"finish";    //write and exit
              default:"error";
            end;

   cmd = namedcmd fby
              case cmd of
               "beginsert": if next C eq '33' then "endinsert"
                           else "moreinsert" fi;
               "moreinsert": if next C eq '33' then "endinsert"
                           else "moreinsert" fi;
               "open"   : "moreinsert";
               "finish"  : "quit";
               default : next namedcmd;
              end;
```

The file **chargen**.

```
      chars = //stream of strings sent to terminal
          CLEAR^HOME^lineconc(initialtext)^HOME fby
          case cmd of
           "moreinsert": C^rhs^back(length(rhs));
           "right":RIGHT;
           "left":LEFT;
           "up":UP;
           "down":DOWN;
           "chdel":stl(rhs)^' '^back(length(rhs));
           "open": DSCROLL(lineno+1);
           "ldel":space(length(rhs))^POSITION(lineno,colno-1);
           "linedel":USCROLL(lineno) ^ if llines eq [] then UP else '' fi;
           "write": if iseod output then BEEP else BEEP fi;
           "quit":if iseod output then eod else eod fi;
           "close":NULL;
           "finish":BOTTOM;
           default: '';
          end;

      lineno = length(ulines)+1;

      colno = 1 fby case cmd of
               "left": colno-1;
               "right": colno+1;
               "endinsert":colno+length(insert);
               "ldel":colno-1;
               "open":1;
               "linedel": if llines eq [] then lineno-1 else lineno fi;
               default:colno;
              end;
```

```
insert = '' fby if cmd eq "moreinsert" then insert^C else '' fi;

rhs = srear(cline,colno-1) ;

initialtext = if filename eq '' then [] else linesof(filename) fi;

filename = arg(1);

output = first filter('cat >'^filename,TEXT fby eod,'s')
        where TEXT is current text;end;

text = lineconc(revulines<>[%cline%]<>llines)
     where
      revulines = r asa u eq []
       where
       ULINES is current ulines;
       u = ULINES fby tl(u);
       r = [] fby hd(u) :: r;
       end;
      end;
```

The file **workingtext**.

```
//the definitions of the variables which represent the
//the current working text

ulines = //list of lines above the cursor
       [] fby
       case cmd of
        "up":tl(ulines);
        "down":cline :: ulines;
        "open":cline :: ulines;
        "linedel":if llines ne [] then ulines else tl(ulines) fi;
        default : ulines;
       end;

llines = //list of lines below the cursor
       tl(initialtext)
       fby
       case cmd of
        "up": cline :: llines;
        "down":tl(llines);
        "linedel": if llines ne [] then tl(llines) else [] fi;
        default : llines;
       end;

cline = // the line the cursor is on
       hd(initialtext)
```

```
fby case cmd of
  "up": hd(ulines);
  "down":hd(llines);
  "endinsert":sfront(cline,colno-1)^insert^
          srear(cline,colno-1);
  "chdel":sfront(cline,colno-1)^srear(cline,colno);
  "ldel":sfront(cline,colno-1);
  "linedel":if llines ne [] then hd(llines) else hd(ulines) fi;
  "open":'';
  default:cline;
  end;
```

The file **escseqs**

```
//the "escape sequences" for the vt100

BEEP = '\7';

CLEAR = '\33[2J';    //clear the screen

HOME = '\33[;H';     // send cursor to upper right hand corner

RIGHT = '\33[C';    //move right

LEFT = '\b';      //move left

UP = '\33M';     //up one row

DOWN = '\33D' ;   //down one row

BOTTOM = '\33[24;1H'; //go to bottom left hand corner

DSCROLL(i) = // control chars to scroll down lines i thru 24
        // cursor left at beginning of line i (now blank)
    '\33[' ^ n ^ ';24r\33[' ^ n ^ ';1H\33M\33[1;24r\33[' ^ n ^ ';1H'
    where
    n = numeral(i);
    end;

USCROLL(i) = // control chars to scroll up lines i thru 24
        // cursor at beginning of line i
    '\33[' ^ n ^ ';24r\33[24;1H\33D\33[1;24r\33[' ^ n ^ ';1H'
    where
    n = numeral(i);
    end;

POSITION(r,c) =   // move cursor to the rth row and cth column
        '\33[' ^ numeral(r) ^ ';' ^ numeral(c) ^ 'H';
```

The file **strings**.

```
//a package of functions for manipulating strings

stl(s) = substr(s,2,length(s));
sfront(s,n) = substr(s,1,n);
srear(s,n) = substr(s,n+1,length(s));

lconc(h) = first s          //concat a list of strings
        where
        H is current h;
         eltH = element(H);
         s = if iseod eltH then '' else eltH^next s fi;
        end;

back(n) = substr(c,1,n)
        where a = '\b\b\b\b\b\b\b\b';
             b = a^a^a^a; c = b^b^b^b; end;
space(n) = substr(c,1,n)
        where a = '       '; b = a^a^a^a; c = b^b^b^b; end;

numeral(n) = s asa k eq 0
        where
        N is current n;
         k = N fby k div 10;
         r = (k mod 10) +1;
         digit = substr('0123456789',r,r);
         s = '' fby digit^s;
        end;

linesof(f) =   //a list of the lines in the file f, each line a string
        first linelist
          where
          F is current f;
           c = filter('cat -u ' ^ F,0,'ci');
           ll = if c eq '\n' then '' else c ^ next ll fi;
           line = ll whenever true fby c eq '\n' ;
          linelist = if iseod line then [] else line :: next linelist fi;
          end;

concup(s) = first t //concatenate a stream of strings
        where
        t = if iseod s then '' else s ^ next t fi;
        end;

lineconc(l) = if iseod l then eod else //concatenate a list of strings
              (concup( element(L)^'\n' ) //with newlines between
              where L is current l; end) fi;
```

The file **gather**.

```
//filters for transforming finite lists into streams and vie versa,
//streams 'terminated' by eod

element(x) = hd(tx)      //the stream of elements of the list x
        where
          tx = if first x eq [] then eod else first x fi fby
             if tl(tx) ne [] then tl(tx) else eod fi;
        end;

gather(x) = first L     //a list of the values in the stream x
        where
          L = if iseod x then [] else x :: next L fi;
        end;

linkup(x) = first L     //concatenate a stream of lists
        where
          L = if iseod x then [] else x <> next L fi;
        end;

ever(p) = first q      //true if p is ever true
        where
          q = if iseod p then false elseif
                  p then true  else
                next q fi;
        end;
```

INDEX

A.P.I.C. Studies in Data Processing
General Editors: Fraser Duncan and M. J. R. Shave

* Out of print.